MEDIEVAL ESSAYS

MEDIEVAL ESSAYS

BY CHRISTOPHER DAWSON

Essay Index Reprint Series

 BOOKS FOR LIBRARIES PRESS
FREEPORT, NEW YORK

BR
253
.D357
1968

Copyright 1954 by Sheed & Ward, Inc.
Reprinted 1968 by arrangement

LIBRARY OF CONGRESS CATALOG CARD NUMBER:

68-58785

MANUFACTURED
BY
HALLMARK LITHOGRAPHERS, INC.
IN THE U.S.A.

ACKNOWLEDGMENTS

The present volume is founded upon my book *Medieval Religion*, which was published in 1934 and has been out of print for eight years. It contains all the six essays which appeared in the earlier work, as well as four unpublished essays, Numbers I, II, VII and X. In addition to these I have included an essay on the decline of the Roman world which first appeared in *A Monument to St. Augustine* and one on Church and State in the Middle Ages which is reprinted by kind permission of Burns and Oates from a volume of lectures on Church and State delivered at Cambridge in 1935 and published in the following year.

I also desire to thank Messrs. Chapman and Hall for their kindness in allowing me to make quotations from the late Charles Scott-Moncrieff's translation of *The Song of Roland* (1919).

Finally I must record the debt that I owe to Mr. Frank Sheed for the help he has given me during the discussion of these essays and for many valuable suggestions and criticisms.

C. D.

15281

CONTENTS

CONTENTS

I

THE STUDY OF
CHRISTIAN CULTURE

THE following essays cover so wide a field in space and time that it may be difficult for the reader at first sight to grasp their connection with one another. True, they all deal with some aspect of "medieval" culture, but the word medieval is in itself unsatisfactory or insignificant. It was coined by post-Renaissance scholars to cover the gap between two periods of positive achievement which were regarded as the only ones worthy of the attention of the educated man—the classical civilization of Greece and Rome and the civilization of modern Europe. But this conception is the very opposite of that on which this book is based. What I am concerned with is not the interim period between two civilizations, but the study of *Christian Culture*—a culture which is not only worthy of study for its own sake, but is the source of the actual sociological unity which we call Europe.

If, as I believe, religion is the key of history and it is impossible to understand a culture unless we understand its religious roots, then the Middle Ages are not a kind of waiting-room between two different worlds, but the age which made a new world, the world from which we come and to which in a sense we still belong.

But the concept of Christian culture is far wider than that of the Middle Ages, not only potentially and ideally but actually and historically. It is true that there have been many Christian cultures and there may be many more. Nevertheless the main stream of Christian culture is one and should be studied as an intelligible historical unity.

1

The present volume does not, of course, attempt to deal with this whole subject. It is limited to particular aspects of the formative process of Christian culture. Even so this formative process involves three distinct phases of evolution and three different cultural situations.

In the first place there is the situation of a new religion in an old culture. This was the situation of Christianity in the Roman Empire of which I write in the essay on "The Age of St. Augustine". This process of conflict and conversion produced the first phase of Christian culture—the society of the Christian Empire and the age of the Fathers. This form of Christian culture was preserved almost unchanged in the Byzantine world, while in the West it provided a kind of classical standard or ideal towards which later ages have looked back.

Secondly there is the situation in which the Church entered the barbarian world not only as the teacher of the Christian Faith but also as the bearer of a higher culture. This double impact of Christian culture on the barbarian world which had its own tradition of culture and its own social institutions produced a state of tension and conflict between two social traditions and two ideals of life which has had a profound influence on the development of Western culture. Indeed it has never been completely resolved, since with the coming of modern nationalism we have seen a conscious attempt to undo the medieval synthesis and to reassert the old pre-Christian national traditions in an idealized form.

In the third place we have the situation in which Christianity inspires a new movement of cultural creativity, in which the new life of the new peoples finds a new expression in consciously Christian forms. This is the medieval synthesis which is the characteristic achievement of the Middle Ages, in the narrower sense of the expression. It would, however, be more correct to describe it as the age of the Western Renaissance for it is essentially the birth of a new world culture. It is to this movement that most of these essays are devoted, since it is the decisive moment in the history of Western culture and since it is possible to study it at first hand in the new vernacular literatures which are its living voice.

Finally I have devoted an essay to the great rival cultures of Western Islam, the influence and importance of which have hitherto been so insufficiently recognized by the Western historians of medieval culture. It is sometimes said that the emphasizing of the Christian character of Western culture makes us blind to the value of other civilizations. I believe that the case is just the contrary. The more we understand Christendom, the more we shall understand Islam, and the more we underestimate the religious element in our own culture the less we shall appreciate the cultures of the non-European world.

At the present time it is exceptionally difficult to realize this affinity between the world cultures because we have become accustomed to think of them primarily in racial and geographical terms; we see Western civilization as the civilization of the white man against the civilization of Asiatics and coloured men. To some extent this was always so and it is easy to find signs of racial antipathy in the Western accounts of the Huns or the Mongols and in Moslem accounts of the Franks. Nevertheless the essential principle of the great world cultures of the past (with the partial exception of India and China) was to be found not in the community of race but in the bond of a common religious faith, or as Moslems and medieval Christians put it, in a common *law*. Both in the North and South, on the Baltic and in the Western Mediterranean, the frontiers of Christendom cut across the geographical and racial frontiers, so that the pagan Lithuanians and the Moslem Spaniards belonged to different cultural and spiritual worlds. While on the other hand, the Christians of Asia, however remote they might be in speech and behaviour, were felt to be in some sense fellow-citizens in the great society of Christendom.

This sense endured longer in the East than in the West. Armenian poets were still composing elegies on the destruction of the Christian Kingdom of Jerusalem[1] when the descendants of the Crusaders themselves were destroying Christendom in the interests of power politics; while at the extreme limit of the Christian world, the little kingdom of Karthli still fought a lonely crusade against overwhelming odds and maintained the tradition of Christian chivalry down to the age of Voltaire.[2] The existence of this culture which was to such a large extent common to East and West and of the great society of Christendom which was its bearer, is one of the main facts of world history which no historian can ignore without falsifying his whole understanding of the past. That it is so largely ignored or forgotten at the present day is one of the most serious faults in our present system of education. No doubt there are many reasons which explain though they do not excuse it.

A secularized society must inevitably be unfavourable to the study of Christian culture, since its own way of life and its beliefs and ideals are totally alien. We see this most clearly in the case of Communist society which is professedly anti-religious and regards the history of Christian culture as nothing but the story of an illusion which has led mankind down a blind alley for 1,700 years. And a similar attitude is also to be found in a less extreme form in the educational theory of democratic idealists like the late Professor Dewey, who believe that education is essentially an instrument for creating a common democratic mentality and that all study must be directed towards sharing the experience of con-

[1] Cf. The elegy on the conquest of Jerusalem in 1187 composed by Nerses Mokatzi in 1622.
[2] The great martyr queen, St. Kethevan, suffered at Shiraz in 1624 and the author of the last heroic epic or *chanson de geste*—the *Guramiani*—survived until the beginning of the nineteenth century.

temporary democratic society and creating new democratic values.

But even before our society had undergone the extreme process of secularization in recent times, the study of Christian culture had never received the attention that it deserved. It was at once ignored and taken for granted; ignored by the Humanists who concentrated their attention on the study of classical antiquity, and taken for granted by the theologians whose energies were devoted to strictly ecclesiastical studies and paid little attention to the non-theological aspects of Christian culture. The Humanists may have been good Christians, and the theologians may have been good humanists, but between them they left vast fields of Christian culture and history uncultivated and disregarded.

The leaders of the Catholic revival in the early nineteenth century—men like Goerres and Ozanam and Montalembert —made a serious attempt to remedy this neglect and to promote the study and appreciation of Christian culture, but their efforts were too sporadic and too uncritical to be entirely successful. The age saw indeed a great renaissance of medieval studies but the ultimate beneficiary was not Christian culture but the modern cult of nationalism which has had such a vast influence on the whole development of modern education and modern historical studies.

It is generally agreed to-day that this influence has not been altogether wholesome. In its extreme forms, as in the nationalist ideology imposed on school and university by National Socialism, it has been one of the most destructive forces that have threatened the existence of Western culture. But even the milder forms of nationalist history, such as prevailed generally in Europe and America in the second half of the nineteenth century, were also unfavourable to the cause of civilization, inasmuch as they tended to widen the gulf that divides nation from nation and to minimize or ignore the elements that are common to Western culture as a whole.

Nevertheless it is useless to look for a remedy to the opposite ideology of Communism with its cosmopolitan ideals of world revolution and the international solidarity of the workers. For it produces just the same subordination of culture to politics and the same compulsory imposition of an exclusive party ideology on society which characterize the rival forms of totalitarianism. Whatever the faults of the old humanist culture, it was wider in sympathy, richer in values and more civilized in its social attitude than the new political faiths. Nevertheless it is hard to see how it can survive in the harsh climate of a world that is subject to the pressures of total war and mass propaganda. It was essentially the culture of a privileged class and of a society that possessed not only leisure, but a kind of moral security which did not depend on political freedom or material wealth but on universally accepted standards of personal honour and civilized behaviour.

From this point of view the world of Christian culture is nearer to our own than is the world of Humanism. The former was always at grips with the problem of barbarism. It had to face the external threat of alien and hostile cultures, while at the same time it was in conflict with barbaric elements within its own social environment which it had to control and transform. And in this work it could not rely on the existence of common standards of civilization or common moral values. It had to create its own moral order before it could achieve an ordered form of civilized existence.

The study of such a culture with its problems, its failures and its achievements, involves a much deeper level of human experience than either the self-centred and self-regarding political ideologies or the self-assured humanism of the Enlightenment. St. Augustine is a better guide for our age than Gibbon or Marx, but he is so remote from us and speaks such an alien tongue that we cannot learn what he has to teach unless we know something of the tradition of Christian culture as a whole. And this is not easy because, as I have said, the study of Christian culture has never hitherto been given a recognized place in university studies or in the curriculum of Western education.

But we cannot afford to neglect it any longer. Though Christians to-day may be only a minority, they are a very considerable minority, and they are quite strong enough to carry out a programme of Christian studies, if they wish to do so. What is needed, it seems to me, is a comprehensive course of studies which would deal with Christian culture in the same integrative and objective way in which the humanist educators dealt with Classical culture. For the Humanist was not merely a grammarian and a philologist, he studied the whole course of ancient civilization from Homer to Marcus Aurelius in all its manifestations—its languages and literatures, its history and institutions, its religion and philosophy, its architecture and art. From the point of view of the scientific specialist, the field of study was too wide; yet as a form of education it was by no means impracticable or ineffective, and has survived down to our own time in such forms as the school of *Litterae Humaniores* at Oxford. And it was, above all, its non-specialized character—the way in which it used the parallel studies of literature and philosophy and history to support and illuminate one another—that was the source of its educational success.

Now it is true that the field of Christian culture is even more extensive than that of Classical culture, since it involves a longer historical development and a larger number of vernacular languages. But this is largely compensated by the fact that every European people possesses its own approach to the common culture of Christendom through its literature and history. I have given a specimen of this approach in my essay on Piers Plowman, and every European literature provides similar opportunities.

Apart from this problem of the vernaculars, a comprehensive study of Christian culture is no more difficult than that of classical antiquity, and it offers the same educational advantages. Professor E. R. Curtius has shown in his book on *European Literature and the Latin Middle Ages* how our ignorance of the common language and literature of Western Christendom has vitiated our interpretation of the origins of our own literary traditions. And the same thing is true in other fields. It is difficult to separate the study of medieval political institutions from that of medieval political ideas, and we cannot understand the latter without a knowledge of medieval philosophy which is part of the central tradition of Christian culture. It is impossible to treat the various national traditions and national cultures as self-sufficient and self-explanatory entities, for they are all of them rooted in the common tradition of Christendom —a tradition which has its own history and its own laws of development. Thus behind all the divergencies and idiosyncracies of the national developments, we have the three great phases of the Christian culture itself which are organically related to one another.

First the growth of the Christian culture on the soil of the Graeco-Roman world which had been fertilized by the accumulated remains of so many older cultures. Secondly its transplantation to the virgin soil of the West, and finally its new flowering in the vernacular cultures of the European world.

Each of these phases has its own social and institutional history, its own form of education and learning and its own literature and art. But the continuity of the tradition as a whole is unbroken and even in the seventeenth century the thought of St. Augustine still exercises a living influence on the thought and life of the new peoples. Nor is this continuity confined to the higher levels of culture. Down to the age of the French Revolution, and sometimes even later, the Church remained the centre of the life of the common people, and even to-day we see in the case of survivals like the Passion Play of Oberammergau how the peasant no less —perhaps even more—than the scholar retained for ages a vital contact with the spiritual and artistic traditions of the Christian culture.

But what is the situation to-day when such survivals, in so far as they still exist, can be regarded as no more than picturesque archaisms? It is clear that contemporary culture can no longer be regarded as Christian, since it is probably the most completely secularized form of culture that has ever existed. Nevertheless the Christian religion still survives and there seems to be little likelihood that it will disappear. In fact it is more widely distributed than ever before. Nor is it confined to the more backward peoples or to the more uneducated sections of society, as was the case with the religions and religious cultures of the past when they were in a state of decline. Indeed to-day Christians take a more active part than they did two centuries ago in the higher cultural activities of society: in science, literature and art.

This anomalous situation offers both obstacles and opportunities for the study of Christian culture. On the one hand it involves the whole subject in a controversial atmosphere, since the secularist is exceptionally sensitive to the intrusion of religion and religious ideas into the field of education which he regards as neutral ground. But on the other hand, the more secularized a society becomes the more necessary is this study, since without it the thought and literature of the past will become increasingly unintelligible to the modern mind.

But for the modern Christian the advantages of this study are obvious since it is the study of his own spiritual tradition. Without it he will suffer from a sense of cultural inferiority and estrangement in the modern world, and the more attached he is to his religion, the greater will be the danger of his adopting a negative sectarian attitude which will narrow his sympathies and contract his social activities. This has always been a danger for religion and not least for Christianity. In the past it has produced a thousand sectarian aberrations, from Tertullian to Jansenius, and from the Puritans to modern pietist groups such as Edmund Gosse described in his own youth; and the danger is no less to-day, though it takes new and less introverted forms. Nevertheless nothing could be more opposed to the nature of Christianity. For the Christian spirit is essentially dynamic and diffusive, penetrating every form of human life and influencing every human activity.

Nowhere do we see this character more clearly than in the development of the culture of Western Christendom. For Medieval Christianity, for all its other-worldliness, its super-naturalism and its moral asceticism, never lost sight of its world mission and its cultural responsibilities, so that there has never been an age in which the transforming power of religion manifested itself so universally in so many different fields. The community of faith expressed itself in the community of thought and the community of life and found media of artistic and literary expression which became the common possession of all the Western peoples.

This simultaneous flowering of Christian culture in thought and art and social life makes the thirteenth century a classical age in the strict sense of the word—one of those ages which in the words of Voltaire "vindicate the greatness of the human spirit and compensate the historian for the barren prospect of a thousand years of stupidity and barbarism". For this reason alone it deserves to be studied as the humanists have studied the age of Pericles or Augustus. But to the Christian it means still more. To him figures like

St. Francis and St. Thomas Aquinas are not just classical types of a culture that has disappeared centuries ago but creative powers whose influence lives on in the spiritual society which produced the Christian culture of the past and will produce the new Christian culture of the future.

The old order of Western Christendom has passed away, but the tradition of Christian culture is inseparable from the tradition of Christian life and of the Christian faith. Consequently our interest in the Christian culture of the past can never be a purely historical or literary one. It is relevant to the problem of Christian culture to-day in spite of the immense changes that have transformed the modern world. Medieval Christendom is the outstanding example in history of the application of Faith to Life: the embodiment of religion in social institutions and external forms; and therefore both its achievements and its failures are worthy of study. No doubt to the secularist the strength of the religious element in medieval culture may only tend to make it more unintelligible, since it is a case of an incomprehensible ideology expressed through a remote and unfamiliar social medium. But the Christian who possesses the ideological key will appreciate the medieval achievement the more in proportion as he recognizes the social limitations of the age. If the semi-barbarous society of feudal Europe could create such a remarkable cultural unity under the influence of Christian ideas, what might the modern world achieve with its vast resources of knowledge and power which are now running to waste or being perverted into instruments of social destruction?

II

THE CHRISTIAN EAST AND THE ORIENTAL BACKGROUND OF CHRISTIAN CULTURE

T HE tradition of higher culture which was created by the ancient Greeks and transmitted by the Roman Empire and the Christian Church to modern Europe was never an exclusively Western one. It arose in the Mediterranean, where the warrior peoples of Europe first came into intimate contact with the higher civilization of the Ancient East, and from the union of these two disparate elements represented by the warrior tribe and the sacred city a new culture was born which proved stronger and more adaptable than either of its constituent elements. In the age of Alexander it spread eastwards across Asia to the Indus and the Oxus; in the age of Cæsar it spread northwards across Europe to Britain and the Rhine; so that by the first century A.D. it had become almost conterminous with the known world.

But this world expansion of Hellenistic culture was too rapid and too superficial to endure. In the East the influence of the subject oriental population gradually undermined and transformed the Hellenistic culture, and in the West the unconquered barbarians of the North destroyed the Roman order and overran the western provinces. Finally, by the eighth and ninth centuries the sphere of Western culture— the society which preserved the traditions of Greece and Rome—had become no more than an island surrounded on every side by the advancing tide of Islamic conquest and barbarian invasion.

Throughout this phase of regression, which lasted for about eight centuries, from A.D. 200 to 1000, the leadership of world civilization passed to the East, and the vital influences that affected Western culture were predominantly of oriental origin. Consequently it is impossible to explain the rise of medieval culture in purely European terms, since we have to look outside Europe to find the source of many of its characteristic institutions and ideas.

This is especially true in the case of the Byzantine Empire, which throughout this period remained by far the greatest European power and the chief surviving representative of higher culture in the West. But while it is difficult to exaggerate the importance of the Byzantine influences on medieval culture, it is no less difficult to exaggerate the strength of the oriental influences on Byzantine culture itself. These are so obvious that many historians have been unable to see anything else and have described Byzantium as a strictly oriental empire which had adopted the Roman name and the Greek language, while remaining utterly remote from the living tradition of Western culture. Today, however, there is a tendency among Byzantine scholars to dispute this view and to emphasize the non-oriental character of Byzantine culture. Thus Professor Norman Baynes has recently asserted that there are no grounds for the view that the Byzantine Empire underwent a process of progressive orientalization, and that "the elements which in their combination formed the complex civilization of the Empire were indeed the Roman tradition in law and government, the Hellenistic tradition in language, literature and philosophy, and a Christian tradition which had already been refashioned on a Greek model".[1]

I do not believe that either of these views can be accepted in its entirety. The fact is that the Byzantine Empire and its culture have a double aspect. From one point of view they represent the last phase of that great movement of conquest

---

[1] In his introduction to *Byzantium: An Introduction to the East Roman Tradition*, edited by N. H. Baynes and H. S. B. Moss, p. xx.

and colonization which had carried Greek culture far into the heart of Asia and had founded Greek cities on the banks of the Indus and as far as Balkh and Khojend. The tide of this great expansion had begun to ebb long before the Byzantine Empire was founded, so that its whole history may be regarded as a long and stubbornly contested rear-guard action of Greek culture against the advancing forces of the East. Nevertheless, from another point of view the Byzantine Empire may be seen as the result of a process of orientalization which had profoundly transformed the character of the Roman Empire and the Greek culture. The old traditions of the classical city-state, with its ideals of freedom and citizenship and autonomy, had given place to a sacred monarchy of the oriental type, and the life of the people found its centre in the Church and the liturgy. The orthodox faith had become the real bond of social unity; and the monastic life, which was the antithesis of the political life of the Greek city, was the typical organ of Byzantine culture.

Hence it is obvious that our attitude to these two alternatives depends to a great extent on our view of the nature of Christianity itself. For no society in history has identified itself more closely with the Christian religion than the Byzantine Empire, and for a considerable period (e.g. in the sixth century) the Byzantine State was practically conterminous with Christendom, while the oriental powers which threatened the existence of the Empire throughout the course of its history, such as Sassanian Persia, the Islamic Khalifate and the Turkish sultanates, were also the enemies of the Christian faith.

On the other hand, it may be argued that Christianity was itself an oriental religion, and that the religious revolution which transformed the ancient world was the main cause of the orientalization of Byzantine culture. But this problem is an extremely complex one which does not admit any easy solution.

In the first place the Jewish background of Christianity sets it apart from the other religious movements in the Roman Empire, oriental no less than Western. No people was more exclusive in its nationalism or more deliberately hostile to the influence of Hellenistic culture. Yet at the same time it held itself no less jealously aloof from the oriental world that surrounded it and from which it was separated by the intransigent monotheism of its prophetic tradition. From this Jewish background Christianity derived a religious literature and a sacred history which were totally different in spirit and in form from the classical tradition, and which gave the primitive Church a sense of social solidarity and historical continuity which set it apart from the surrounding Gentile world.

On the other hand, the direct association of Christianity with Judaism and its Palestinian background had already come to an end in the apostolic period. As soon as Christianity began to expand it spread northwards and westwards into the centres of Hellenistic culture. Christianity as a new world religion was born not in Judaea but in the great cities of the Mediterranean world—Antioch and Ephesus, Thessalonica and Corinth, Rome and Alexandria. Wherever Hellenism was strongest, there also Christianity took root and flourished, and nowhere was it stronger or more precocious than in the original homelands of Greek culture in Ionia and on the shores of the Aegean.

But in the later stages of its development, when Christianity began to expand inland from the Mediterranean cities, its progress was far more rapid in the East than in the West. The non-Hellenized or semi-Hellenized population of the eastern provinces accepted the faith readily, whereas in the West Christianity remained for centuries a religion of townsmen. Pontus in northern Asia Minor was already almost a Christian country early in the second century, and not long afterwards the little Aramaic kingdom of

Edessa in northern Mesopotamia became the first Christian
State.

Finally in the third century A.D. a great change took place
in the social life of the Empire. The revival of Persian power
under the Sassanians and the military and economic crisis
of the Roman Empire altered the balance of power in favour
of the East and led to the decline of the Hellenistic city
and its civic culture.

The late Sir William Ramsay has shown in detail how
this change changed the character of Anatolian society.[1] As
the Greek cities and the privileged citizen class declined, the
status of the peasantry improved, owing to the reorganization of the tenants of the great imperial estates on a non-
urban basis. Nevertheless, this did not mean the complete
orientalization of Anatolian culture, since the process of
Hellenization was continued under a new form. As Sir
William Ramsay wrote: "The East absorbed the European,
but the new product spoke the language of Europe and was
in other ways altered in character."

It was in this region and in this society that the new
Christian Byzantine society found its strongest support. In
spite of their remoteness from Europe and the Mediterranean, the Christians of Pontus and Cappadocia played
a leading part in the formation of the new culture. Above
all the great Cappadocian Fathers, St. Basil, St. Gregory of
Nyssa and St. Gregory Nazianzen and their disciple Evagrius
of Pontus were the spiritual leaders who completed the work
begun by Origen and Eusebius of Cæsarea and achieved
that synthesis between Greek intellectualism and oriental
spirituality which gave the Orthodox Church and the Byzantine culture their distinctive character.

Both spiritually and materially Christian Asia Minor was
the foundation of the Byzantine Empire. Even in the age of

[1] e.g. in *The Cities of St. Paul, Luke the Physician* and *Studies in the History and Art of the Eastern Provinces.*

decline Trebizond survived Constantinople, and Pontus remained a Christian country long after the Turks had overrun the Balkans.

Nevertheless, the identification of the Byzantine Empire with Christendom was never so complete as it appeared in the eyes of Byzantine patriotism and Greek orthodoxy, for between the East and the West there existed a wide transitional zone which was Christian in faith but oriental in speech and culture. This zone extended eastwards far beyond the frontiers of the empire, while on the west it crossed the Byzantine frontier and included a considerable part of the eastern provinces. It is here that we must look if we wish to understand the real nature of oriental Christianity and the channels through which it influenced Western culture.

Throughout the early Middle Ages and the preceding centuries the frontier between East and West was not the frontier between the Eastern and Western Churches in the modern sense; it ran far to the east and south—in Armenia and Mesopotamia, in Syria and in Egypt. In these lands the native peoples possessed a much stronger sense of nationality than those of Asia Minor and were the heirs of a great tradition of ancient civilization. Here the Eastern Empire was an alien intrusive power, whose relations to the conquered peoples were not unlike those of the modern European colonial powers in the East. No less than the modern European, the Greek, alike in Hellenistic and Byzantine times, was characterized by a boundless faith in the superiority of his own culture. It is true that the Greeks were comparatively free from racial intolerance. They freely admitted members of the subject races to citizenship and social equality. But they did so only in so far as the subject peoples became denationalized and adopted the Greek language and culture. Unlike the English in India, the Greeks never took the trouble to learn the language of the subject peoples. All the knowledge—and it was not inconsiderable—which they acquired concerning oriental culture was due to the work of oriental scholars who wrote in Greek, like Manetho and Berosus and Sanchoniathon.

The most remarkable example of this cultural dualism is the case of Egypt, where the two peoples and cultures lived side by side for a thousand years without ever blending with one another or producing a common culture. From first to last Alexandria was the greatest city of the Hellenistic world and the most active centre of Greek literature and learning. But at its gates and below the surface of the ruling society the immemorial life of Egypt, which was old when Hellas was born, still maintained its separate existence.

All the efforts of the Ptolemies and their successors to Hellenize Egypt and to spread the influence of Western culture merely touched the surface of society and left the mass of the subject population isolated in their own unchanging world. The wealth and culture of Alexandria were a superstructure based on the servile exploitation of the masses, and the higher it was raised the more heavily it pressed on the necks of the subject population.

It was only with the coming of Christianity that this state of things was changed. As Christianity spread from Alexandria to the population of the Χώρα, and finally to southern Egypt and the Thebaid, which was the stronghold of the native Egyptian tradition, the barrier which separated the two nations was broken down and Egypt was once more united in a common spiritual unity. This revival manifested itself in the birth of a new Christian-Egyptian vernacular literature, which originated in the Thebaid and the region of Akhmīm, and gradually spread northwards to the Fayyum and to Lower Egypt.

It is true that Coptic is the poorest and least original of all the oriental Christian literatures and the one which had least direct influence on Byzantine culture. But, in spite of the literary poverty of the Coptic tradition, it is impossible

to exaggerate the importance of the Egyptian contribution
to medieval culture, for it was in the Egyptian desert among
the representatives of the despised and oppressed native
population that there arose the new institution of Christian
monasticism and the new ideals of Christian asceticism
which were destined to have such a vast influence on the
future of both Byzantine and Western culture.

Here at last we find something entirely oriental in spirit,
without any affinity with Hellenic or Western traditions.
The primitive monasticism of Scete and Nitria and the
Thebaid represents a clean break with the spirit of Hellenic
culture. It was a departure—*anachoresis*—from the city to
the desert, from the life of the citizen to the life of the
solitary, from the enjoyment and adornment of human life
in the theatre and gymnasium to a state of total abnegation
and physical austerity which scarcely provided for the bare
necessities of existence.

As the Jews had escaped from their bondage in Egypt
and gone out into the wilderness to find a new law in
Sinai, so the monks left civilization to meet God alone in
the desert and to find a new way of life according to the
Spirit.

The new movement spread with extraordinary rapidity
all over the known world from Persia to the British Isles,
and wherever it went it carried with it the documents and
traditions of early Egyptian monasticism—the Lives of the
Fathers, the *Apothegmata* or Sayings of the Elders, and the
Rule of St. Pachomius, who founded the cenobitic life at
Tabbenesi in the Thebaid about A.D. 330.

The agents of this diffusion were men of diverse origin
and nationality who for the most part had come to Egypt
to learn the new way of life from the words and examples
of the desert monks. Such were St. Basil himself, who
became the spiritual master of Byzantine monasticism,
Palladius the Galatian, the author of the most vivid and

popular account of Egyptian monasticism for the Greek-speaking public, and St. John Cassian, who performed the same service for the Latin world. The monasteries established by St. John Cassian and St. Honoratus on the French Riviera became a secondary centre of diffusion whence the influence of Egyptian monasticism penetrated the whole of the West even beyond the limits of the Empire. In Wales and Ireland, above all, monasticism became identified with Celtic Christian culture, and the great monastic *familiae* of the sixth century, which followed a common rule and obeyed a common arch-abbot, like those of Bangor, Clonard and Iona, bear a remarkable resemblance to their Egyptian and Pachomian archetypes.

It was, however, in Palestine and Syria and Mesopotamia that the influence of Egyptian monasticism was felt earliest and most strongly, and the *lauras* of the Syrian desert and the monasteries of Tur Abdin and Mount Izla in Mesopotamia soon became populated by thousands of monks, some of whom, like St. Simeon Stylites, outdid even the monks of Egypt in the rigours of their asceticism. Here, no less than in Egypt, the monastic movement represents the reassertion of a purely oriental type of spirituality against the dominant Hellenistic culture, so that when we read the *Religious History* of Theodoret we find ourselves in a world that is nearer to that of the Indian *saddhu* than to that of the European ecclesiastic, in spite of the fact that Theodoret himself was an accomplished Hellenist.

Nevertheless, in Syria the division between Greek and oriental culture was far less rigid than it was in Egypt. The forces of Hellenism were not concentrated in a single centre like Alexandria, but were spread abroad over the land in a hundred Greek cities which stood like islands in an oriental sea. The policy of the Seleucid monarchy towards the subject population had always been more liberal than that of the Ptolemies in Egypt, and this difference of policy was maintained in Roman and Byzantine times. Consequently the culture of Syria was largely bilingual, and Greek-speaking Syrians played an important part in its diffusion. Thus the Syrian world provided the main channel through which Greek culture penetrated into the oriental world and through which oriental influences permeated Byzantine culture. It embraced, on the one hand, representatives of the most advanced type of Græco-Byzantine culture, like Theodoret of Cyrrhus, and, on the other, independent centres of Aramaic culture, like the School of the Persians at Edessa and Nisibis, whence in turn the Aramaic version of Christian culture was diffused throughout the Persian Empire, and ultimately to Central Asia and to India and China.

It is comparatively easy to trace this Eastern development, since it was a literary and ecclesiastical one, due to the cultural activity of the Syrian scholars and the missionary activity of the Patriarchate of Seleucia-Ctesiphon. The Western diffusion is much more difficult to follow, since the Byzantines were as unwilling as their classical predecessors to admit their literary debt to the "barbarians", or even the existence of any "barbarian" culture at all. But there can be no question of the importance of the influence of Syrian monasticism and the cult of Syrian saints, like St. Simeon Stylites or of St. Sergius the Megalomartyr, whose basilica at Rosapha on the banks of the Euphrates was a great centre of pilgrimage for the whole of the Christian East. One of the earliest Arabic poets describes the Beni Taglib riding into battle under the banner of St. Sergius, and his fame spread westwards to Constantinople and Rome. Here, as in so many other cases, the channels through which oriental influences reached the West were not literary but religious ones: they were the pilgrimage routes, the famous sanctuaries and the oriental monastic colonies, like the great monastery of the Akoimetoi on the Bosphoros, which was of purely Syrian origin.

Nevertheless, literary influences were not altogether absent, though they reached Byzantium at second hand through the medium of the mixed Græco-Syrian culture of the cities. It was in this way that the liturgical poetry of the Byzantine Church was transformed by the influence of the rhythmical style of Syrian religious verse. Above all, both Byzantine and Latin religious thought owed a very heavy debt to the writing of the unknown Syrian mystic who used the name of Dionysius the Areopagite and was accepted by St. Maximus the Confessor and almost all subsequent theologians as the authentic voice of apostolic tradition.

Similarly the homilies attributed to Macarius the Great, which were very widely diffused and had an immense influence on Byzantine mysticism, were in reality the work of a Syrian, Symeon of Mesopotamia, who was himself influenced by the ideas of the Messalian sect. And finally, at a later date, the revival of Byzantine mysticism which was initiated by St. Symeon the New Theologian at the beginning of the eleventh century and attained its full development with Gregory of Sinai and the Hesychasts of the fourteenth century, owes a great deal to the influence of a Nestorian monk of the seventh century, Isaac of Ninive, who was transformed by his editors and translators first into a Monophysite and finally into an Orthodox saint.

It is difficult to exaggerate the importance of this spiritual tradition in the history of the Orthodox Church. Indeed, when modern writers like Kireyevsky, and Khomyakov in the past, and Berdyaev and Bulgakov in our own days, write of the essential character of Orthodox Christianity and the contrast between Byzantine mysticism and Latin rationalism, it is undoubtedly this tradition that they have in mind. Nevertheless, it is only Byzantine by adoption and it was never completely representative of Byzantine culture. Throughout their history the Byzantines prided themselves on their inheritance of Greek culture, and the

Byzantine humanists, like Michael Psellos and John Italus in the eleventh century, and Theodore Metochites and Nicephorus Gregoras in the fourteenth, were perhaps more authentic representatives of Byzantine culture than the mystics and ascetics.

Throughout the Middle Ages these two elements coexisted and sometimes came into sharp conflict with one another, as in the case of the condemnation of John Italus in the eleventh century, and the controversy between Barlaam and Gregory Palamas in the fourteenth. And thus Byzantine culture had two different aspects, each of which represented a different historical tradition and left a different legacy. On the one hand there was the oriental tradition of asceticism and mysticism which was transmitted by Byzantine monasticism to medieval Russia and was responsible for all that was deepest and most spiritual in Russian Christianity. And on the other hand there was the tradition of humanist culture which the Byzantines had inherited from ancient Greece and which they passed on in the later Middle Ages to modern Europe, not through Russia and the other Orthodox peoples, but through Italy, by the agency of men like Manuel Chrysoloras and Cardinal Bessarion, who restored the classical link between the Greek and the Latin worlds.

But in the other direction, beyond the Byzantine Empire to the east, there existed the world of Aramaic Christian culture, which extended from Mount Taurus through northern Syria and Mesopotamia and Persia onwards indefinitely into the furthest recesses of the Asiatic continent. This, and not the Byzantine world, was the true centre of oriental Christian culture, but it never created an independent Syriac national state or developed a political life of its own, owing to the unfavourable historical conditions which caused it to be divided and overshadowed by the dominant cultures of Byzantium and Persia and Islam. It was only in the Church that the Syriac national culture could find expression, and therefore it is not surprising that their desire to assert their independence should have led them to separate themselves from the Church of the Byzantine Empire even at the cost of schism and heresy.

But although the Aramaic-speaking world never achieved political independence, its missionary activity created a whole constellation of daughter churches and cultures. Some of these, like the Christian Turkish culture of Central Asia —the medieval kingdom of Prester John—have vanished without a trace. Another, the Church of Malabar, still survives as an isolated relic of a lost world. But north of Mesopotamia, in Armenia and Georgia, the development of Christian culture which was originally derived from the East Syrian Church was marked by a remarkably strong consciousness of national independence.

Indeed, Armenia provides óne of the first examples in history of a conscious policy for the development of a national culture. For, as the late Père Peeters has shown,[1] the origins of the Armenian literature and script are directly due to the deliberate effort of the leaders of the Armenian people to save their religion and nationality from being absorbed by the Persian Empire. In order to achieve this end they despatched a cultural mission to the centres of Syrian Christian culture at Samosata and Edessa under the leadership of St. Mesrop the Teacher, who, with the help of Syrian scholars, invented the Armenian script and alphabet and laid the foundations of a national Christian literature.

Thenceforward for fifteen hundred years the Armenian literature and script have been the bulwarks of Armenian nationality and religion. During its great age, in the ninth and tenth centuries, the Armenian kingdom was also the

[1] Cf. Paul Peeters, S. J., *Orient et Byzance: le tréfonds oriental de l'hagiographie byzantine* (1950), p. 25; and *Pour l'histoire des origines de l'alphabet arménien* in *Rev. des études arméniennes*, vol. ix, pp. 203–37.

bulwark of the whole of Eastern Christendom against Islam, and when it was destroyed by the short-sighted imperialism of Byzantium the Armenian national spirit was strong enough to survive the Seljuk conquest and re-create a second Armenian state in Cilicia and Commagene. Here it came into contact with the Latin West through the crusading states, and no oriental people showed themselves more tolerant and receptive of Western influences than the Armenians. Western saints like St. Thomas of Canterbury were commemorated by the medieval Armenian Church, and the Western coronation rite was translated into Armenian by St. Nerses of Lampron for the crowning of Leo the Great in 1157.[1]

At the same time the medieval Armenians were equally at home in the oriental world. Haythum I (1226–69) was in friendly relations with the Mongol Empire and visited the court of the Great Khan at Karakorum in person. He attempted to organize a common front against Islam between the Mongols, who were at that time in close relation with the Nestorian Christians of the East, and the crusading states of the West, which were in close relations with Armenia. These ambitious schemes, which were carried on by Haythum's successors, Leo III and Haythum II, failed owing to the lack of support of Western Christendom and the decline of the crusading movement. Nevertheless, they show that in the thirteenth century oriental Christianity was still an important factor in international politics. There is no more interesting document in the history of the relations of East and West than the account of the embassy of the Syrian monks from China, Mar Yaballaha and Rabban Sauma, who were sent to the West in 1287 by Arghun Khan in order to forward this alliance and who visited Rome and Paris and Bordeaux. At the same time Western missionaries were visiting central Asia and China

[1] Peeters, *op. cit.*, p. 194.

and establishing archbishoprics at Pekin in 1308 and at Sultanieh in Persia in 1318. If this twofold movement towards the integration of Eastern and Western Christendom had prospered it might have changed the course of history by establishing a channel of Christian intercourse across the Old World from Paris to Canton.

Unfortunately it marks an end and not a beginning. Although a few far-seeing minds in the West, like Roger Bacon and Raymund Lull, Philip de Mezières and Marco Sanuto, Gregory X and John XXII, had some inkling of the importance of the Christian East, Western Christendom as a whole was too divided by political and ecclesiastical rivalries to make a full use of its opportunities. The conversion of the Mongols to Islam deprived the Armenian kingdom of its external support, and the growth of Moslem intolerance which culminated in the disastrous reaction of Tamerlane destroyed the influence and even the existence of Syrian Christianity in Central Asia. The last king of Christian Armenia died in exile in Paris in 1393, and three years afterwards the last great army which Western Europe sent to the succour of Eastern Christendom was completely destroyed at Nicopolis on the Danube. There was no longer any question of the eastern expansion of Christianity. Even the cradle-lands of Christianity and Hellenism in Asia Minor and Greece were lost, and Constantinople became the capital of a new non-Christian empire which was even wider and more extensive than the Byzantine Empire had been in the age of Justinian. For two hundred years and more the tide of Moslem conquest continued to flow, until the horse-tail standards had been carried to the walls of Vienna[1] and Moscow[2] and Hungary, the bulwark of Western Christendom, had become a Turkish province.

These catastrophic events mark the end of medieval civilization. The Islamization of the Byzantine Empire and

---

[1] In 1529 (and again in 1683).   [2] In 1570 and 1571.

the disappearance of the oriental background of the older Christian world changed the character of European culture, which was forced to turn westwards and face towards the Atlantic. The oriental stream of culture which had fertilized Europe since the beginning of history had dried up, and for four hundred years the West was left to itself to create new ways of life and to make a new world.

III

THE CHRISTIAN WEST AND THE FALL OF THE EMPIRE

S T. AUGUSTINE has often been regarded as standing outside his own age—as the inaugurator of a new world and the first medieval man, while others, on the contrary, have seen in him rather the heir of the old classical culture and one of the last representatives of antiquity. There is an element of truth in both these views, but for all that he belongs neither to the medieval nor to the classical world. He is essentially a man of his own age—that strange age of the Christian Empire which has been so despised by the historians, but which nevertheless marks one of the vital moments in the history of the world. It witnessed the fall of Rome, the passing of that great order which had controlled the fortunes of the world for five centuries and more, and the laying of the foundations of a new world. And Augustine was no mere passive spectator of the crisis. He was, to a far greater degree than any emperor or general or barbarian war-lord, a maker of history and a builder of the bridge which was to lead from the old world to the new.

Unfortunately, although there is no lack of historical evidence, the real importance of this period is seldom appreciated. Ever since the Renaissance the teaching of ancient history has been treated as part of the study of the classics and consequently comes to an end with the age of the Antonines, while the teaching of modern history is equally bound up with the nationalist idea and begins with the rise of the existing European peoples. Consequently there is a gap of some five hundred years from the third to the seventh century in the knowledge of the ordinary educated person. It lasts from the collapse of the old Empire

in the third century A.D. to the break-up of the reconstituted
Eastern Empire in the seventh century under the stress of
the Mohammedan invasions. This is the period of the Christian Empire, the Empire of Constantine and Justinian, the
age of the Fathers and of the great councils. It deserves to
be studied as a whole and for its own sake, instead of piece-
meal and from conflicting points of view. Hitherto the
secular historians have confined themselves to one side of
the evidence and the ecclesiastical historians to the other,
without paying much attention to each other's results. We
have to go back to the days of Tillemont to find an historian
who is equally competent in both fields. The modern historians of the period have shown themselves notably un-
sympathetic to its religious achievements. The greatest of
them—Gibbon and the late Professor Bury—were free-
thinkers with a strong bias against Christianity, while the
remainder, from the days of Finlay and Burckhardt and
Gregorovius to Seeck and Stein and Rostovtzeff in our time,
all write from a secularist point of view. This is peculiarly
unfortunate, not only because by far the larger part of the
historical evidence has a religious character, but still more
because the whole historical development becomes inexplic-
able when viewed from a purely secular standpoint. To
neglect or despise the religious achievement of the age is as
fatal to any true understanding of it as a complete disregard
of the economic factor would be in the case of nineteenth-
century Europe. For the real interest and importance of that
age are essentially religious. It marks the failure of the
greatest experiment in secular civilization that the world
had ever seen, and the return of society to spiritual principles.
It was at once an age of material loss and of spiritual recovery, when amidst the ruins of a bankrupt order men
strove slowly and painfully to rebuild the house of life on
eternal foundations.

This vital revolution owes nothing to the coming of the

new peoples. It was already accomplished while the Roman Empire was intact and the Eternal City was still inviolate. Yet it was this change rather than the material collapse of the Roman state which marks the real break between the ancient classical civilization and that of the Byzantine and medieval world.

Rome had won her world empire by her genius for military and political organization, but her positive contribution to culture was comparatively small. She was rather an agent in the expansion of culture than its creator. Her part was that of the soldier and engineer who cleared the way and built the roads for the advance of civilization. The cosmopolitan culture which became common to the whole Roman Empire was itself mainly the creation of the Hellenic genius. It had its origins in the life of the Greek city-state and had already acquired the character of a world civilization in the great states of the Hellenistic world. Alexander the Great and his successors had made it their mission to spread this civilization throughout the lands that they had conquered. All over the East, from the Mediterranean and the Black Sea to the Oxus and the Indus, countless cities sprang up which in their constitution, their social life, and their buildings were modelled on the pattern of the Greek city. And each of these cities became a centre of diffusion for Western culture. The peasants no doubt continued to live their own life and served their new masters as they had served so many conquerors in the past, but the upper and middle classes were by degrees drawn into the privileged society and were either completely Hellenized or at least acquired a superficial veneer of Greek manners and culture. A single type of urban civilization gradually came to prevail throughout the Hellenistic world.

Rome in her turn took on this inheritance from the great Hellenistic monarchies and carried on their work. But she did so in a strictly practical and utilitarian spirit. At first, indeed, her attitude was entirely selfish, and she organized the world only to exploit it. Roman capitalists, money-lenders, slave-dealers and tax-gatherers descended on the East like a swarm of locusts and sucked the life out of the dependent communities. Every Roman, from the aristo-cratic capitalist like Brutus or Lucullus down to the meanest agent of the great financial corporations, had his share in the plunder.[1] The age of the Republic culminated in an orgy of economic exploitation which ruined the prosperity of the subject peoples and brought Rome herself to the verge of destruction.

The crisis was averted by the foundation of the Empire. Julius Cæsar and Augustus put an end to the misrule of the capitalist oligarchy and the tyranny of military adven-turers and returned to the Hellenistic ideal of an enlightened monarchy. The provinces recovered their prosperity, and alike in the Hellenistic East and the Latin West there was a fresh expansion of urban civilization. For two centuries the ancient world enjoyed an age of continuous material progress.

Everywhere from Britain to Arabia and from Morocco to Armenia wealth and prosperity were spreading, new cities were being founded, and the more backward peoples were adopting a higher form of civilization. And nowhere was this process more striking than in Africa, where even to-day the stately ruins of so many Roman cities still remain to impress the modern tourist with their evidence of vanished civilization. Even a comparatively remote and unimportant town like Timgad, in North Africa, possesses public build-ings and monuments finer than those of many a modern city of vastly superior wealth and population. It had its theatres and amphitheatres in which free spectacles were

[1] It is a characteristic that Brutus, who was regarded in later times as a model of republican virtue, quarrelled with Cicero because the latter was forced to reduce the interest on Brutus's loans to the impoverished cities of Cilicia from forty-eight per cent to a beggarly twelve per cent!

provided for the entertainment of the people. It had porticoes and basilicas where the citizens could attend to public
business or idle away their leisure time. It had baths and
gymnasia, libraries and lecture halls, and temples which
were not, like our churches, destined solely for religious
worship, but were the centre of civic ceremonial and public
festivities. There has probably never been an age in which
the opportunities for living an enjoyable and civilized existence were so widely diffused. For the ancient city was not,
like the average modern town, a factory or a place of business; it existed for the enjoyment of its citizens and it was
the centre of an active communal life, lived in public and
at the public expense.

This was most strikingly exemplified at Rome itself, where
the Greek democratic principle of the right of the citizen to
be fed and amused at the expense of the state had been
carried to its extreme conclusions. These rights were the
only remaining privilege of the Roman democracy, which
had completely lost all share in the government of the
Empire, but, so far from disappearing with the loss of
political rights, they continued to expand down to the last
period of the Empire. The corn dole had been limited by
Augustus to some 200,000 citizens, but even so it involved
a vast organization, the traces of which are to be seen in
the remains of the great public corn depots at Ostia, and
the setting aside for the use of the capital of the chief
corn-growing areas of the Mediterranean world—Egypt
and Sicily. Moreover, in the course of time the free distribution of other articles such as oil, wine and bacon were
added to the corn dole. Gifts of money had been common
even in republican times, and during the reign of Augustus no less than six distributions of between £2 and £3 10s.
per head were made to between 200,000 and 320,000
persons.

No less important was the amusement of the people. The

games of the circus and the amphitheatre involved enormous expenditure and occupied a considerable part of the year. Apart from the special festivals, which might last as long as a hundred days on end, the regular games took up sixty-six days a year in the time of Augustus, and had increased to a hundred and seventy-five days by the fourth century.

Finally, vast sums of public money were absorbed by the public buildings. To some extent this expenditure served ends of real value, above all in the case of the great aqueducts which ensured to Rome a better water supply than that of most modern capitals. For the most part, however, it was entirely unproductive. The Colosseum—which has stood for eighteen centuries as a symbol of the material power of imperial Rome—was created to serve the brutal amusements of the Roman populace. The imperial palaces and fora, with their temples and libraries and porticoes, provided a sumptuous background for the social life of the Court and the capital. But the most characteristic monuments of the imperial period are the thermæ, which continued to increase in size and splendour down to the age of Diocletian and Constantine. They were not mere public baths in our sense of the word, but true palaces for the people, of vast size, containing baths and gymnasia, lecture-rooms and libraries, and adorned with the masterpieces of Greek and Hellenistic art. Public building on such a scale far surpassed anything that the modern world has yet seen. Imperial Rome became a city of gold[1] and marble, a worthy incarnation of the *Dea Roma* whom her subjects worshipped. And the same ideal was pursued by all the cities of the Empire according to their capacity. Each tried to surpass its neighbour in the splendour of its public buildings and

[1] She was literally a "golden city", for the growing scarcity of precious metal which characterized the later Empire is attributed by historians in part to the enormous quantities of gold which were used to gild the roofs and domes of the temples and public buildings of Rome.

the number of its games and festivals. Not only millionaires, like Herodes Atticus, but every citizen of moderate wealth, used his money unstintingly in the service of his native city, either by building baths, theatres and porticoes, or by providing public spectacles or endowments for educational and charitable purposes.

All this testifies to a high level of material culture and to an admirable development of public spirit on the part of the citizen class, but from the moral and spiritual point of view it was less satisfactory. All the vast development of material prosperity and external display had no spiritual purpose behind it. Its ultimate end was the satisfaction of corporate selfishness. The religious element in ancient culture, which had been the inspiration of civic patriotism in the fifth and sixth centuries B.C., had almost disappeared from the cosmopolitan civilization of the imperial age. The temples and the gods remained, but they had lost their spiritual significance and had become little more than an ornamental appendage to public life and an occasion for civic ceremonial. For the educated, the only real religion was philosophy—a philosophy which provided high moral ideals for the élite, but which was incapable of influencing the mass of society.

The true religion of society was not the philosophic paganism of men like Marcus Aurelius or St. Augustine's correspondent, Maximus of Madaura, but the cult of material pleasure and success. Christianity had more to fear from Trimalchio than from Julian, and the real Antichrist was not Apollo, but Belial, "the prince of this world". And this is fully recognized by the majority of Christian writers from the time of St. Paul down to the fifth century. St. Augustine himself, in a well-known chapter of *The City of God,* reveals the naked materialism which lay behind the opposition of pagan society to Christianity, and shows that it was as irreconcilable with the old Roman traditions as with Christian teaching. Its ideal was not civic virtue and patriotism, but to have a good time and bigger and better shows. "They do not trouble," he writes, "about the moral degradation of the Empire; all that they ask is that it should be prosperous and secure. 'What concerns us,' they say, 'is that everyone should be able to increase his wealth so that he can afford a lavish expenditure and can keep the weaker in subjection. Let the poor serve the rich for the sake of their bellies and so that they can live in idleness under their protection, and let the rich use the poor as dependants and to enhance their prestige. . . . Let the laws protect the rights of property and leave men's morals alone. Let there be plenty of public prostitutes for whosoever wants them, above all for those who cannot afford to keep mistresses of their own. Let there be gorgeous palaces and sumptuous banquets, where anybody can play and drink and gorge himself and be dissipated by day or night, as much as he pleases or is able. Let the noise of dancing be everywhere, and let the theatres resound with lewd merriment and with every kind of cruel and vicious pleasure. Let the man who dislikes these pleasures be regarded as a public enemy, and if he tries to interfere with them, let the mob be free to hound him to death. But as for the rulers who devote themselves to giving the people a good time, let them be treated as gods and worshipped accordingly. Only let them take care that neither war nor plague nor any other calamity may interfere with this reign of prosperity.' "[1]

This indictment of the spirit of hedonism and materialism which dominated Roman society runs through all the writings of the Fathers and is supported by many non-Christian writers. Even allowing for the exaggerations of the moralist, there can be little doubt of its substantial truth. Nor was this spirit confined to great cities such as Rome and Antioch and Carthage; it was also characteristic of

[1] Condensed from *De Civitate Dei*, II, xx ; cf. *Ep.* cxxxviii, 3, 14.

provincial sociey, as St. Jerome testifies in a characteristic sentence[1] about his own countrymen. It is a mistake to suppose that the age of the Empire was a religious one because it was marked by so many new religious movements. The mystery religions and the tendency towards mysticism and asceticism are a proof of the religious bankruptcy of society which drove the religious-minded to seek spiritual life outside the life of the city and of society in an esoteric ideal of individual salvation. Even Stoicism, the one sect of the time which inculcated a disinterested ideal of social duty, was fundamentally an unsocial and individualistic creed. The reigning culture had become almost completely secularized, and the religious and the social instincts were becoming opposed to one another.

The one exception to this tendency is to be found in the Jewish tradition, and that was the one religious tradition which had preserved its independence in face of the cosmopolitan Hellenistic culture. The attempt of the Seleucid kings to Hellenize Judaea had led to the great national rising of the Maccabean period, which was nothing less than a crusade against Hellenism, and though the Roman Empire succeeded in breaking down the material resistance of the nation, it could not overcome their spiritual opposition. The Jews remained a people apart, and refused to submit to the dominant culture or to share in the life of the city. The primitive Church inherited this tradition. The Christians claimed, no less than the Jews, to be a people apart—"a chosen race, a royal priesthood, a holy nation". But this claim no longer involved any political aspirations. Throughout the centuries of persecution the Christians remained faithful to the teachings of St. Peter and St. Paul and submitted to the imperial government as a power ordained of God. St. Clement's noble prayer on behalf of princes and

---

[1] "In mea enim patria, rusticitatis vernacula, deus venter est et de die vivatur, sanctior est ille qui ditior est."—*Ep.* vii, 5.

rulers would not be out of place in the altered circumstances of a Christian society.

But this political loyalty to the Empire as a state only throws into stronger relief the irreconcilable hostility of Christianity to the imperial culture. The Church was to a great extent an alternative and a substitute for the communal life of the city-state. It appealed to all those elements which failed to find satisfaction in the material prosperity of the dominant culture—the unprivileged classes, the poor and the oppressed, the subject oriental populations, and above all those who were dissatisfied with the materialism and sensuality of pagan society and who felt the need for a living religion on which to base their lives.

Consequently it was inevitable that Christianity should come into conflict with the pagan government and society. To the ordinary man the Christian was an anti-social atheist, "an enemy of the human race", who cut himself off from everything that made life worth living. To the authorities he was a centre of passive disaffection, a disloyal subject who would not take his share of the public service or pay homage to the emperor. The Christian, on his part, regarded the official worship of the emperor as a supreme act of blasphemy—the deification of material power and the setting up of the creature in place of the Creator. So long as the Empire confined itself to its secular function as the guardian of peace and order, the Church was ready to recognize it as the representative of God, but as soon as it claimed an exclusive allegiance and attempted to dominate the souls as well as the bodies of its subjects, the Church condemned it as the representative of Antichrist. Thus the denunciations of the Apocalypse are as integral a part of the Christian attitude to the Empire as St. Paul's doctrine of loyal submission. To St. John the official cultus of the emperor, as organized in the province of Asia, is the worship of the Beast, and Rome herself, the *Dea Roma* of the state religion,

is the great harlot enthroned upon the waters, drunken with
the blood of the saints and the blood of the martyrs of Jesus.
It is, however, important to notice that Rome is not described as a conquering military power, but as the centre of
a luxurious cosmopolitan culture, the great market in which
all the merchants of the earth congregate. It is the triumphant materialism of Rome, not her military and political
oppression, which is denounced in the Apocalypse.

Nothing can give a more vivid impression of the failure
of material civilization to satisfy the needs of the human
soul than St. John's vision of the arraignment of the great
heathen world power before the eternal justice by the souls
of its innocent victims. Ancient civilization had set itself
in opposition to the religious spirit and had alienated the
deepest forces in the mind of the age, and thereby its ultimate doom was sealed. There is a remarkable passage in one
of the sermons of St. Gregory in which he looks back from
the disorder and misery of the age in which he lived to the
material prosperity of the world in which the martyrs had
suffered. In his own days the world seemed dying. "Everywhere death, everywhere mourning, everywhere desolation."
In the age of Trajan, on the contrary, "there was long life
and health, material prosperity, growth of population and
the tranquillity of daily peace, yet while the world was still
flourishing in itself, in their hearts it had already withered".[1]
In cordibus aruerat—that was the innermost secret of the
fall of ancient civilization. It had lost its roots in the human
soul and was growing more and more empty and sterile.
The vital centre of the society of the future was to be found,
not in the city-state, but in the Christian *ecclesia*.

Are we, then, to conclude with Renan that the rise of
Christianity was the real cause of the decline of the Empire
—that "Christianity was a vampire which sucked the life-

---

[1] St. Gregory, *Hom.* xxviii.

blood of ancient society and produced that state of general enervation against which patriotic emperors struggled in vain"?[1] Certainly the victory of Christianity does mark a most profound and vital aspect of the decline of the old culture, but it does not follow that it was directly responsible for it. The cosmopolitan urban culture of the later Empire broke down through its own inherent weaknesses, and even before the victory of Christianity it had already failed to justify itself on sociological and economic grounds.

In spite of its apparent prosperity and its brilliant outward appearance, the vast development of city life under the Empire was out of all proportion to its real strength. It was an elaborate superstructure built on relatively weak and unstable foundations. For the urban civilization of the imperial age was essentially the civilization of a leisured class, a society of consumers, which rested on a foundation of slave labour and rural serfdom. The vast civic expenditure on public buildings and public games was unproductive and entailed an increasing drain on the economic resources of the Empire. And at the same time the process of urbanization led to a similar exhaustion of human resources. For the citizen class was extremely sterile and had to be constantly recruited by new elements usually drawn from the class of freedmen. Moreover, neither the upper nor the lower classes of the city provided suitable military material, and the Empire came to rely more and more on the rural population, especially the natives of the recently conquered and less civilized provinces, for its supply of troops.[2]

The Roman Empire and the process of urbanization which accompanied it were, in fact, a vast system of exploitation which organized the resources of the provinces and concentrated them in the hands of a privileged class. The system

[1] Renan: *Marc-Aurèle*, p. 589.
[2] Cf. Rostovtzeff: *Social and Economic History of the Roman Empire* (1926), pp. 332–3.

worked well so long as the Empire was expanding, for there was no lack of new territory to urbanize and new masses of cheap slave labour with which to cultivate it. But the close of the period of external expansion and internal peace at the end of the second century put an end to this state of things and the Empire was left with diminishing resources to face the growing menace of external invasion and internal disruption. In spite of its apparent wealth and splendour, the urban society of the Empire had no reserve forces either of men or of money, and it was unable to face the crisis. The wealthy provincial bourgeoisie, which had been the backbone of the Empire in the second century, was financially ruined and lost its hold on the government. Power passed to the soldiery who belonged by origin to the peasant class and had no sympathy with the civic tradition.[1]

Thus the third century witnessed a social and constitutional revolution of the most far-reaching kind. The great break in the history of the ancient world—the end of the old society and the inauguration of a new order—took place not in the age of St. Augustine, when the barbarians conquered the western provinces and the unity of the Empire was destroyed, but more than a century earlier, in the age of military anarchy which followed the fall of the house of Severus. When the Illyrian soldier-emperors succeeded in stemming the tide of anarchy and beating back the enemies of Rome, the Empire which they re-established was no longer the same state. The old civic society was moribund, and neither the Senate, nor the Italian citizen body, nor the provincial city-states, were any longer strong enough to form a satisfactory basis of government and administration. Only the army and the imperial power itself had survived as living forces. But the emperor was not only the first magis-

[1] According to Rostovtzeff (op cit., ch. xi), the motive force of this revolution is to be found in the class conflict between the peasant soldiery and the urban bourgeoisie, which he compares to the class conflict of bourgeois and proletariat in our own times.

trate of the Roman republic, he was also the representative of the great Hellenistic monarchies which had themselves inherited the absolutist traditions of the oriental state. In the East, and above all in Egypt, the organization of society was entirely different from that of the Græco-Roman world. Instead of a free citizen class, based on slave labour, practically the whole population consisted either of serfs or officials and priests. The institutions of the city-state, private property and slavery hardly existed. The whole economic life of Egypt was directly controlled by the state, and every class was bound to its special task. It was, in fact, a great system of state socialism, in which the state was the one landowner and organized the manufacture and distribution of goods by means of state monopolies and state factories and warehouses.

It was from this source that the new principles were derived on which Diocletian and his successors based their work of reorganization. The imperial office itself acquired the characteristics of an oriental kingdom. The emperor ceased to be primarily the *princeps* of the Roman state and the commander-in-chief of the Roman armies and became a sacred monarch surrounded by the ceremonial and solemn ritual of an oriental court. "The Sacred Palace" became the centre of government and the apex of a vast official hierarchy. The Empire was no longer a federation of city-states, each of which was a self-governing unit, but a centralized bureaucratic state which controlled the life of its members down to the minutest detail. Society was based on the principle of compulsory state service, and every class and occupation was subjected to state regulation and tended to become a fixed hereditary caste. The trades which were most essential to the public service, especially those connected with the food supply, were organized as hereditary guilds which were corporately responsible for the fulfilment of their obligations. The same principle was applied even

more strictly to the land, on which the state depended in the
last resort alike for its food supply and its revenue. Consequently the government did all in its power to prevent land
going out of cultivation. The peasant, whether a slave or a
freeman, was bound to his holding and was forbidden to
abandon its cultivation or to migrate elsewhere. If a holding
became derelict, and no owner could be found, the neigh-
bouring land-holders were jointly responsible for its cultivation and taxes. In the same way, the members of the citizen
class became corporately liable for the payment of taxes on
the whole city territory, and were bound to their *curia*—
their town council—just as the peasant was bound to his
land, so that a citizen who attempted to escape his financial
burdens by entering the army or migrating elsewhere was
liable to be arrested and sent back to his *curia*, like a run-
away slave.

Under these conditions the old civic ideal of the leisured
classes passed away and was replaced by that of the servile
state. The urban aristocracy lost its economic prosperity and
its social prestige, and its place was taken by the members
of the official hierarchy and by the great landowners who
stood outside the *curia* and who were strong enough to hold
their own against the exactions of the tax-gatherers and the
oppression of the bureaucracy. Society tended more and
more to return to an agrarian foundation, and the city-state
was no longer the vital centre of the whole social structure,
as it had been during the eight classical centuries of Mediterranean culture.

But this social revolution involved no less fundamental
changes in the relations of the Empire to religion. The old
official cultus was essentially bound up with the institutions
of the city-state, and now that these had lost their vitality
the state was in danger of being left without any religious
foundation. The new unitary state required a religion of a
more universal character than the polytheistic cults of the

city-state possessed, and, as a matter of fact, we observe throughout the third century a tendency towards a vague semi-philosophic monotheism in pagan society.[1] This tendency finds expression in the worship of the sun, which was adopted by Aurelian and his successors as the tutelary deity of the Empire. No doubt it owed much to Syrian and Persian influences, but we see in the writings of Julian[2] how easily it adapted itself to the ideals of contemporary philosophic speculation and how well suited it was to serve as a principle of inspiration in the religious life of the age and as the official cult of the new orientalized monarchy.

Nevertheless, this solution was not destined to prevail. For Constantine, instead of contenting himself with the vague solar monotheism which had been the religion of his house, made an abrupt break with tradition and found a new religious basis for the Empire in an alliance with the outlawed and persecuted Christian Church. It was an act of extraordinary courage, and it is not altogether surprising that many historians, from the time of Gibbon to Ferdinand Lot in our day, should regard it as an act of madness which endangered the stability of the Empire by sacrificing the interests of the most loyal and influential part of the citizens in order to conciliate an unpatriotic minority. Yet it is possible that Constantine, even as a statesman, was more farsighted than his critics. The Church was the one living creative force in the social and spiritual life of the age. It brought to society just those elements of freedom, private initiative and co-operative action of which the Empire itself stood most in need.

The life had gone out of the civic organization, and citizenship meant little more than the obligation to pay taxes. The citizenship of the future was to be found in the Church. It

---

[1] Cf. especially the hymn of the army of Licinius to the *Summus Deus* which has been preserved by Lactantius: *De mort. persecut.* xlvi, 6.
[2] *Oratio* iv.

was a far wider citizenship than that of the old city-state, since it was open to all, even to the slave, and the poor enjoyed a specially privileged position. They were the *plebs Christi*, the people of Christ, and the wealth of the Church was in a very real sense "the patrimony of the poor". In the same way the functions of the city magistrates as the representatives and protectors of the people passed to the magistrates of the new society—the Christian bishop. While the former had become mere puppets in the hands of the bureacracy, the latter was the one independent power in the society of the later Empire. The choice of the bishop was the last right which the people preserved, and we know from countless instances how eagerly they availed themselves of it. A man who had the gift of leadership and who was trusted by the people was liable to be elected, whether he wished it or not. In the case of St. Ambrose we see a high secular official, who was not even baptized, being chosen bishop of the most important see in North Italy by popular acclamation and ordained in spite of his personal wishes. Even more strange is the case of Synesius, a Neo-platonist and a man of letters who was chosen bishop of Ptolemais in Lybia mainly on account of his patriotism and as a bold defender of the rights of his fellow-citizens.[1]

The Christian bishop was, in fact, the dominant figure in the life of the time. His position was something entirely new, for which no precedent can be found in the old religion of the city-state or in the priesthoods of the oriental mystery religions. Not only did he possess enormous religious prestige as the head of the Christian Church, but he was the leader of the people in social matters also. He occupied the position of a popular tribune, whose duty it was to defend the poor and the oppressed and to see that the strong did not

[1] In the case of St. Augustine's successor we have an instance of a more regular and ecclesiastical type of election, and the report of the proceedings which has been preserved in St. Augustine's letters (ccxiii) shows how closely the procedure resembled that of a civic assembly.

abuse their power. He alone stood between the people and the oppression of the bureaucracy. He was not afraid to withstand an unjust law or to excommunicate an oppressive governor, and the life and correspondence of St. Ambrose or St. Basil or Synesius or St. Augustine himself shows how frequently a bishop was called upon to intervene between the government and the people, and how fearlessly he performed his duty. On one occasion it is recorded that the prætorian prefect was so offended by St. Basil's freedom of speech that he declared that he had never in his life been spoken to in such a manner. "No doubt," replied St. Basil, "you have never met a bishop."

In the same way, it was the bishop rather than the city magistrate who inherited the civic tradition of popular oratory. While the Forum and the Agora were silent, the Churches resounded to the applause and exclamations of crowds who were still swayed by the voice of the orator. In St. John Chrysostom's homilies *On the Statues,* delivered to the people of Antioch when the fate of their city hung in the balance, we hear the last echo of the great Hellenic tradition of oratory which goes back to the golden age of Athenian democracy. And if the sermons of St. Augustine lack the classical grace of his great Syrian contemporary, they are no less interesting as examples of genuine popular oratory adapted to the simpler and less refined tastes of an ordinary provincial audience.

The Church was also taking the place of the state as the organizer of charity and of the support of the poor. Every church had its *matriculum,* or list of persons in receipt of regular relief, and enormous sums were spent in every kind of charitable work. All over the Empire, hospitals, orphanages and hostels for travellers were being built and endowed; so that the basilica was often the centre of a whole quarter which lived by and for the Church. Thus the Church stands out in this dark age as the one hope of humanity both spiritually and materially. It saved the individual from being entirely crushed under the pressure of the servile state and it opened to him a new world of social and spiritual activity in which the free personality had room to develop itself.

Hence, when the final collapse of the imperial government in the West took place the bishop remained the natural leader of the Roman population. He was the representative of the old secular culture as well as of the new spiritual society, and it was through him, above all, that the continuity of Western civilization was preserved.

> *Comme aux jours de scandales*
> *Un vieil évêque en sa ville assiégée*
> *Par des Alains, des Goths ou des Vandales*
>
> .   .   .   .   .
>
> *Son esprit las porte un double fardeau*
> *Derrière lui sur le mur noir et froid*
> *La vieille louve allaite les jumeaux*
>
> *Et devant lui Jésus meurt sur la croix.*[1]

In the fourth century, however, these diverse traditions were still far from being completely reconciled with one another. There were, in fact, three distinct elements—and even three distinct societies—in the culture of the later Empire.

There was the new religious society of the Christian Church, with its tradition of independent spiritual authority; there was the city-state, with its Hellenistic traditions of intellectual and material culture; and there was the Empire itself, which more and more was coming to represent the oriental tradition of sacred monarchy and bureaucratic col-

[1] R. Salomé: *Notre Pays*, p. 52.

lectivism. The Church no longer held itself entirely aloof from secular society, but it had not yet succeeded in Christianizing it. The civic culture remained pagan in spirit and, to a great extent, in outward form. But while the Church remained hostile to the paganism and immorality of civic life, as seen above all in the public shows and the games of the amphitheatre, she could not refuse to recognize the value of the classical tradition in its intellectual aspects. The Fathers were, almost without exception, men who had passed through the schools of rhetoric and whose minds were steeped in classical literature. St. Basil and St. Gregory Nazianzen had studied at the university of Athens, the centre of pagan culture; St. John Chrysostom was the most brilliant pupil of Libanius, the greatest heathen professor of his time; St. Augustine was himself a professional teacher of rhetoric; while St. Jerome is, of all his generation, the most typical representative of the rhetorical tradition in all its strength and weakness.

Consequently the patristic culture is a blend of Christian and classical elements. The writings of St. Ambrose are as full of reminiscences of the classics as those of a Renaissance scholar. The two Apollinarii, St. Gregory Nazianzen, Paulinus and Prudentius did their best to create a Christian literature based upon classical models. It is true that in the case of St. Augustine we see a gradual evolution from the Christian humanism of Cassiacum to the anti-Pelagian severity of his later years. But it is easy to exaggerate the change, since he continued to realize the educational value of classical literature and to acknowledge his sympathy with the Platonic tradition. Nor must we attach too much importance to the famous vision in which St. Jerome was condemned as "a Ciceronian and not a Christian". After all, as he himself observed, when Rufinus taxed him with inconsistency, it was only a dream, and in spite of his visionary experience he ultimately returned to his Plato and Cicero.

This fusion of the old culture with the new religion was of incalculable importance for the future of Europe. Although the secular culture of the ancient city passed away with the city itself, the patristic culture lived on in the Church. The course of studies which St. Augustine had described in his treatise *On Christian Doctrine* became the programme of the monastic schools, and bore fruit in men like Bede and Alcuin. Thanks to the work of the Fathers and of their age, the medieval world never entirely lost touch with the tradition of ancient civilization.

In the same way the relations between the Church and the imperial order were becoming more intimate in this period. Although the Church condemned the cruelty and the oppression of the weak which were so prevalent during the later Empire, she was wholly favourable to the principles of authority and hierarchy on which the imperial order was based. The ideal of a world state which should secure universal peace and the reign of law was thoroughly in harmony with Christian principles; indeed, the political unity of the world empire seemed to be the natural counterpart of the spiritual unity of the Catholic Church. Hence we find a new attitude to the Empire in the Christian literature of the fifth century—an appreciation of the positive services which Rome had rendered to the cause of humanity and a realization of the common unity of Roman civilization—*Romania,* to use Orosius's expression—as something greater and more permanent than even the political structure of the imperial state. At the beginning of the fifth century the Spaniard Prudentius already anticipates Dante's belief in the providential mission of the Roman Empire as a preparation for the world religion of Christianity. "In all parts of the world," he writes, "men live to-day as members of the same city and children of the same hearth. Justice, the forum, commerce, the arts and marriage unite the inhabitants of the most distant shores; from the mingling of so many different bloods, a single race is born. Such is the fruit of the victories and triumphs of the Roman Empire: thus has the road been prepared for the coming of Christ."[1]

But this new far-seeing spirit of Christian patriotism was confined to a small aristocratic circle, to men of letters like Prudentius and Paulinus of Nola. The average man who felt the heavy hand of the tax-gatherer and the quarter-master could not take so wide a view. The pessimism and defeatism of Salvian is no doubt inspired by moral preoccupations, but he also expresses the criticism and discontent which were widespread in the society of the time. The Church, as the representative of the poor and the oppressed, could not be a whole-hearted supporter of the existing order. In the West, at least, the adherents of the old religion still claimed to be the true representatives of the national Roman tradition, and attributed all the misfortunes of the Empire to its abandonment of the service of the gods. It was natural that patriotic Romans, like Symmachus, should feel that the destinies of Rome were inseparably bound up with the religion of Numa and Augustus. To them the new religion, like the new capital, was an oriental *parvenu,* fit only for slaves and foreigners. A true Roman, they felt, could not abandon the temples and altars which had become doubly sacred from their glorious past.

In fact, even at the end of the fourth century the situation of Christianity in the West was still not altogether secure. Many of the highest positions in the Empire were in the hands of pagans, and the prætorian prefect, Flavian Nicomachus, took advantage of the revolt of Arbogast and Eugenius in 392–394 to reinstitute pagan worship and to reconsecrate the city by a solemn lustral purification. More-

---

[1] Prudentius: *Contra Symmachum,* 582–91. Cf. *Peristephanon,* II, 419 *seq.* The same idea appears in the anonymous *De Vocatione Gentium,* II, xvi, and is developed at greater length by St. Leo, *Sermo* lxxxii. It had, however, already appeared in the East, though in a less specifically Roman form, in the writing of Eusebius (esp. *Theophany,* III, i–ii) and in the Apology of Melito of Sardis.

over, the events which followed the victory of Theodosius only served to justify the criticism of the pagans. The reign of the miserable Honorius witnessed a continuous series of disasters, and if, as Claudian hoped, the conservative party could have found an able leader in the person of Stilicho, it is possible that there might have been yet another pagan reaction.

But this was not to be. Stilicho fell, and his fall was followed by that of Rome itself. To pagan and Christian alike it seemed the end of all things—in St. Jerome's words, "the light of the world was put out and the head of the Empire was cut off". It is true that Alaric's raid on Rome was not in itself decisive; it was an episode in a long-drawn-out tragedy. Every year the tide of barbarism rose higher and fresh territories were overwhelmed. It is the tendency of modern historians to minimize the importance of the invasions, but it is difficult to exaggerate the horror and suffering which they involved. It was not war as we understand it, but brigandage on a vast scale exercised upon an unwarlike and almost defenceless population. It meant the sack of cities, the massacre and enslavement of the population and the devastation of the open country. In Macedonia the Roman envoys to Attila in 448 found the once populous city of Naissus empty save for the dead, and they were forced to camp outside. In Africa, if a city refused to surrender, the Vandals would drive their captives up to the walls and slaughter them in masses so that the stench of their corpses should render the defences untenable.

"The mind shudders," wrote St. Jerome, "when dwelling on the ruin of our day. For twenty years and more, Roman blood has been flowing ceaselessly over the broad countries between Constantinople and the Julian Alps, where the Goths, the Huns and the Vandals spread ruin and death. . . . How many Roman nobles have been their prey! How many matrons and maidens have fallen victims to their lust! Bishops live in prison, priests and clerics fall by the sword, churches are plundered, Christ's altars are turned into feeding-troughs, the remains of the martyrs are thrown out of their coffins. On every side sorrow, on every side lamentation, everywhere the image of death."[1]

And this was in 396, when the storm was only beginning. It was to last, not for decades, but for generations, until the very memory of peace was gone. It was no ordinary political catastrophe, but "a day of the Lord" such as the Hebrew prophets describe, a judgment of the nations in which a whole civilization and social order which had failed to justify their existence were rooted up and thrown into the fire.

.   .   .   .   .

It was in this age of ruin and distress that St. Augustine lived and worked. To the materialist, nothing could be more futile than the spectacle of Augustine busying himself with the reunion of the African Church and the refutation of the Pelagians, while civilization was falling to pieces about his ears. It would seem like the activity of an ant which works on while its nest is being destroyed. But St. Augustine saw things otherwise. To him the ruin of civilization and the destruction of the Empire were not very important things. He looked beyond the aimless and bloody chaos of history to the world of eternal realities from which the world of sense derives all the significance which it possesses. His thoughts were fixed, not on the fate of the city of Rome or the city of Hippo, nor on the struggle of Roman and bar-barian, but on those other cities which have their founda-tions in heaven and in hell, and on the warfare between "the world-rulers of the dark æon" and the princes of light. And, in fact, though the age of St. Augustine ended in ruin and though the Church of Africa, in the service of which he spent his life, was destined to be blotted out as completely as if

[1] *Ep.* lx; cf. *Ep.* cxxiii, written in 409 on the destruction of Gaul.

it had never been, he was justified in his faith. The spirit of Augustine continued to live and bear fruit long after Christian Africa had ceased to exist. It entered into the tradition of the Western Church and moulded the thought of Western Christendom so that our very civilization bears the imprint of his genius. However far we have travelled since the fifth century and however much we have learnt from other teachers, the work of St. Augustine still remains an inalienable part of our spiritual heritage.

IV

THE SOCIOLOGICAL FOUNDATIONS OF MEDIEVAL CHRISTENDOM

THE study of medieval religion is of primary importance alike for those who wish to know something of the history of Christianity and for those who wish to know something of the history of Europe. We cannot understand the religious problems of the world today unless we understand something of their roots in the history of the past, and we cannot understand the secular history of modern Europe unless we understand something of that long thousand-year process of change and growth which we name the Middle Ages. Those thousand years saw the making of Europe and the birth and rebirth of Western culture; they also witnessed the creation of that socio-religious unity that we call Christendom, and the gradual penetration of our culture by Christian beliefs and Christian moral and intellectual standards. They have left an indelible imprint on both our social and religious life. They have helped to make us what we are, whether for good or evil, and even those who know and care nothing about medieval religion and culture are themselves the unconscious heirs of medieval traditions.

It is true that the continuity of the European tradition was apparently broken by the conscious reaction against medieval culture and religion which occurred in the age of the Renaissance and the Reformation. The Humanists regarded the Middle Ages as a "dark age" of Gothic barbarism, while to the Reformers they seemed an age of spiritual darkness and superstition which hardly deserved to be called Christian at all. Both parties agreed in wishing to cut out the last thousand years of history and to start again from classical culture, on the one hand or from primitive Christianity, on the other.

Nevertheless, this break with the past was far less complete than the makers of it believed. The Reformers and their successors the Puritans were not early Christians but post-medieval men who had a great deal in common with their immediate ancestors, while in the case of the Renaissance it is becoming increasingly clear that the new thought of the new age, whether it be the philosophy of Descartes, the science of Copernicus, the drama of Shakespeare, or the poetry of Spenser, has far closer links with the medieval past than their makers themselves realized. Thus the sixteenth-century reaction against the Middle Ages did not really destroy the continuity of our culture, or wipe out our debt to the Middle Ages; what it did do, however, was to place an artificial barrier between the European mind and medieval culture and religion, and to make the appreciation of the latter impossible for centuries. This was not peculiar to Protestant Europe, it was almost equally characteristic of Catholic countries in the post-Renaissance period, and it was not until the coming of the Romantic movement in the nineteenth century, and of the new school of history that had its origin in Romanticism, that a genuine appreciation of medieval culture became possible. In fact the Protestant prejudice against medieval religion seems to have been a less serious factor than the intellectual and æsthetic prejudices of Humanism.

In other words, the real cause of modern misunderstanding and lack of appreciation of the medieval tradition has been cultural rather than religious. No doubt it is always difficult to understand the religion of the past without some knowledge of contemporary culture, but this is, above all, the case in periods like the Middle Ages, when religion and civilization were so closely united that religious institutions were the main organs of culture and almost every form of social activity possessed a religious sanction. In order to understand the religion of such an age, it is not enough to study it theologically in its essential dogmas and religious principles; it is also necessary to study it sociologically with reference to the changing complex of social traditions and cultural institutions into which it became incorporated. The social form of a religion depends not only on the inner logic of its moral doctrine but on the type of culture with which it is united, and also on the way in which its union with the culture is achieved.

In the first place, a religion may grow up, as it were naturally, with the life of a people, so as to seem inseparable from it. This is the normal process in the case of primitive cultures, and it is often the case with more advanced types of civilization, as with the Greeks and the Romans.

In the second place, a religion may enter a fully formed culture from without, as Buddhism entered China or as Islam conquered Persia in the seventh century. Finally, we have the case of a religion already fully formed entering a culture which is still in process of formation and thus itself becoming one of the constituent elements of the new culture that is growing up.

The history of medieval Christianity is the classic example of this third process, and it is exceptionally worthy of study not only on account of its influence on the development of the modern world but also owing to the peculiar complexity of the process itself and the number of factors that are involved. For Christianity did not come to the peoples of northern and western Europe out of the void, as Islam came to western Asia in the seventh century: it already had a long history behind it. To the Northern barbarians Christianity was the religion of the Roman Empire and to them it stood for the Latin order with all its heritage of law and civilization. To the Romans themselves, however, even in the fifth century, Christianity was comparatively a newcomer. It came to them from the Hellenistic East, its mother tongue was Greek and its theological development was mainly the work of the Greek Fathers and the Greek councils. And, finally, the Greek-speaking world itself possessed a double tradition. The schools of Athens still maintained what they believed to be the pure Hellenic tradition of culture and looked on Christianity as a modern intruder, while the Christians themselves claimed to be the spiritual heirs not of Greece but of Israel, and of an historic religious tradition which had its roots deep in the past of the ancient East.

All these currents of religious and social tradition met in the main stream of Catholic Christianity which now flowed out into the barbarous West. Was this great river of sacred tradition to become lost in the swamps and forests of the North? or was it destined to irrigate the virgin soil and make it capable of bearing as rich a spiritual harvest as the highly cultivated lands of the eastern Mediterranean? That was the great problem which the early medieval Church had to face, and its essential preoccupation was how to preserve its spiritual inheritance so that nothing was lost and so that the same faith and the same life should be followed by the Northern barbarians, as by the educated classes of the later Roman Empire.

Many different views have been held as to the measure of success which the Church attained in carrying out this task, but there can be no question of the vast moral effort that it entailed or that this effort was one of the great formative spiritual powers in the making of Western culture. At first sight it might seem that the task was almost a hopeless one, for the German warrior and the Celtic peasant looked on the world with other eyes than did the civilized Roman magistrate or the Greek scholar or the oriental ascetic, and there was nothing in their culture and their social traditions that could help them to understand the religious thought and the moral ideals of the civilized Christian world of the patristic age. Thanks, however, to the existence of the Church and the ecclesiastical order, Christianity was not abandoned passively to the influences of its social environment. It had its own principle of order, its own social organs and its own civic traditions. Christianity was not merely a doctrine and a life; it was above all a society, and it was the organic unity and continuity of the Christian society which preserved the spiritual identity of the Christian religion. Had it not been for the existence of this firm juridical and institutional organization, there can be little doubt that Christianity would have changed its nature in changing its social environment and would have become to all intents and purposes a different religion.

We can trace the beginnings of such a development in the Arianism of the Goths and the Vandals, which was due to political rather than theological causes and which seemed likely to become the national religion of the Germanic peoples. Even in the short period of their existence these churches seem to have acquired a distinctive national type of organization. Their clergy were attached to the chief and to the army rather than to diocesan sees, and St. Ambrose describes the Gothic bishop, with his barbaric necklaces and arm bands, going before the army like the priests of the old heathen cult whose place he had taken.[1] Modern German writers such as Stutz[2] and von Schubert regard this "nationalization" of Christianity as typical not only of the Gothic Arians but of the Germanic peoples in general, and as supplying a key to the changes in ecclesiastical organization and institutions which marked the new age. No doubt other influences were at work. For example, the development of lay ownership of churches and abbeys, which these writers

[1] *Ep.* 10, cap. 9.
[2] V. Stutz, *Geschichte des Kirchlichen Benefizialwesens,* i, 1895, and his articles *Eigenkirche, Eigenkloster* in Hauck's *Realenzyklopaedie,* 1913.

regard as a typically German institution, like the private sanctuary of Nordic paganism, seems rather to be due to the tendency of landlords in the Roman Empire no less than in the barbarian kingdoms to treat the churches on their domains as private property.[1]

Nevertheless, the differences in sociological structure that distinguished the barbarian kingdoms from the old imperial society could not fail to have an effect upon the Church itself. The Church of the Empire had been a Church of the cities. Its organization was based upon the municipal system, and the bishop played an even more important part in the life of the city than the civil magistrates themselves. The larger the city, the greater, as a rule, was its ecclesiastical importance, as for example in Egypt, where Alexandria was the one great ecclesiastical centre and its bishop exercised almost absolute control over the whole country.

Among the Germanic and Celtic peoples, however, social conditions were entirely different. City life was non-existent, and the only units were the people or the tribes and their subdivisions.

Here the Church could find no fixed centres on which to concentrate its action and from which to radiate its influence. It was forced either to create such centres for itself through the foundation of monasteries which in the Celtic countries became the basis of the whole ecclesiastical organization, or else to make the tribal territory or petty kingdom itself an episcopal see, as we find in many cases in Anglo-Saxon England.

In the Frankish kingdom, where the city and the city territories survived, the Church was able to preserve its old basis of organization, but even here the decay of urban life and the disappearance of the old provincial organization

[1] Cf. Lesne, *Histoire de la propriété ecclésiastique en France*, i, 70–8 (1910).

destroyed the cohesion and autonomy of the hierarchy and brought them into dependence on the royal power. The Church became more and more closely bound up with the life of the State. It ceased to be simply a province of the international Christian society and became a territorial Church (or what the Germans call a *Landeskirche*). This development was not, however, entirely due to the growing dependence of the Church upon the State; it also involved a corresponding dependence of the State upon the Church. The trained bureaucracy which had been the strength of the later Roman Empire no longer existed, and the clergy was the only remaining class which could provide the State with educated councillors and administrators.

In all the Western kingdoms the bishops took a leading part in the royal councils and national assemblies, while in England and Spain the kings and secular magnates also took part in the ecclesiastical councils; indeed in Visigothic Spain the great councils of Toledo were true national assemblies which exercised legislative and judicial functions even in secular affairs. In Gaul the Merovingian kings, for all their violence and tyranny, recognized what they owed to the support and co-operation of the Church and paid their debt by lavish grants of territory and all kinds of fiscal and judicial privileges. It has been calculated that by the close of the seventh century the Church owned no less than a third of the soil of France, and whatever may be the exact proportion there can be no doubt about the enormous agrarian wealth of the Church or of the change in social and economic conditions that this involved. The Church had ceased to be urban and had become agrarian. All over western Europe it had sunk its roots deep in the soil. The bishops had become great territorial magnates who governed their estates like princes and levied not only tithes and ecclesiastical dues but also tolls and taxes.

Obviously the royal power could not afford to neglect

so vast a source of wealth and power. From the beginning the Frankish rulers attempted to control episcopal elections for their own ends until in the eighth century bishoprics and abbacies were used by Charles Martel in order to provide his relatives and partisans with rich benefices even though they were laymen. This marks perhaps the lowest point to which the Frankish Church descended. It had become so closely identified with the territorial State that it had lost its spiritual autonomy and seemed bound to be swamped by the flood of barbarism in which it was sinking.

It was clear that the territorial Church did not possess sufficient inherent vitality to react against its barbaric environment and to create a genuinely Christian culture. For this it was necessary that there should be a reassertion of the universalist principles that were of the very essence of Western Catholicism—a revival alike of the ecclesiastical order and of the ecclesiastical culture, both of which had been impaired by the centrifugal development of the national or territorial Churches of the West. The reassertion of these principles was due to the intervention of the Papacy, which had retained its position as the organ of unity and the guardian of Catholic tradition in spite of the fall of the empire. Rome still remained nominally a part of the empire and thus held an intermediate position between East and West, between the Byzantine and the Germanic worlds. But while the Papacy enjoyed immense prestige in the West both as the heir of the traditions of imperial Rome and as the Apostolic See of St. Peter, it had no power to make its authority effective and consequently was little more than the shadow of a great name in the ecclesiastical affairs of the new kingdoms. It is true that the Bishop of Arles held the title of Vicar of the Holy See and thus supplied a link and a channel of communication between Rome and the Frankish Church. But Arles was itself little more than a relic of the Roman past and had no real importance for the territorial Frankish Church. Between that Church and Rome stood not the Apostolic Vicar but the Frankish monarchy. No reform was possible without the consent of the latter, and since the royal interests were bound up with the existing abuses the problem of reform was not an easy one.

There was, however, a third element in the Western Church which provided the Papacy with the assistance of which it stood in need. Without the help of the monks the Papacy could never have made its authority effective in the West, while without the Papacy, the monks could have had little influence in the ecclesiastical organization of the territorial Churches. It was the union of these two powers which determined the evolution of the medieval Church and restored its universal character. Purely oriental in its origins, the monastic life had been adapted to the needs of Western society and to the spirit of the Latin tradition by the work of St. Benedict, and it was the biographer of St. Benedict, the great monastic Pope, St. Gregory, who first enlisted the monks in the service of the universal Church by entrusting to them the mission to the Anglo-Saxons which was the starting point of a new era in the history of the Western Church. Already in the North the Irish monks had begun to combine the monastic life with an active missionary propaganda, both in Britain and Gaul, and Anglo-Saxon monasticism inherited their traditions as well as those of St. Benedict and St. Gregory. But it was the Roman and Benedictine traditions which gave the new movement its organizing power and its spirit of Christian universalism. The Celtic monks on the continent had striven to emancipate their monasteries from the control of the local bishops and to make them independent of the territorial Church organization, but the Anglo-Saxons brought this autonomous tradition into direct relation with the centre of Catholic unity.

They were a disciplined army under the orders of the Holy See for the service of the universal Church.

The climax of this development is to be seen in the work of St. Boniface, which marks an epoch in the history both of the territorial Churches of northern Europe and in that of the Papacy. For at the very moment when these new prospects were opening to the Papacy in the West, its traditional connection with the East was being threatened by the iconoclastic policy of the Isaurian emperors. Gregory II, the greatest of the Popes between Gregory I and Nicholas I, showed a remarkable insight into the significance of what was taking place. In his letters to the Emperor Leo III, the genuineness of which has recently been vindicated by Professor Caspar, he appeals from the verdict of the Emperor and the civilized Byzantine world to the new Christian world that was coming into existence in the West, and in order to show his independence of the former he announced his intention of leaving Rome on a journey "to the innermost lands of the West" in order to baptize the princes of the newly converted nations that were bringing the first fruits of their faith to the see of Peter.[1]

This journey never actually took place, but even if the Pope had visited Germany in person he could not have associated himself more decisively with the work of St. Boniface than he had already done in 722 when he con-

---

[1] "The whole West", he writes, "has its eyes fixed on our poor person, and though we are unworthy of it yet they have great confidence in us and in him whose image you would destroy and abolish, the Holy Apostle Peter whom all the kingdoms of the West reverence as a god upon earth." "You know your empire cannot insure control of Rome, apart from the city itself, on account of the nearness of the sea and the ships, but the Pope has only to depart three miles from Rome and he has no more to fear from you. It grieves us that the savages and barbarians are becoming tame while you, the civilized, are becoming barbarous. The whole of the West brings the fruits of its faith to the Prince of the Apostles, and if you send troops for the destruction of the images of St. Peter, look to it. We warn you beforehand that we are innocent of the blood that you will shed. Be it on your own head." Cf. Caspar, *Geschichte des Papsttums*, ii, 656–62, and more fully in *Zeitschrift für Kirchengeschichte*, vol. 52, pp. 29 *seq.* (1933).

secrated Boniface as bishop for Germany at large in immediate dependence on the Holy See, and gave him a mandate for the conversion of Germany. This mandate was still further extended by Gregory II's successors, who made Boniface their legate and personal representative and charged him not only with the organization of the German Church but also with the reform and reorganization of the territorial Church of the Frankish kingdom as a whole. Thus St. Boniface had a double mission to fulfil, and the way in which he carried out his immense task almost gives him the right to be called the founder of medieval Christendom. In Germany he was the creator of a new Christian order, not only by the formation of the new German sees, but still more by the introduction of Anglo-Saxon monks and nuns and their establishment as colonists of Christian culture in the newly converted territories of central Germany. In Gaul he was the apostle of Catholic universalism and canonical order, and the reformer of the secularized and territorialized Church of the Frankish kingdom.

But while his apostolate in Germany was amazingly fruitful, his efforts for the reform and reorganization of the Frankish Church were only partially successful. The keystone of his programme of reform was the restoration of the old metropolitan organization and the centralization of the Church by the direct subordination of the metropolitans to Rome. As he wrote to the Archbishop of Canterbury after the great Pan-Frankish reform council of 747: "We decreed and acknowledged in our synod that we would preserve to the end of our lives Catholic faith and unity and subjection to the Roman Church; that we would be subject to St. Peter and his vicar; that we should convoke a synod every year; that the metropolitans should seek their palls from the Holy See, and that in all things we desired to follow the precepts of St. Peter, according to the canons, so as to be numbered among the sheep entrusted to him. . . . We decreed that it was the business of a metropolitan in accordance with canon law to examine the conduct of the bishops subordinate to him and their care for their people; and that he should warn the bishops on coming from the synods to meet the priests and abbots in his own diocese and to enjoin them to keep the decrees of the synod. And each bishop, if there is anything in his diocese that he has been unable to correct or amend, should bring it before the archbishop in the presence of all at the synod, in the same way as the Roman Church bound us with an oath to do when we were ordained, that if I saw priests or people wandering from the way of God and was unable to correct them, I should always faithfully point it out for correction to the Apostolic See and the vicar of St. Peter. For so, if I am not mistaken, all the bishops should make known to the metropolitan whatever they are unable to correct in their people, and he in like manner to the Roman pontiff, and so they will be clear of the blood of lost souls."[1]

The realization of such a programme would have cut across the existing organization of the territorial Church and would have deprived the State of the *de facto* control over the Church which it actually enjoyed. The interests of the Frankish State were opposed to the direct subjection of the metropolitans, and through them of the national Church, to the authority of Rome, yet, as Boniface himself recognized, it was only by the favour and help of the temporal power that the work of reform and evangelization could be carried on. "For without the protection of the prince of the Franks," he writes to Bishop Daniel of Winchester, "I can neither rule the people nor defend the priests or the deacons, the monks or the handmaidens of God, nor without his mandate and fear can I forbid the rites of the pagans in Germany and their sacrilegious idolatry."[2] And thus

[1] S. Boniface, *Ep.* 78.   [2] S. Boniface, *Ep.* 63.

the final result of Boniface's work was a compromise, which secured the reform of the Frankish Church, and its closer union with Rome, but which did so, not by the canonical machinery of metropolitans and provincial synods and the appellate jurisdiction of the Holy See, but by the direct co-operation of the temporal power and through its controlling influence on the territorial Church.

In fact Boniface was the unwilling agent of that alliance between the Papacy and the Frankish monarchy which did so much to determine the course of medieval history, but which was fatal to Boniface's own ideal of ecclesiastical independence. It led to the separation of the Papacy from the Byzantine Empire and to the conversion of the Frankish monarchy into the Holy Roman Empire. It abolished the national particularism of the territorial Churches and restored the universalism of the Roman tradition. But it did so not by freeing the Church from secular control, but by the transformation of the territorial Church into an imperial Church and by a still more intimate fusion between the ecclesiastical and the territorial systems.

As we have seen, there were two fundamental elements in early medieval culture: the barbarian peoples and the Catholic Church. One found its organizing principle in the Germanic monarchies, the other in the Roman see. According to the ideas of Gregory the Great and St. Boniface, these two powers should co-operate with one another for the conversion of Europe and the creation of a Christian order, an ideal which was at least partially realized in Anglo-Saxon England during the seventh and eighth centuries and in the realm of the Franks during the co-operation of Boniface and Carloman. With the foundation of the Carolingian Empire, however, the universal Church no longer had to deal with a number of local monarchies but with a single power which itself claimed to represent the principle of Christian universality and Roman order. The Catholic

Church found its secular counterpart in the Holy Roman Empire; indeed something more than that, for the Carolingian State was itself a quasi-religious unity which asserted its sacred character and tended to regard the Church as nothing more than its theological and liturgical organ. The Carolingian Church was thus the State-Church of a Church-State. It had been freed from the worst abuses of the territorial system only because the secular power had become conscious of its ecclesiastical responsibilities and had itself acquired an almost ecclesiastical position. It was in fact the territorial Church regularized and universalized to such a degree that the Papacy itself had been subordinated to its principles. Charlemagne was able to complete the Bonifacian reforms and to restore the canonical organization of metropolitans and provincial councils, because he himself now stood at the apex of the ecclesiastical pyramid, and the Pope was under his control.

But though the Carolingian system militated against the independence of the Church and the effective supremacy of the Holy See, it nevertheless helped to strengthen both the Christian and Latin elements in Western culture. It created a new social unity in which the Germanic and Latin elements were combined organically instead of coexisting as two independent traditions, as had been the case in the earlier Germanic kingdoms. Here again the influence of monasticism was of the highest importance. The Carolingian abbeys were, apart from the royal palace, the only real centres of culture in the empire. And their culture was almost entirely a Latin one, founded on the traditions of the Western Fathers and the old schools of rhetoric, as transmitted through the influence of Cassiodorus and Columbanus and the monastic schools of England and Ireland.

Thus throughout the darkest period of the Middle Ages the Western Church preserved its intellectual tradition almost unimpaired, and the contemporaries of the Vikings possessed all and more than all of the patristic learning of the contemporaries of St. Gregory. No doubt the monasteries were themselves exposed to the danger of secularization, but to nothing like the same extent as the rest of the Church. While the parish priest might be an ignorant peasant and the bishop a territorial magnate, who lived the same life as the secular nobility of his time, the monk, if he was to remain a monk at all, had to preserve his social and spiritual identity. The territorial Church was a Christian hierarchy artificially superimposed on an alien social foundation and almost absorbed by it, but the monastic society was Christian in its essential social constitution and governed its whole life, at least in theory, not on the usages of its social environment but on the written law of the Benedictine Rule. As Dom Ursmer Berlière has written: "The Benedictine abbey was a little state which could serve as model to the new Christian society which was arising from the fusion of conquered and conquering races, a state which had religion for its foundation, work restored to honour as its support, and a new intellectual and artistic culture as its crown."[1]

It is characteristic of medieval religion that its spiritual ideals found expression in a definite sociological organism. The spiritual life was not a vague aspiration, or an abstract idea; it was a *life* in the full sense of the word, an organized pattern of behaviour which was embodied in distinct institutional forms and possessed an autonomous economic existence, which rendered it at least potentially independent of its social environment.

Thus whenever the territorial Church tended to become a part of the machinery of the territorial State or to be overwhelmed by its barbaric environment, as occurred alike in the seventh and the tenth centuries, the monasteries

[1] U. Berlière, *L'Ordre Monastique*, p. 41.

preserved the principle of an autonomous Christian order which again and again proved to be the seed of new life for the whole Church. For the modern historian the great importance of monasticism may seem to lie in its services to culture, in its preservation of the tradition of letters and of classical literature. But from the point of view of medieval religion it is the essential monastic ideals of asceticism and otherworldliness and fidelity to the Rule that are the important matters, for it was these that gave it its spiritual independence, its powers to resist the pressure of its environment and to initiate movements of religious reform. That is why in the tenth century Cluny is of more importance than Reichenau or St. Gall in spite of their greater culture and artistic activity, and why in the twelfth century Clairvaux is, in turn, more important than Cluny.

Now this monastic ideal of spiritual independence and of the strict observance of the Benedictine Rule had a natural affinity with the traditional Roman ideal of ecclesiastical independence under the sovereignty of the papacy and of the strict observance of the canon law. As Dr. Coulton writes, "[the monks] formed of all ecclesiastical bodies, that one whose general interests and ideals coincided most exactly with that of the papacy. They were truly a papal militia; *schola servitii* with a *lex sub qua militat*. What the military colonies were to the Roman Empire, the monasteries will now be to what we may call the papal empire".[1] And as Gregory the Great first called in the monks to help in the conversion of the new peoples and Gregory II and his successors allied himself with Boniface and the Anglo-Saxon monks for the conversion of Germany and the reform of the Frankish Church, so now Gregory VII allied himself with Cluny and with the monastic reformers of Lorraine and Italy in order to achieve his vast

[1] G. Coulton, *Five Centuries of Religion*, i, p. 217.

plan for a movement of universal reform and for the freeing of the Church from its bondage to the empire and the territorial system.

The struggle of the Investitures was an attempt to reverse the whole development of the territorial Church from its roots in the rights of patronage and advowson and the lay proprietorship of ecclesiastical benefices (the principle of the *Eigenkirche*) to its consummation in the ecclesiastical imperialism of the Carolingian and Saxon emperors. It aimed, whether consciously or unconsciously, at undoing the work of Charlemagne, at cutting through the dense growth of custom and prescription that bound Church and State together and at reconstituting the Church as a free and universal spiritual society under the sovereignty of the Apostolic See with its own code of laws and its own independent legislative and judicial system.

Such a programme could only be realized on condition that the Church as a whole was animated by the same spirit of uncompromising unworldliness and ascetic fervour that characterized the movement of monastic reform. And to a considerable extent this was actually the case. The great reforming Popes—Leo IX, Gregory VII, Urban II, and many more—were themselves monks and found their allies and helpers among the leaders of the monastic reform or their disciples—St. Peter Damian, Humbert of Moyenmoutier, St. Gerald of Ostia, St. Hugh of Cluny, St. Anselm of Lucca and St. Anselm of Canterbury. Moreover, their work resulted in imparting to the medieval Church as a whole something of the monastic spirit, as we see, above all, in the enforcement of the celibacy of the clergy, which did so much to set apart the clergy as a separate body whose interests were bound up not with their family or their locality but with the ecclesiastical order of which they formed part. The best of the medieval prelates, men such as Anselm, and Thomas of Canterbury, and Hugh of Lincoln—to quote examples from this country alone—were patterns of asceticism and of all the monastic virtues, and the fact that such men could hold the highest offices in the Church is enough to prove that the reforming movement was not without fruit.

Nevertheless, the full programme of the reformers was incapable of complete and immediate realization. It was impossible to reverse the whole development of the last five centuries by any changes, however revolutionary. It would have involved a fight to the death, not only with the State Church of the Empire, but with the whole feudal world of Western Europe. The only way in which it could have been achieved was through the solution which was accepted for a moment by the unworldly idealism of Pascal II in the Concordat of Sutri: that is to say, by the Church's renunciation of all the endowments and privileges which it held of the secular power in return for the renunciation by the empire of its rights of investiture and control over ecclesiastical appointments—in other words, the separation of Church and State. Such a drastic solution, however, aroused the opposition of all the vested interests in the imperial Church and was almost immediately abandoned by both parties. The solution that was actually reached by the Concordat of Worms was a compromise which left the roots of the problem untouched, a temporary truce which allowed the combatants to organize their forces before taking up the struggle again.

The conflict had, however, brought an immense gain of prestige to the Papacy and a corresponding loss to the Empire. Henceforward there was no question as to the international unity of the Church or the supreme authority of the Holy See. The Investiture controversy was much more than a mere quarrel about ecclesiastical benefices: it involved new social principles and ideals that transformed the whole character of European society. For the first time the unity of Christian Europe, which had been implicit in the earlier medieval development, found explicit recognition in an international organization that was really effective and genuinely international. The Holy Roman Empire, especially in the age of Charlemagne, had, it is true, attempted to realize this ideal, but it had failed owing to the inherent weakness of the medieval State. The Church and the Church alone possessed the power and authority necessary to unite the semi-barbaric peoples of Europe in a universal society. The medieval Church was not a group of individuals, united by common religious opinions, like a modern sect; it was a true *kingdom* with its own constitution and its own laws, it embraced a much larger part of human life and imparted a far wider citizenship than did the fragmentary and barbarous feudal State. It undertook far greater social responsibilities, inasmuch as all that we now think of as "the social services", the care of the poor and the sick, and the protection of the weak, belonged to its province instead of to that of the State. Above all, it was the true organ of culture. Education, thought, literature and art all existed primarily in and for the Church, and it was the representative of the tradition of Latin civilization and order, as well as of the Christian ideals of charity and brotherhood.

Even in political matters the Papacy came to exercise a kind of international authority, as the supreme court of appeal and source of justice. It established a kind of protectorate over the lesser kingdoms and the outlying territories of Christendom, as, for example, in Spain and Hungary, whose rulers took a special oath of allegiance to the Pope as "Knights of St. Peter" and vassals of the Holy See. And though this did not involve any direct political control, it emphasized the new position of the Papacy as the head of Christendom and the president of a sort of Christian league of nations.

Nevertheless, these things were not the ends for which the reformers themselves had fought. Nothing could be more unhistorical than the traditional idea of Gregory VII as an ambitious ecclesiastical politician like Boniface VIII or Julius II. He was, above all, a reformer, and a champion of the spiritual freedom of the Church, and his ideals were fundamentally the same as those which Augustine set forth in *The City of God*. He was inspired not, as a modern historian has said, by "magnificent visions of ecclesiastical grandeur" but by a profound sense of the degradation of the secularized Church of his age and the urgent need of reform.

"I cry, I cry and I cry again," he writes in his final appeal to the Christian world in 1084. "The religion of Christ, the true faith, has fallen so low that it is an object of scorn not only to the Devil but to Jews and Saracens and pagans. . . . These keep their law, as they believe it, but we, intoxicated with the love of the world, have deserted our law." "Every day we see thousands of men go to death for the sake of their lords, but if a few are found to resist the wicked, men do not help them but regard them as fools and madmen." "I have laboured with all my might that the Holy Church, the Bride of God, our mistress and our mother, should recover her honour and remain chaste, and free and Catholic."[1]

Thus the reforming movement was at once revolutionary and conservative. It broke with the tradition of the Carolingian Empire and the territorial Church in the name of canonical principles and of patristic and apostolic ideals. But, in the circumstances of the age, this led to revolutionary innovations in the relation between Church and State and to the active intervention of the spiritual power in the social life of Christendom. The distinction and independence of Church and State, of the spiritual and temporal powers,

[1] *Mon. Greg.* 572, etc.

was recognized in theory as it had been in patristic times. But the concrete situation had been entirely changed by the territorialization of the Church on the one hand, and by the desecularization of the State on the other. In the patristic age the Church, for all its power and privileges, was a secondary society that existed in the Roman Empire in the same way as the Church exists in the modern State; as St. Optatus writes: "The State is not in the Church, but the Church is in the State; that is, in the Roman Empire." But in the Middle Ages this relation was reversed, and it could really be said that the State was in the Church. The latter was the primary and fundamental social reality, and the State was merely a subordinate institution charged with the office of preserving peace and order. This conception, which is of fundamental importance for the understanding of medieval ideas, was clearly recognized by medieval canonists and theologians but proved extremely difficult to apply to the complex realities of the feudal state. For the symmetry and completeness of medieval social theory was contradicted by the inextricable confusion of ecclesiastical and secular rights and jurisdictions that characterized the actual conditions of medieval society. The Holy Roman Empire was one attempt to achieve a synthesis, the papal theocracy was another. Neither was completely successful. The ideal of Catholic universalism could not make the realities of the territorial system conform to strict canonical principles, while the territorial Church, in spite of its centrifugal tendencies, could not deny the validity of these principles or refuse allegiance to the universal ideals that were inherent in the Catholic tradition. This unresolved tension explains the ultimate disruption of medieval Christendom. Yet, at the same time, it is an essential condition of the religious achievement of the Middle Ages. The Middle Ages were not the ages of Faith in the sense of unquestioning submission to authority and blind obedience. They were ages of spiritual struggle and social change, in which the existing situation was continually being modified by the reforming energy and the intellectual activity that were generated by the contact between the living stream of Christian tradition and the youthful peoples of the West.

V

CHURCH AND STATE IN THE
MIDDLE AGES

IT is impossible to understand the history of the medieval
Church, and its relations with the State and to social
life in general, if we treat it in the analogy of modern
conditions. The Church was not only a far more universal
and far-reaching society than the medieval State, it possessed many of the functions that we regard as essentially
political. As F. W. Maitland used to insist, it is difficult
to find any definition of a State which would not include
the medieval Church, while the State under feudal conditions often lacked prerogatives and functions without
which we can hardly conceive a State existing.

In the modern world the Church is regarded as essentially a voluntary society of limited membership and limited
functions, while the State is the fundamental fact that dominates every aspect of social life and leaves little room for
any independent activity. The chief problem for us is how
to safeguard that minimum of social autonomy without
which neither the spiritual society of the Church nor natural
social organisms like the family can fulfil their functions.
In the early Middle Ages, however, the State had neither the
physical power nor the moral prestige to make such universal claims. It was sufficiently occupied with the problems
of bare existence. It occupied a precarious position between
the universal society of the Church, which possessed a
monopoly of the higher culture, and the lesser territorial
units which possessed so large a measure of local autonomy
as to leave few political prerogatives in the hands of the
nominal sovereign. Accordingly, in the Middle Ages the

75

ultimate social reality was not the national kingdom, but the common unity of the Christian people of which the State itself was but the temporal organ and the king the divinely appointed guardian and defender.

Thus to the medieval mind the distinction was not between Church and State as two perfect and independent societies, but rather between the two different authorities and hierarchies which respectively administered the spiritual and temporal affairs of this one society, as Stephen of Tournai puts it in a well-known passage: "In the same city and under the same king, there are two peoples and two ways of life, two authorities and two jurisdictions. The city is the Church —the king is Christ. The two peoples are the two orders in the Church—the clergy and laity. The two ways of life are the spiritual and the bodily. The two authorities are the priesthood and the kingship. The two jurisdictions are the divine and human laws."[1]

Of course, Church and State retained their formal distinction. Indeed from one point of view there was a far greater sociological difference between the two societies than there is today, since they inherited distinct cultural traditions and historical backgrounds. The Church looked back to the civilized past and preserved the tradition of Latin culture and of the Roman order, while the medieval State was the heir of the barbarian conquerors and represented the social traditions and institutions of the Germanic peoples —Franks, Saxons, Lombards and Visigoths. Thus medieval society has a twofold aspect. On the one hand, there was the ideal unity of Christendom which united all the baptized as a single people and family against pagan barbarians of the North and the civilized Moslem world to the South, and on the other there was the centrifugal tendency of

---

[1] *Cf.* Carlyle, *History of Political Theory,* ii, 198 and iv, 166. This passage is quoted by M. Maritain in *Primauté du Spirituel* in such a way as to suggest that the city is humanity and that the two peoples are the Church and State, but this is not what Stephen of Tournai says.

national and local particularism which divided Western
Europe into a confused mass of warring principalities.

It is, however, important to remember that these two
aspects of medieval society are not to be identified simply
with the ecclesiastical and political categories in the narrower
sense. The medieval king was not merely the representative
of the old barbarian national monarchies; he was also an
officer in the Christian society, who stood in a peculiarly
close relationship to the Church and was consecrated by
religious rites. However much the reforming canonists might
insist on the essential distinction between the royal and the
sacerdotal unctions, the medieval monarchy possessed a
sacred and quasi-sacerdotal character which it never entirely
lost until the end of the old regime at the close of the
eighteenth century.

This religious conception of the State and the royal office
found its most complete expression in the Carolingian
Empire, which had so vast an influence on the subsequent
development of medieval culture. The Carolingian Empire
was the most complete political expression of these unitary
and universalist tendencies of which we have spoken. It was
regarded by Charlemagne and his successors and their
ecclesiastical advisers not merely as a Frankish imperial
State, nor even as the revival of the Roman Empire in the
West, but as the political organ and counterpart of the
Catholic Church. In the words of Charlemagne's letter to
Leo III, the emperor is "the representative of God who has to
protect and govern all the members of God"; he is Lord and
Father, King and Priest, Leader and Guide of all Christians.

This unitary conception of Christian society naturally
tended under a strong emperor to result in a kind of
Cæsaropapism like that of the Byzantine Church. The
emperor was regarded as the apex of the pyramid of
Christian society, the culminating point at which the ecclesiastical and civil hierarchies converged. The Carolingian

Empire, however, unlike the Christian Empire of the East, possessed no trained bureaucracy or class of lawyers and was consequently far more dependent on the assistance of ecclesiastics in the task of civil administration than was the Byzantine State. Alike in the Carolingian Empire and its Germanic successor, the bishops were the mainstay of the government, and the ecclesiastics of the royal *capella* under the archchaplain formed the imperial chancery and the central organ of administration. Thus, on the one hand, the emperor was continually interfering in purely ecclesiastical matters in virtue of his general prerogative as defender of the faith and overseer of ecclesiastical order, while, on the other hand, the clergy took a leading part in the secular administration of the Empire. Under such conditions the distinction between Church and State tended to become blurred and effaced. The Church was a State Church and the State was a Church State, membership of the latter involved membership of the former and the personnel of government was practically the same. Moreover, this state of things was not peculiar to the Empire. Similar conditions obtained in Anglo-Saxon England and in Capetian France. In both the principal advisers and ministers of the king were churchmen. In England bishops and abbots sat along with secular magnates in the Witan and the shirecourt and enacted secular and ecclesiastical laws jointly with them, while in France the king owed much of his influence to his control of bishoprics and his position as lay abbot of some of the richest and most important monasteries.

Thus the Carolingian or unitary conception of the relations between Church and State tended at once towards the secularization of the former and the clericalization of the latter. Bishops and abbots became great secular magnates who administered justice in their own courts and led their own soldiery into battle, and at the same time the Church became involved in the feudal development of society so that ecclesiastical benefices and offices were treated in the same way as lay fiefs and were used by princes to endow their relatives and followers.

The history of the medieval Church consists largely of a series of attempts to remedy this state of affairs and to emancipate the spiritual power from lay control and exploitation by a return to the traditional principles of canonical order. The first of these attempts was the reform of the Frankish Church by St. Boniface, but it took place in the eight century, before the foundation of the Empire and the rise of the feudal state. The second was the reforming movement of the Carolingian period which has been dealt with exhaustively, so far as the control of church property is concerned, by Emile Lesne in the second volume of his History of Ecclesiastical Property in France.[1] This movement was directed primarily against the secularization of abbeys and church property and in defence of the rights of the bishops against the metropolitans, on the one hand, and the royal power, on the other. Partly owing to the limited character of its objectives, it failed to achieve any lasting success, and its most important result was the forgery of the False Decretals and the false capitularies which had so great an influence on the subsequent history of canon law.

Incomparably more important was the third movement of reform which culminated in the work of Gregory VII and the great struggle of the Investitures. Considered from the ecclesiastical point of view this Gregorian movement was a reformation in the strict sense of the word, an attempt to return to the purer tradition of the ancient Church and to restore strict canonical discipline. But it had no less revolutionary consequences in the political sphere, since it involved new conceptions regarding the relations between the temporal and spiritual power. The reformers inherited

[1] E. Lesne, *Histoire de la propriété ecclésiastique en France*, vol. II. Pub. in three parts, 1922–8.

the same unitary conception of Christian society that the Carolingians had already possessed. But whereas the latter regarded the Emperor as the supreme head of the whole Christian people and the bond of unity between Church and State, the new reformers proclaimed the absolute transcendence and superiority of the spiritual power and demanded that the temporal power should be subordinated to the spiritual, in the same way as the body is subordinated to the soul.

Thus the essential principle of the reforming movement was the same as that which has inspired the whole development of canon law in medieval and modern times—that is to say, the constitution of the Church as a free and universal spiritual society under the sovereignty of the Apostolic See, with its own code of laws and its own independent legislative and judicial system. But owing to the special circumstances of medieval society it was impossible to maintain this principle without at the same time claiming a large measure of control and responsibility in regard to the temporal power. Given the unitary conception of Christian society, the programme of the reformers involved the substitution of the Pope for the Emperor as *de facto* head of Christendom and leader and judge of the Christian people. From the modern point of view there is an immense gulf between these two sides of the reforming programme, but the reformers themselves were hardly conscious of it and we find in their writings the claim to spiritual freedom and the claim to supremacy over the temporal power treated as inseparable parts of a single whole. Thus, in the famous propositions, known as the *Dictatus Papae,* which seem to have been drafted by Gregory VII himself in 1075, we find claims like that of the right of the Pope to use the imperial insignia, to depose Emperors and to release subjects from their oath of allegiance to unjust rulers asserted at the same time and, as it were, in the same

breath with strictly canonical principles like the supreme
authority of the Holy See, the irreformability of papal
decrees, and the power of the Pope to depose or absolve
bishops.

In the same way the imperialist writers do not restrict
themselves to defending the purely political prerogatives of
the temporal power, to rejecting the right of the Pope to
depose rulers or to use the temporal sword against their
opponents. They in their turn claim for the Emperor the
right to interfere in purely ecclesiastical matters, not merely
in the appointment of bishops, but even in the affairs of the
Papacy, so that the Emperor was the ultimate arbiter in the
government of the Church, and had the right to control
the election of the Pope and to depose him if he was
unworthy, as in the famous example of the Synod of Sutri
when Henry III deposed the three claimants to the Papacy
and substituted his own nominee.

Thus the struggle between the Empire and the Papacy
concerning the investitures was involved in an almost inextricable confusion which renders it very difficult for the
modern student to judge both parties fairly. It is a profound mistake to read into the history of the early Middle
Ages that opposition between the claims of the national
monarchy and the universal jurisdiction of the Papacy
which was characteristic of the age of the Renaissance and
the Reformation. It was not the new political State with its
ideals of centralized administration and its strongly developed national consciousness that was the enemy which
Gregory VII and his successors had to combat, but rather
the old Carolingian and Ottonian tradition of the Christian
Empire with its universal claims and its theocratic ideal. It
was not until the Church had asserted her claim to freedom
from secular control that the State became conscious of its
proper mission and was able to vindicate its political autonomy. The revival of Roman law which played so great a

part in the medieval political renaissance and the development of the European State was itself the sequel and consequence of the revival of canon law which accompanied the reforming movement. The revival of Roman law was never regarded as a danger by the Roman Church. On the contrary, it was the Papacy that was the first to assimilate the principles of the legal renaissance and it found in them an invaluable instrument for carrying out its task of legal reorganization and centralization. Civilians and canonists were not enemies or even rivals; they were allies in the task of rationalizing and clarifying the complex tangle of political and ecclesiastical relations that constituted medieval society. Indeed the creators of the new State and the new law were themselves for the most part churchmen, as, for example, Roger of Salisbury, Hubert Walter and Henry of Bracton in England.

Moreover, Roman law was in itself regarded as more akin to canon law than it was to the customary law of the feudal State; in the words of an early jurist, it was a sacred thing, *res sanctissima,* and our own John of Salisbury treats the attempt of King Stephen to suppress the teaching of Roman law in England as an act of sacrilegious tyranny like the destruction of the Books of the Law by Antiochus. "This view of the Roman law as a sacred thing," writes Prof. Clement Webb, "is connected with John's deep sense of the spiritual significance of the unity of Christian civilization under the universal Roman law and the universal spiritual jurisdiction of Peter's successor, as a divine ordinance against the separatist tendencies of the different national kingdoms whose ultimate salvation was to be found in force rather than in reason or revelation."[1]

It is true that the Empire no less than the Church stood at least in theory for this ideal of unity and that the Roman

[1] Article on "The Policraticus of John of Salisbury", in *Church Quarterly Review,* Vol. lxxi, p. 341 (1911).

law might well have been used as a weapon by it in its great conflict with the Papacy: indeed it was actually so used by one of the earliest anti-papal pamphleteers—Peter Crassus of Ravenna. Nevertheless, the real strength of the imperialist position lay in its appeal to the theocratic ideals of the Carolingian monarchy; and the new Empire was so thoroughly Germanic and un-Roman in constitution and tradition that the authentic legal tradition of the old Empire as represented by the *Corpus Juris,* remained utterly alien to it in spirit. The Roman Church, on the other hand, had a real affinity and sympathy with the traditions of the civilized Latin world and despised the Germanic Empire as an alien barbaric power. A good example of this attitude is to be seen in Bonizo of Sutri, one of the leading Italian canonists and a supporter of the Gregorian reform. As M. Fournier points out: "This enthusiastic Gregorian professes a real admiration for the Empire, not the Empire of the Carolingians and their successors, but the Empire of antiquity. He regards the Roman Empire as a gigantic monument, erected by ancestors who have spread the glory of Italy far and wide, and he opposes this glory to the state of the Empire in his time ruined by the deplorable anarchy into which its German masters had allowed it to fall—*barbaris servit & suis non utitur legibus.*[1]

Thus it was the Papacy and not the Empire which first applied the revived science of law to the task of government. The development of canon law on scientific principles by Gratian and his successors gave the whole system of ecclesiastical government a rational legal basis such as the medieval State did not as yet possess. While the latter was still feebly

[1] Fournier and Le Bras, *Histoire des Collections canoniques en Occident,* ii, p. 148. Compare Alfanus of Salerno's noble Horatian ode to Hildebrand, the representative of the greatness of Rome against the forces of barbarism.

> *Quicquid et Marius prius*
> *Quodque Julius egerant*
> *Maxima nece militum*
> *Voce tu modica facis.*

groping after the rudiments of an administrative order, the Church was already constituted as an organized international society, complete with a centralized government, a written code of laws and an elaborate system of appellate jurisdiction and representative and legislative assemblies.

The result of this development was to make the Papacy an effective power in the public life of Europe and to give it an international prestige which far outweighed that of the empire or any of the feudal kingdoms. Even in its greatest days under Charlemagne or Otto I or Henry III the power of the Empire had rested in the last resort on its military strength and it was incapable of exerting its influence effectively in Italy, for example, without repeated military expeditions which had much of the character of a barbarian invasion. The superiority of the Papacy, on the other hand, was both moral and intellectual, and even the powers which fought against it were incapable of resisting its spiritual prestige.

While the Holy Roman Empire gradually lost its old position as the representative of the unity of Christendom and became an unwieldy and disorganized mass of feudal territories, the Papacy became the head of Christendom in every sense of the word and exercised an effective super-political authority over the peoples of Western Europe. This authority was not confined to the ecclesiastical sphere: it extended to every side of social life and human activity. It judged the affairs of kingdoms, it organized crusades against the infidel and the heretic, and excommunicated and deposed rulers who had offended against the common law of Christendom. In fact, the medieval Papacy combined two distinct but related functions. It was the ruler of the Church in the strict sense, the representative of Peter and the head of the ecclesiastical hierarchy, but it was also the leader and judge of Christian society in the widest sense—the president of a kind of European league of nations and the supreme authority in international law.

This twofold aspect of the medieval Papacy finds its most complete expression in the pontificate of Innocent III, who is often regarded as the greatest of the medieval popes. On the one hand, he completed the organization of the medieval Church according to the principles of the new canon law, and the great Lateran Council of 1215 marks the final triumph of the programme of ecclesiastical reform that had been initiated under Leo IX and his successors. But, on the other hand, he was the head and ruler of Christendom, who realized the ideal of the unity of Christian civilization under a single head far more completely and effectively than Charlemagne or Otto the Great.

In the words of the Bible which he took as the text of his sermon on the day of his consecration, he was "set over the nations and over the kingdoms to pluck up and to break down, to destroy and to overthrow, to build and to plant. . . ." He judged between nation and nation, between kings and peoples, between the rival claimants to the Empire, between the King of France and the King of England and between the latter and his rebellious subjects. These two aspects of the papal authority were not, however, distinguished by Innocent III himself as different in kind or principle. Both of them were derived from the claim of the Pope to be Vicar of God on earth. In the words of Innocent, the Pope was the judge of the world, "set in the midst between God and Man, below God and above Man"; he is "the representative of Him to whom the earth belongs with all that it contains and all its inhabitants"; he is a priest after the order of Melchizedek, at once priest and king who unites in his person the fullness of all power and authority.

It is obvious that so wide a claim to universal authority leaves little room for the modern distinction between the two autonomous orders and societies of Church and State.

But I have already pointed out the medieval conception of Christian society was essentially a unitary one. State and Church were not two independent organisms but different orders or functions in a single society of which the Pope was the head. Yet at the same time this did not mean that the two orders were confused or identified with one another. The prince had his own proper function in Christian society and his own rights within the sphere of its exercise. The authority of the Pope was a super-political one, which transcended that of the king without destroying it.

This is what the Pope means when he replies to Philip II's protest against his intervention in the quarrel with King John that he is not judging about the fief but about sin. In other words, he intervenes in a political quarrel because moral issues are at stake of which he is the divinely appointed guardian. Nevertheless, this distinction did not involve any serious limitation on the *plenitudo potestatis* of the Papacy, since the royal office according to medieval ideas was essentially a moral one. The king, like the priest, was an officer in the one Christian society, though his office was essentially lower and limited to temporal affairs. Consequently, the secular power was little more than a feeble reflection of the spiritual. To quote Innocent III again: "As the moon derives its light from the sun to which it is inferior alike in quantity and quality, in position and in effect, so too the royal power derives the splendour of its dignity from the power of the Pope."[1] And in another passage he writes: "Princes and kings each have their separate province or kingdom, but Peter is supreme over all alike in the extent and fullness of his power, for he is the Vicar of Him whose is the earth and the fullness of it."[2] And again: "Christ left to Peter not only the universal Church, but the whole world to govern."[3]

[1] Migne, vol. ccxiv, col. 377.
[2] *Op. cit.*, vol. ccxvi, p. 4, col. 1013.
[3] *Op. cit.*, vol. ccxiv, col. 759.

Here the papal claim seems to transcend the limits between the spiritual and temporal spheres and to involve a universal and all-embracing supremacy which is theocratic in the strict sense. Nevertheless this claim is already implicit in St. Bernard's famous image of the two swords both of which belong by right to Peter though the use of the material sword is delegated to the State and exercised by it under the Church's discretion—*ad nutum sacerdotis*. This passage is all the more significant because St. Bernard was by no means a "curialist" in the later sense of the word. He was acutely conscious of the worldliness and corruption of the Church of his age and of the temptations to ambition and avarice that accompanied the growing power of the Curia. Yet for all his outspoken criticisms there is no more fervent supporter of the universal claim of the Papacy than St. Bernard.

Anti-papal controversialists sometimes make use of the passage from *De Consideratione* in which he exorts the Pope to regard himself as one of the bishops and not their master, and the Holy See as the mother not the mistress of the Churches. Yet this very passage, taken in its entirety, is perhaps the most sublime expression of the ideal of the supremacy of the spiritual power that has ever been written. The Pope, he says, should be "the hammer of tyrants, the father of kings", "the dispenser of laws and canons", "the Light of the world, the Vicar of Christ, the Christ of the Lord, and, last of all, the God of Pharaoh. Understand what I say. When power and wickedness go hand in hand we must claim something for you more than human. Let your countenance be on them that do evil. Let him who fears not man nor dreads the sword, fear the breath of your anger. Let him think that he who incurs your wrath, incurs the wrath not of a man but of God".[1]

[1] *De Consideratione*, IV, vii.

This clearly expresses the fundamental preoccupation which determined the attitude of medieval Catholicism towards the relations between Church and State: the need for some power to defend the cause of justice and the Law of God against the forces of violence and disorder which were rampant in medieval Europe. It is the same preoccupation which dominates the whole life of Gregory VII and finds so poignant an expression in the letters of that great Pope. Nevertheless we must not shut our eyes to the lower and more materialistic conceptions of the theocratic ideal that go far to justifying the criticisms of its opponents. In the eleventh century the cause of the Papacy was defended not only by the disinterested idealism of Gregory VII but by the gross and hateful fanaticism of Manegold of Lutterbach, and in the later period the apologists of the papal *plenitudo potestatis* did not confine themselves to the high spiritual ground of St. Bernard but resorted to the false Donation of Constantine in an attempt to give a formal legal justification for a claim which essentially transcended the whole sphere of politics and required a religious justification if it was to be justified at all.

The fact is that throughout the earlier part of the Middle Ages and down to the emergence of Thomism there was an inevitable confusion between the temporal and the spiritual orders which led to tragic misunderstanding and conflicts. The struggle between the Papacy and the Empire was not a struggle between the Church and the secular State such as we know today. It was a conflict between two parallel forms of the same ideal, between the ideal of a theocratic empire and that of a theocratic church, each of which was inspired by the same vision of an all-embracing Christian society—the City of God on earth.

It is needless to point out how vast was the gulf between this grandiose vision of a universal order and the semibarbaric anarchy of feudal Europe. And the tragic irony

of the contrast was heightened by the fact that these conflicting idealisms were so often used to serve the ends of
selfish ambition.

Similar conditions obtained in Italy, though there it was
the cities rather than the feudal princes which exploited
the situation. There the conflict between the Papacy and
the Empire ultimately developed into a sordid and ferocious
struggle between rival parties and factions in which the
principles for which each side ostensibly stood disappeared
under a complicated growth of civic feuds and vested
interests. It was impossible to take the spiritual issues of
the conflict very seriously when the whole alignment of
the conflicting forces was so obviously determined by the
political and financial interests of the different cities and
classes and when the use of spiritual penalties, such as ex-
communication and interdict, had become so common that
they had begun to lose their effect. Above all, the new
conditions of Italian city life had caused the problem of
the relations of Church and State to assume an altered
character that made the old claims of the theocratic empire
irrelevant. The whole issue was being fought out anew on
the restricted stage of city politics and it made little difference to the result whether the city in question nominally
belonged to the papal or the imperial factions. At the very
moment when the Papacy seemed to have attained a final
and crushing victory over the Empire the secular power
was successfully asserting its independence in the political
microcosm of the city-state. Yet this did not necessarily
mean that the spiritual power of the Church was weakened,
for, though the bishops might lose their political privileges
and the abbeys their lands, the Church found new and
more potent means of asserting her influence through the
evangelism of the new preaching orders and the action
of the lay religious confraternities, such as the Humiliati
and the Third Orders.

At the same time the rise of the new Christian philosophy of St. Thomas at last provided a solid intellectual foundation for the ideal of an autonomous State which does not transcend its proper sphere by theocratic claims. Already in the twelfth century the canonist Huguccio, the teacher of Innocent III, had taught that "both the power of the Pope and that of the Emperor is from God and neither is dependent on the other", but even this principle did not prevent infinite misunderstandings with regard to the proper functions and limits of the two powers. Since the law of nature is also the law of God, men tended to merge the sphere of natural right with that of Christian revelation, as we see in the opening words of Gratian's *Decretum*: "Natural law is that which is contained in the law and the Gospel": and thus to make the Church equally responsible for both. It was left for St. Thomas to define clearly and exhaustively the idea of an autonomous natural order and a natural law and to lay down the principle that "the divine right, which is of grace, does not destroy the human right which is of human reason" (*S.T.*, II–IIæ, Q. x, art. 10). Elsewhere in the commentary on the Sentences he seems to draw the obvious political corollary of this principle when he states that "in matters of civil good, it is better to obey the secular power than the spiritual".[1] Nevertheless, it was centuries before this principle was worked out in detail and made the basis of the classical Catholic doctrine of the two *societates perfectæ*. St. Thomas himself, in the passage to which I have just referred, qualifies his principle by adding: "Unless perchance the secular power is conjoined with the spiritual as in the Pope who holds the summit of both the spiritual and secular power alike, by the ordering of Him who is both Priest and King."[1] Thus, too, we find that the most eminent disciple of St. Thomas in the following generation, Ægidius Romanus, is

[1] In II Sent. dist. XLIV, Q. ii, art. 2.

at the same time the most uncompromising advocate of the theocratic claims of the Papacy in their most totalitarian form. Although he admits that the two powers are distinct, at least in theory, he makes them both alike dependent on the Pope as their ultimate source. For since God is the source of all authority and since there is neither law nor justice save in obedience to Him, it follows that all rights whether political or economic, are ultimately dependent on the authority of God's vicar on earth, and the prince who rebels against the Pope thereby destroys the basis of his own derived and delegated power. And thus the unitary conception of society is no longer restricted to its historic basis, the actual society of Western Christendom, but is extended to the world in general and to humanity as a whole. The kingdoms of the heathen are nothing more than organized robberies with no higher sanction than the reign of force, for outside the Church there is no justice and without justice there is no legitimate authority, whether spiritual or temporal.

Thus the first effect of the new philosophy was to accentuate the universalist tendencies in medieval social doctrine, and we see the same thing on the imperialist side in the case of Dante, that other disciple of St. Thomas. Never, in fact, did the vision of unity that haunted the memory and inspired the imagination of the medieval world receive fuller and nobler expression than in the work of the great Ghibelline poet. But though Dante was profoundly Christian and Catholic it is no longer to the Church that he looks for his ideal of unity as the thinkers of the earlier Middle Ages had done, imperialists no less than papalists. For Dante, the ideal unity was not that of the Church but of humanity, and the Roman Empire was its divinely predestined servant and instrument. Thus the claims of the Empire are based not on its ministerial office towards the spiritual power, but, as he puts it, "on the necessity of human civilization", which cannot realize its essential and natural ends without the peace and order which only political unity can give. Thus the State—at least that ideal and universal State which is the Roman Empire—has not merely an independent foundation in natural right, it has a providential mission towards the human race which is analogous in the natural order to the mission of the Church in the order of grace. Indeed Dante goes farther still and claims for the State its own peculiar grace, so that there are two chosen peoples and two holy cities.

This Messianic idealism inspires the whole of Dante's work and finds its earliest and clearest expression in the Fourth Treatise of the *Convivio,* where he sets forth the high mission of the Roman people, which rests not on force or conquest but on the divine vocation and election. "For since," he writes, "there never was nor ever shall be, a nature more sweet in the exercise of lordship, more firm in its maintenance nor more subtle in acquiring it than the the nature of the Latin folk (as may be seen by experience) and especially that of the hallowed people in whom the high Trojan blood was infused, God chose that people for such office." "And if we consider her more advanced youth when she was emancipated from the guardianship of royalty by Brutus the first Consul even until Cæsar the first supreme prince, we shall find that she was uplifted not by human but by divine citizens into whom was inspired not human but divine love, in their love of her. And this could not, nor might not be, save for some special end, purposed by God in so great an infusion of Heaven." "Wherefore we need demand no more in order to see that a special birth and special progress thought out and ordained by God, was that of the holy city. And verily I am of firm opinion that the stones that are fixed in her walls are worthy of reverence and the soil where she sits more worthy than man can preach or prove."[1]

[1] *Convivio,* trans. Wicksteed, Treatise iv, chs. 4 and 5.

This exaltation of the State as such, with its idealization of ancient Rome and its intense Latin patriotism, is almost unique in medieval literature and is much farther removed from the main tradition of medieval thought than the theocratic totalitarianism of Ægidius Romanus and his successors, though it is even more dependent on Thomism in its philosophical presuppositions. Nevertheless, though it had no direct influence on the main current of medieval thought, it is profoundly significant from the historical point of view, since it embodies in an individual synthesis the diverging tendencies of medieval thought and Western culture. While, on the one hand, it looks back to the medieval ideal of a universal society and to the tradition of Charlemagne and the Holy Roman Empire; on the other, it looks forward to the Renaissance, to the national monarchy and to the new humanist culture. Looked at superficially, Dante's thesis may seem to differ little from the old theocratic imperialism. There is much in Dante's *De Monarchia* which recalls Jordan of Osnabrück's apologia for the Empire, even to the latter's extreme conclusion "that as the Roman Church is the Church of God so the Roman Empire is the kingdom of God". Yet when we look deeper we see that with Dante the whole character of the imperialist theory is changed by being brought into relation with the Thomist doctrine of natural law and the Aristotelian social theory, on the one hand, and with the new political consciousness and lay culture of the Italian city state, on the other. It marks a definite break with the unitary theory of society which had dominated the previous five centuries, though the revolutionary character of the change was obscured by the fact that Dante's political hopes were still fixed on the universal Empire of the past and not on the national monarchy of the future. By an unfortunate fatality the country of St. Thomas and Dante, the one country of medieval Europe which was far enough advanced in culture to acquire complete political self-consciousness, lacked the historical conditions for national self-determination, and consequently Dante's intense Italian patriotism was forced to ally itself incongruously with its natural enemy, the alien power of Germanic imperialism. On the other hand, where historical conditions were favourable to the rise of the national monarchy, as in France and England, the state of culture was not sufficiently advanced for the Church to disentangle herself from her political commitments and for the State to fulfil its own proper functions without the Church's help. Consequently in northern Europe the relations between Church and State were still dominated by the old unitary conception of society, which now tended to find national forms of expression, a state of things which prepared the way for the ultimate dissolution of religious unity and the rise of the national Churches in the sixteenth century.

VI

THE THEOLOGICAL DEVELOPMENT
OF MEDIEVAL CULTURE

THE transformation which religion underwent in passing from the ancient to the medieval world was, as we have seen, mainly a sociological one. It was not accompanied by any revolutionary change in doctrine such as those that took place at the Reformation, or even those which marked the breaking away of the oriental Churches from the Church of the Empire. In matters of dogma medieval religion is characterized, above all, by its conservative spirit. It had inherited from the patristic age an enormous mass of theological learning, and its chief problem for centuries was how this learning was to be preserved and assimilated. Hence the impersonal note that marks the theological literature of the early Middle Ages. As the Abbé Tixeront writes: "They did not believe that it was possible to renew or to advance the progress of doctrinal exposition, after the geniuses that had preceded them. They classify, they codify, they give their correspondents solutions and explanations; they hold councils for the reform of morals, but they remain rather on the surface of dogma. And one cannot be surprised when one considers the times in which they lived. It was no small thing in such an age and in such an environment merely to preserve the past and to instruct the terrible neophytes who were entering the Church in the elements of the catechism."[1]

Hence the student of medieval religion has constantly to be on his guard against confusing patristic and medieval thought. There are, of course, popular writers who do not attempt to make any distinction, and who are prepared

---

[1] J. Tixeront, *Histoire des dogmes*, iii, 324.

to treat the whole development of Catholic thought from the age of Tertullian and Cyprian to that of Bossuet as "medieval". But even scholars who fully realize the immense gulf that divides the ancient from the medieval world are often careless in this respect and describe ideas or beliefs as characteristic of the Middle Ages when they are in reality only the medieval echoes or repetitions of pure patristic tradition. Indeed, the development of early medieval thought was so overshadowed by that of the patristic age that it is by no means easy to distinguish its original features. It is, however, important to remember that the expression "Medieval Catholicism" is commonly used to describe three phrases of religious development which are in point of time as far from one another as we ourselves are from the Reformation.

First, there is the religion of the later Roman Empire, which we may call Patristic Catholicism. Secondly, there is the religion of the Dark Ages, the age of the conversion of the barbarians. Thirdly, there is the religion of the twelfth to the fourteenth centuries, which are often regarded as the central period of the Middle Ages but which were also, as Père Mandonnet and Prof. Haskins have pointed out, essentially an age of the renaissance of European culture.

Moreover, we must also remember that in none of these periods was Catholicism or any form of Christianity the only European religion; in each of them it had rivals to contend with, and rivals which changed from age to age.

In the first age the ruling classes were still largely pagan and the Fathers of the Church had to meet the criticisms of highly educated men who despised Christianity as an upstart oriental superstition that was a stranger to the glorious traditions of classical civilization, while at the same time they had to combat the attacks of numerous heretical sects, Arians, Donatists, Priscillianists and the rest, as well as the still more fundamental challenge of the Manichean dualism.

In the second age the scene has entirely changed. Heresy is practically non-existent in the West, the old educated paganism is dead, and the Church has herself become the representative of the traditions of classical culture in so far as they survive. But paganism is still strong, and threatens the Church, both from within and from without: from within, by the masses of uninstructed and half-converted peasants and barbarians who had found themselves Christians, as it were without knowing it, owing to the conversion of their landlords and chieftains; from without, by the warrior peoples of the North and the East, whose attacks again and again threatened to destroy the new Christian culture that had been painfully and laboriously built up in the West.

Finally, in the third age, Catholicism has emerged victorious, and the Church has become the mistress and teacher of Western society. Nevertheless, her position is not uncontested. The revival of trade and town life was accompanied by a new current of Manichean influence from the East through the Balkan peninsula; while the movement for ecclesiastical reform, in spite of its fundamental orthodoxy, contained explosive elements which sometimes attained an unorthodox and revolutionary character, as, for example, with the Waldenses and the Franciscan Spirituals. Moreover, the expansion of Christendom brought the Church into contact and conflict with the thought of the Moslem world, which in the twelfth century still possessed a strong centre of diffusion in south-western Europe. Indeed, the most influential European thinker of the age was not a Christian but the Spanish Moslem, Averroes. Thus once more, as in the patristic age, the representatives of Christian thought had to meet the criticism of highly educated antagonists who were their equals or even their superiors in philosophic and scientific equipment. In fact, it was not until the second half of the thirteenth century that Western

Christendom had attained a sufficiently high level of culture to meet the Moslem philosophers on their own ground.

In this extended sense the history of medieval culture covers a thousand years and throughout that period the development of Catholic thought was characterized by a remarkable unity and continuity.

In each of the three phases of this development, however, Catholic theology possesses distinctive features that are determined by the conditions I have just referred to. The patristic age was the creative period of Western theology and finds its fullest expression in the personality and work of St. Augustine. The second age was the age of traditionalism *par excellence,* and its typical representatives are Gregory the Great and St. Isidore and the Venerable Bede; while the third age was the age of scholasticism—of the systematic dialectical reorganization of the whole traditional material—a work which was begun by Anselm and Abelard and Peter Lombard and which achieved complete expression in the great philosophical synthesis of St. Thomas Aquinas. It is possible to say without exaggeration that whatever was given in the first phase of this development was preserved in the second and was incorporated into the organic unity of scholastic theology in the third. Nothing was lost. All the materials that lie scattered in the writings of the Fathers—in sermons and commentaries and controversial treatises—are to be found again built up into the imposing and symmetrical edifice of thirteenth-century scholastic theology.

This organic development was, however, a process that was limited by the frontiers of the Latin-Christian culture and the Western tradition. It did not include Greek-Christian culture and the tradition of the Eastern Church except in so far as these were already incorporated in the teaching of the Latin Fathers. Throughout the Middle Ages East and

West followed a separate line of theological development, and this goes far to explain the division of the Churches and the growing alienation of the Eastern and Western minds. From the first the theological interests of the two halves of Christendom had been different, and while the Christian East was passionately absorbed in the great Christological controversies that tore the Byzantine Church and Empire asunder, the West was far more interested in questions of ecclesiastical order and moral discipline such as those which gave rise to the Novatian and Donatist heresies. It was not until the time of the Pelagian controversy that a theological issue of the first importance arose in the West, and even here the centre of interest was predominantly moral in comparison with the speculative metaphysical problems that absorbed the Greek mind.

These interests continued to characterize the theological development of the Eastern and Western Churches. Theology in the West found its centre and principle of organization in the doctrine of Grace; the sacraments are conceived primarily as Means of Grace, and the Christian life is the Life of Grace. In the East theology is the doctrine of the Consubstantial Word. The sacraments are conceived as mysteries of illumination, and the Christian life is seen as a process of deification by which humanity is assimilated to the immortal nature of the Divine Word. Thus the tendency of Western theology finds its representative and embodiment in St. Augustine, the Doctor of Grace, whose influence dominates the whole medieval development, while the typical representative of Eastern theology is to be found in Origen, who continued to influence the development of Greek Christian thought through the medium of Athanasius and the great Cappadocian fathers, Basil and the two Gregories. There is, however, a striking difference in the fortunes of these two great names, for while St. Augustine remained and still remains the acknowledged Father of Western

LEWIS AND CLARK COLLEGE LIBRARY
PORTLAND, OREGON 97219

theology, Origen was disowned and abandoned by his spiritual descendants and his writings were proscribed as heretical. Indeed, by a strange paradox, the writings of the greatest of the Greek Fathers survive to a great extent only in Latin translations and in Western MSS. which are incomparably more numerous than the Greek MSS. of those parts of the original text of his writings that still remain. This points to an aspect of medieval Western culture which is seldom sufficiently recognized—namely, its openmindedness and its readiness to incorporate foreign elements in its intellectual tradition. For while the Orthodox East was too proud of its high culture and its wealth of theological learning to learn anything from the West,[1] the Latin world remained open to oriental influences and was fertilized by intellectual and spiritual elements drawn from outside.

This is to be seen not only in the wholesale translation and adaptation of Greek theological works which marked the patristic age itself, the age of Rufinus and Jerome and Marius Victorinus, of Hilary and Ambrose, but also in later periods. Even the Dark Ages did not pass without some fresh additions to the intellectual patrimony of the West, notably the translations of the works of the Pseudo-Dionysius, which were of epoch-making importance in the development of the religious thought of the Middle Ages. Finally, in the third period the new developments in Western theology and the immense progress realized by the scholastic movement are closely connected with a new stream of oriental influences, due to the mass of new material brought into the Latin world by the translators of the twelfth and thirteenth centuries. The greater part of this material was scientific and philosophical, but in addition to this main stream of Aristotelian and Arabic influence there

---

[1] The first important translations from Latin into Greek were made by Maximus Planudes, who translated Boethius, St. Augustine on the Trinity and perhaps also the *Summa Theologica* of St. Thomas, about the end of the thirteenth century.

were also a number of translations of the works of the Greek Fathers which had a direct influence on Western theology.

The most important of these was the treatise of St. John Damascene on The Orthodox Faith, the third part of his great theological summa, *The Source of Knowledge*, which is a systematic and authoritative summary of the whole Greek theological tradition. This work was first translated into Latin by Burgundio of Pisa in the middle of the twelfth century and almost immediately, in spite of the attacks of a few bigoted traditionalists, became one of the standard authorities of Western theology, owing to its partial utilization by Peter Lombard in his *Sentences*. It was translated yet again by Robert Grosseteste in the thirteenth century and was used extensively by St. Thomas and the other great scholastics.

This work, together with other translations from the Greek, above all the Pseudo-Dionysian writings with the comment of St. Maximus which were translated again and again during the Middle Ages, had an important effect on Western theology. It led the scholastics—above all, St. Bonaventure and St. Thomas—to revise and complete the Augustinian doctrine of grace in the light of the teaching of the Greek Fathers and thus to create a synthesis of the two great theological traditions of the East and the West. While preserving the broad lines of the Augustinian doctrine, they laid a much greater emphasis on the ontological character of the supernatural order. While Augustine conceives grace primarily as an act of divine power that moves the human will, Thomas considers it, above all, under its essential aspect of the new spiritual principle which transforms and renews human nature by the communication of the Divine Life: in other words, the state of deification of which the Greek Fathers habitually speak. It is not merely a power that moves the will but a *light* that illuminates the mind and transfigures the whole spirit. This combination of the Augustinian tradition with the characteristic doctrine of the Greek fathers is perhaps the greatest theological achievement of the scholastic period, though it is usually little noticed in comparison with their philosophical synthesis. Although it was not always fully accepted or fully understood by the later scholastics, it became the basis of classical Catholic theology, and when the great theological struggle of the Reformation came it was at once the centre of the Protestant attack and the rallying point of the Catholic defence.

Moreover, the influence of Greek religious thought was not confined to the theological schools and to the learned tradition; it had a direct influence on the religious life of the West, owing to the rise of the new schools of mysticism which were intimately connected with the scholastic development. These owed even more than scholasticism in general to the new elements of Byzantine thought imported into the West by the works of the Pseudo-Dionysius and by other neo-Platonic treatises such as the *Liber de Causis* and the *Introduction to Theology* of Proclus, which last was translated by William of Moerbeke, the Flemish Archbishop of Corinth and the friend of St. Thomas. Mysticism was no new religious phenomenon in medieval Europe. The neo-Platonic influences which reached the West in an undiluted form in the thirteenth century were already present from the beginning in Marius Victorinus and Macrobius and Boethius and, above all, in St. Augustine himself. The latter united his neo-Platonic doctrine of contemplation and illumination with a highly individual and essentially Christian mysticism of dynamic charity which became the characteristic note of Western mysticism, in the same way as the closely allied Augustinian doctrine of grace became characteristic of Western theology as a whole.

As Abbot Butler has shown in his work on Western mysticism, this Augustinian mystical tradition is carried on by St. Gregory and St. Bernard, the two most influential spiritual writers of their respective periods, and dominates the spiritual life of the Western Church down to the age of scholasticism.

The mysticism of St. Augustine is intensely personal and possesses a psychological and introspective character that is lacking, or at least extremely rare, in the mysticism of the Christian East. In this respect it is very significant that the great mystical classic of the Eastern Church should be the work of an unknown author who hides his personality under the name of the Areopagite, while the fountain head of Western mysticism should be the great spiritual auto-biography in which St. Augustine makes his own inner life the key to the deep things of God. And these divergent tendencies continued to distinguish the spirituality of the Eastern and Western Church. Eastern mysticism remained impersonal and rarely expressed itself in religious auto-biography or self-revelation, save in Russia during recent centuries; while in the West, from the time of St. Augustine to our own days, spirituality has always tended to possess a highly individual and personal character, and spiritual autobiographies have been the classics of Western mysticism.

But while the mysticism of St. Augustine is one of the most fundamental and permanent elements in the religious tradition of the West, its influence reached its climax in the twelfth century before the coming of the oriental influences to which I have just referred. The twelfth century was a period of immense spiritual and cultural vitality. It has been called the age of the medieval renaissance, but it was a renaissance that was not only intellectual but also religious. If it produced humanists like John of Salisbury, philosophers like Abelard and Bernard of Tours, and poets like Chrétien of Troyes, its greatest, and, on the whole, its most representative figure was an ascetic and mystic, St. Bernard of Clairvaux, the last of the Fathers.

The mysticism of St. Bernard and the whole Cistercian school, above all that of his friend and disciple, William of St. Thierry, is profoundly Augustinian. It is, like St. Augustine's, a mysticism of charity—*theologia cordis*—but to an even greater degree, since with St. Bernard the affective and voluntarist element completely overcomes the neo-Platonic intellectualism which still retained its influence over St. Augustine's mind. To St. Bernard love is better than knowledge, since it reaches beyond knowledge and is its own cause and end. *"Amor praeter se non requirit causam, non fructum. Fructus ejus, usus ejus. Amo quia amo; amo ut amem. Magna res amor, si tamen ad suum recurrat principium, si suae origini redditus, si refusus suo fonti, semper ex eo sumat unde jugiter fluat. Solus est amor ex omnibus animae motibus, sensibus atque affectibus in quo potest creatura, etsi non ex aequo, respondere auctori vel de simili mutuam rependere vicem."*[1]

This is the theme of St. Bernard's sermons on the Canticles, which is one of the classics of medieval religious literature and which had an immense influence on the development of Western mysticism. The allegorical interpretation of Canticles as an epithalamium on the mystical marriage between the human soul and the Divine Word, has its roots deep in the tradition of the Eastern Church with Origen and Methodius of Olympus, and Gregory of Nyssa. But it was through St. Bernard that it first became completely incorporated in the Western spiritual tradition, passing on through Richard of St. Victor and St. Bonaventure to St. John of the Cross

[1] *In Cantica*, lxxxiii, 4: "Love seeks no cause nor end but itself. Its fruit is its activity. I love because I love, I love that I may love. Love is a mighty thing, if so it returns to its own principle and origin, if it flows back to its source and ever draws anew whence it may flow again. Love is the only one of all the senses, movements and affections of the soul, by which the creature can answer to its creator and repay like with like."

and the mystics of the seventeenth century, both Catholic and Protestant. This is one of the aspects of medieval spirituality that is least sympathetic to the modern mind, which is apt to regard the mystical Eros as a perversion of, or a substitute for, sexual passion. But the medieval Christian, whether philosopher or mystic, viewed the matter from a diametrically opposite point of view. To him, divine love was the reality and human love the shadow. The cosmic process has its origin in the overflowing of the love of God which is the act of creation and finds its motive force in the desire by which all creation seeks to return to its source. And hence sexual passion is but a blind and perverted form of the universal force which finds its true, conscious and normal expression in the love of God.

This philosophy of love, which is implicit in the whole thought and life of St. Bernard, had been developed in its full metaphysical implications by the Pseudo-Areopagite in his treatise on the Divine Names.

"By all things", he writes, "is the Beautiful and the Good, desired and loved and chosen to be loved; and because of it and for its sake those that are lower love those that are higher by attraction, and those that are of the same rank love their equals in communion, and the higher love the lower by forethought and kindness, and each loves its own by coherence; and all things by desiring the Beautiful and Good do and will whatsoever they do and will. Further it may be truly said that the very Cause of all things, by reason of the overflow of His Goodness, loves all, creates all, perfects all, holds all together, turns all to Himself; and the Divine Love is the Good and of the Good and by reason of the Good. For that Love itself, working the good of existing things, pre-existing overflowingly in the Good, did not suffer Him to remain in Himself without fruit, but moved Him to creation, by the overflowing which is generative of all things."

"And let us not be afraid of this name of Love [Eros] or be perturbed by what anyone may say against it. For the theologians seem to me to treat the words Charity and Love [Agape and Eros] as equivalent, and preferred to reserve love in the absolute sense for divine things, on account of the misplaced prejudice of the vulgar. For though Love in Itself is spoken of in the divine sense not by us only, but by the Oracles [the Scriptures] themselves, the multitude, not comprehending the oneness of the divine name of Love, fell away, as might be expected of them, to a divided, material, and partial conception of love, which is not true love, but a shadow of Love itself, or rather a falling away from it."[1]

Thus the devotional mysticism of St. Bernard and his school, especially William of St. Thierry, finds its philosophical complement in the mystical metaphysics of the Pseudo-Areopagite, and it was the union of these two traditions which gave birth to the great development of speculative mysticism in the later Middle Ages. The earliest contact between the two traditions took place in the twelfth century with Hugh and Richard of St. Victor. It is true that the works of the Pseudo-Areopagite had been accessible in the West ever since the ninth century, when they were first translated by Hilduin of St. Denys. But apart from the outstanding exception of John Scotus Erigena, whose mystical neo-Platonism had singularly little influence either on his contemporaries or his successors, the Dionysian writings had no real importance for Western thought until the sudden awakening of interest in the twelfth century, which shows itself in the successive commentaries on the book of the Celestial Hierarchies, produced by Hervé of Deols, 1110–30, by Hugh of St. Victor about 1137, and by John Sarrazin, who died in 1180. But even in the case of Hugh of St. Victor the Dionysian influence is slight, and on the whole the Victorine school belongs to the same Western

[1] *The Divine Names*, iv, 10, 12.

Augustinian tradition as the Cistercian school with which they are so closely allied, until we come to the time of Thomas of St. Victor, afterwards Abbot of Vercelli, about 1225, who fused the tradition of the school of St. Victor with the teachings of the Pseudo-Dionysius, which he did so much to popularize by his translations and adaptations.

It was, however, among the great scholastics of the thirteenth century that the influence of the Pseudo-Dionysius and the neo-Platonists attains its complete development. Indeed, so far from scholasticism and mysticism being two hostile and contradictory forces in medieval thought, we may justly describe the introspective mysticism of the later Middle Ages, especially the school of Eckhart, Tauler and Ruysbroeck as "scholastic mysticism", since it is as closely bound up with the scholastic development of the thirteenth and fourteenth centuries as is Thomism itself. In fact, these two movements had a common source in the teaching of St. Albert the Great, who was the teacher both of St. Thomas on the one hand and of Ulrich of Strasburg on the other, from whom in turn the tradition was handed on through Dietrich of Freiberg to Eckhart, who was universally acknowledged as the founder and master of the great school of fourteenth-century German and Flemish mysticism. No doubt it is possible to contrast the neo-Platonism of this school with the Aristotelianism of St. Thomas, so as to make them appear completely opposed to one another. But we must remember that the Aristotelianism of St. Thomas was profoundly impregnated with neo-Platonic elements, and that the Dionysian writings were themselves one of the main formative influences on St. Thomas's thought, while on the other hand Eckhart and Tauler and the rest were themselves students of Aristotle and St. Thomas, and regarded the latter as the great theologian of their order.[1]

[1] Cf. G. Théry in his *Introduction Historique* to Tauler's Sermons, tr. Hugueny, vol. i, 192–7. Paris (1927).

In Eckhart the Dionysian current, reinforced by further neo-Platonic elements derived from Proclus and the Arabs, reaches its extreme development and seems to pass the utmost bounds of orthodoxy and to bring the medieval theological development to a conclusion not far removed from the pure monism of the Vedanta. Nevertheless, as Denifle pointed out long ago, Eckhart is not an oriental pantheist nor a modern idealist; he is a medieval Dominican and a scholastic, and in order to understand his views it is necessary to put them in their historical context and relate them to the intellectual *milieu* in which they originated. Thus when Eckhart asserts that God is all, that creatures are sheer nothing and that it is a fallacy to speak of God as good, he is merely expressing in paradoxical and unguarded language the commonplaces of the Dionysian theology which are to be found in a more balanced but no less complete form in the standard works of Ulrich of Strasburg and of St. Thomas himself.

But whatever may be thought of Eckhart, there can be no question as to the fundamental and entire orthodoxy of his disciples, John Tauler, Henry Suso, Henry of Nordlingen, and John Ruysbroeck, through whom the mystical metaphysics of Pseudo-Dionysius and Eckhart became one of the great sources of spiritual life and inspiration for the later medieval Church. The Friends of God, as they were called, gained adherents among every class throughout the Rhineland and Lower Germany. They included not only learned Dominican theologians, like Tauler, and nuns like the members of the Dominican communities at Töss and Unterlinden, but also secular priests, like Henry of Nordlingen, knights of the Teutonic Order such as Nicholas von Laufen, the Strasburg banker Rulman Merswin, and even peasants and uneducated lay people. Thus the *via negativa* of the medieval mystic, which seems to the outsider to lead to a pantheistic nihilism that leaves no room for any social or moral activity, actually inspired one of the great popular religious movements of the Middle Ages.

It is a striking example—perhaps the most striking instance in history—of the way in which abstract theological thought may affect religious life and social action, and it is the more remarkable when we consider how unfavourable were the circumstances of the time and place for the development of such a highly intellectualized and esoteric type of religion.

But while this mystical movement represents one of the peaks of the medieval religious development, it was by no means the only or the most important one. The movement which had the greatest influence on medieval religion and medieval culture was not the speculative mysticism of the Dominicans but the evangelical piety and the devotion to the Humanity of Jesus that found its supreme expression in the life of St. Francis. This movement has far less connection with the scientific theology of the schools than the other, though one of its most notable representatives, St. Bonaventure, was also one of the greatest scholastic theologians. It was pre-eminently practical, emotional and human, owing nothing to learned tradition or metaphysical ideas, but springing directly from the heart and from personal experience. The greatest religious achievement of the Middle Ages is not to be found in the imposing edifice of its ecclesiastical organization, or in its work of intellectual synthesis, but in its deepening of the spiritual life by a new type of religious experience which had a profound influence on Western Christianity.

One of the most original and suggestive of modern writers on medieval religion, the late Pierre Rousselot, has written of this change as follows: "St. Augustine had considered the struggle for truth and holiness, before all, as a personal affair between the individual soul and God; it is by that

that he had so to speak 'interiorized God'. But he had not in the same way interiorized Jesus. The humanity of Christ remains with him rather in the background. The great novelty of the Middle Ages, their incomparable religious merit, was the understanding and love, or rather one may say, the passion of the humanity of Christ. The Incarnate Word, *homo Christus Jesus,* is no longer only the model to be imitated, the guide to be followed, and on the other hand, the uncreated light that enlightens the interior of the soul; he is interior, even in respect of His Humanity; He is the *spouse* of the soul, who acts with it and in it; He is the friend."[1]

Now this new development of the religious tradition of the West, this new type of Christian sensibility, had already made its appearance in the early twelfth century with St. Bernard. In his teaching the Humanity of Jesus acquires a new significance. In place of the severe figure of the Byzantine Christ, throned in awful majesty as the ruler and judge of men, St. Bernard prefers to dwell on the human likeness of Jesus, the human suffering of His Passion and the human weakness of His Infancy. *"Arbitror Jesum et Joseph, virum Mariae, super genua frequenter arrisisse,"*[2] he writes; and again: "O man, why do you dread the face of the Lord? . . . Say not, like Adam, 'I heard His Voice and I hid me,' for behold He is a speechless infant, and the voice of a child crying is more to be pitied than feared."[3]

This was a new note in Christian literature and one which was to be repeated in countless meditations and hymns, such as the famous *Jesus dulcis memoria* and the *Salve caput cruentatum.* Nor is their influence confined to the Catholic world, it was also the principal inspiration of the Moravian and Methodist hymn writers and of their Christocentric piety. And all this tradition has its source in St. Bernard

[1] *Christus,* ed. V. Huby (1916), pp. 1119–20.
[2] *In Cantica,* xliii, 5.
[3] *Serm. in Nat. Dom.,* i, 3.

and his disciples; above all, the English Cistercians, such as Aelred of Rievaulx, the author of the little treatise *On Jesus a boy of twelve years old*, Isaac of Stella, Gilbert of Hoyland, and Stephen of Sawley.

But it was in St. Francis of Assisi that this new spiritual culture bore its final and most perfect fruit. He is the embodiment in flesh and blood of the new spirit of Western Christianity. Hitherto, though Christianity had been the great formative power in Western culture, it had been a foreign power that was still, as it were, something external to the nature of Western man, its real centres of life were in the monasteries, those camps of the disciplined *militia Dei*, which were scattered over the half-pagan soil of Europe like fortresses in a newly conquered territory. With St. Francis, for the first time we see Christianity breaking through the barriers of race and social tradition and achieving an organic and complete expression in Western man. There is no longer any conflict or inconsistency between religion and culture, between faith and life. The whole man is Christian, and the Christian spirit is united with the Western nature as intimately and inseparably as the union of soul and body.

Nothing could be more spontaneous, less artificial and "cultured" than the genius of St. Francis, yet he is the final fruit of a long process of spiritual cultivation. He marks the coming of age of Christian Europe and the birth of a new consciousness. And hence it is no accident that his advent should have been followed by the appearance of a new Christian art and poetry which, as Walter Pater wrote, "gave visible feature and colour and a palpable place among men to the regenerate race".

It is true that this European renaissance failed to fulfil the spiritual promise of its beginnings, just as the Byzantine culture failed to justify the promise of the earlier Christian centuries. The fourteenth century was an age of deception and disappointment, the age of the Black Death, and the Great Schism, and the Hundred Years War. It saw the partial disruption of the unity of Christendom and the decline of that movement of spiritual reform which had been the soul of medieval culture. From the tenth to the thirteenth century the movement of European culture under the urge of a powerful religious impulse had been centripetal, towards unity and towards the ideals of Catholic universalism. From the beginning of the fourteenth century this tendency is reversed and a centrifugal movement sets in which ultimately culminates in the Reformation and the complete destruction of the religious unity of Christendom. The territorial element in the Church once more reasserted itself as opposed to the tradition of Catholic universalism, whose claims now seemed irreconcilable with the prerogatives of the new national monarchies.

The causes of this change are complex and obscure, since they involve a number of both sociological and religious factors. On the one hand, the renaissance of Western civilization itself strengthened the centrifugal tendency by the new life that it brought to the national cultures. In the early Middle Ages, the nations had been the *gentes,* the descendants of the barbarian tribes that had invaded the empire, while the Church represented the traditions of Roman order and higher civilization. But now this duality of culture had been overcome and the peoples of the West were full of the pride of youth and the consciousness of their latent powers. The State was no longer a confused tangle of feudal and regional units engaged in perpetual war. It had achieved political order, and, in the Western kingdoms at least, national unity. And consequently, when they had overcome the anarchy and separation of feudalism, they felt that the Church, with its international system of jurisdiction and finance and its vast territorial endowments, was a rival that interfered with the full realization of their ideals of sovereignty and autonomy.

But, on the other hand, this nationalist tendency was reinforced by influences of a purely religious character. In the earlier conflicts between Church and State Rome stood for the cause of ecclesiastical reform and spiritual freedom, and the great spiritual reformers, Humbert of Moyenmoutier, St. Peter Damien, St. Anselm, St. Bernard, St. Francis and St. Dominic, were the champions of the Papacy. In the fourteenth century, however, this was no longer the case. The defeat of the Papacy in its first great conflict with the national monarchy, represented by Philip the Fair, had led to its removal from Rome to Avignon, an event which did more than anything else to destroy its supernational prestige. The result was that the reformers themselves began to abandon the cause of the Papacy and to look for help either to the secular power, as did Dante and William of Ockham and the Spiritual Franciscans, or, like Gerson and d'Ailly and Langenstein, to the territorial Church and to the ecclesiastical parliamentarism of the Council of Constance, which, in Dr. Figgis's phrase, "attempted to turn into a tepid constitutionalism the divine authority of a thousand years".[1]

Finally, in the Hussite movement we see the reforming spirit separating itself altogether from the Catholic tradition and coalescing with the spirit of nationalism to produce a great explosion of revolutionary feeling, which already betokens the end of the medieval order.

Thus the breach between the papacy and the spiritual reformers is the vital cause of the decline of the medieval Church and is one of the main factors in the dissolution of the medieval unity and the transformation that passed over Europe in the later Middle Ages. We can trace its influence in later medieval poetry, in Dante and Petrarch and Langland, no less than in theological literature proper.

[1] *From Gerson to Grotius*, p. 35.

But its earliest manifestation is to be found in the extreme wing of the Franciscan Order, the followers of John Peter Olivi and Angelo Clareno, and the disruption of the Franciscan movement is the first symptom of the approaching disruption of medieval Christendom. If the Franciscan movement had fulfilled the promise of its beginnings, it might have played the same part in the later medieval Church as the monastic reformers had done in the Church of the eleventh and twelfth centuries. Actually we see the beginnings of such a development in the missionary activity of the friars, both in Europe and Asia, and in the part that they took in the university movement and in the life of the medieval city. Never, in fact, had the prospects of Christendom seemed more hopeful or its spiritual ideals nearer to their realization than in the thirteenth century. Men believed that they were on the threshold of great events, and they saw in St. Francis the herald of a new age. The extreme form of this apocalyptic tendency is represented by the followers of Joachim of Flora, who announced the coming of the Third Kingdom and the Eternal Gospel. But it was by no means confined to them. It finds expression in most of the great minds of the age, in St. Bonaventure and Mechtild of Magdeburg, in Roger Bacon and Ramon Lull and Dante. Thus St. Bonaventure, who was no Joachimist but rather the representative of the opposite tendency in the Order, regards St. Francis as the type of the new seraphic order of spiritual men, and as the herald of the time "when the city of God will be built up and restored as it was in the beginning in the likeness of the Heavenly City and when the reign of peace will come".[1]

And when St. Bonaventure died he may well have believed that his hopes were about to be realized, for the moment of his death coincided with a last triumph of the ideals of Catholic universalism and spiritual reform. Gregory X,

[1] *In Hexaemeron*, xvi, 30.

perhaps the best, if not the greatest, of the thirteenth-century Popes, had dedicated himself to the cause of peace. He had broken with Charles of Anjou, the evil genius of the Papacy, and had ended the long feud with the Empire; and he now summoned the greatest of all the medieval councils to Lyons in 1274 to restore the unity of Christendom by the extinction of the still older schism with the Greek Church and to carry on the work of ecclesiastical reform with the help of the greatest thinkers of the age. St. Thomas, it is true, died on his way to the Council, while St. Bonaventure himself died during its session, but he could say his *Nunc dimittis,* for he had taken part in the final negotiations with the ambassador of the Byzantine emperor, and had preached at the bi-lingual Mass which celebrated the reunion of East and West.

Nor were the Greeks the only orientals to be present at the Council. Its cosmopolitan importance was marked by the presence of an embassy from Abagha, the Khan of the Tartars, who had been sent to conclude an alliance with the Christians against the Sultan of Egypt, the last independent Moslem ruler. It seemed as though the power of Islam, which had threatened the very existence of Christendom for so many centuries, was itself destined to destruction and that Asia would once more be thrown open to Christianity. Indeed, thanks to the favour of the Mongol princes, it was possible for the Franciscan, John of Montecorvino, to visit the Far East and to found missions and bishoprics in India and China.

Nevertheless, the promise of a new age of Christian unity and progress was doomed to disappointment. The Council of Lyons marks an end, not a beginning. In thirty years all these brilliant prospects were ruined. The union of the Churches had vanished with the death of the emperor who had procured it. The last remnant of Christian dominion in Palestine had disappeared, and the Mongol rulers of

Persia, instead of destroying Islam, had themselves become
Moslems. The spiritual inspiration of the Franciscan movement had become obscured by the sterile controversies
between the parties of the stricter and the laxer observance.
Finally, the Papacy itself had suffered a tremendous defeat
at the hands of the French monarchy and was about to go
into exile at Avignon, thus forfeiting the traditional prestige
that had made Rome for so many centuries the spiritual
capital of the Christian world. Thus the thirteenth century,
for all its great religious achievement and its brilliant cultural
development, proved fatal to the ideal of spiritual unity
that was the centre of the medieval religious development.
The age of St. Francis and St. Louis became the age of
Boniface VIII and Philip the Fair. Men felt, with Dante,
that they had lost a great opportunity and had made a great
refusal, but they were no longer able to find a rallying
point that would unite them in the common cause. Hence,
though the fourteenth century was an intensely religious age,
it was no longer spiritually constructive. It was essentially
an age of transition in which the new forces that were to
destroy the medieval order were already active.

VII

THE MOSLEM WEST AND THE ORIENTAL BACKGROUND OF LATER MEDIEVAL CULTURE

THE history of the early Middle Ages is remarkable for its discontinuous character; indeed, at first sight it seems to consist of a series of false starts. As soon as one set of conquerors have established themselves successfully in their new territory and have begun to repair the devastation they have caused and to build an ordered society, a fresh movement of conquest takes place and all is to do over again. Thus in Italy the work of Theodoric was undone by Justinian, and the work of Justinian by the Lombards; in Ireland and Northumbria the achievements of the new Christian culture were ruined by the Viking raiders; while the Carolingian Empire itself, the most imposing political creation of the early Middle Ages, is hardly established before it begins to fall to pieces, leaving Western Christendom more derelict and more devoid of order than ever before.

But with the coming of the eleventh century European history seems to find a new principle of continuity and a new unity of direction. From the moment when the first barons fenced their earthen *mottes* and raised their rude keeps of wood or stone Western culture has gone on steadily expanding until it has conquered the world and subdued nature itself to serve its ends. It is true that the final stages of this expansion have been so swift and so revolutionary in their effects on human existence that it is difficult for us to realize that they have any organic relation to the society and culture of medieval Europe. We are separated from our own past not only by the changes of the sixteenth century —the Renaissance and the Reformation—but still more

117

by the great threefold revolution, scientific, economic and political, which has transformed the face of the world. Nevertheless these changes, vast as they are, form part of a single cultural process, and there is no such breach of social continuity between their different phases as we find, for example, between Moslem and Christian Spain or between Roman Britain and Saxon England.

No doubt this continuity of development is a commonplace of modern historical teaching, but that teaching still retains inevitably a national bias which falsifies its general perspective. Historical continuity is conceived primarily as a continuity of national development, and modern historical research for the last century and more has been conducted along national lines. In other words, the successful states have written history in their own honour, and the more important is a state today the greater is the place that it occupies in the history of the past. And the same is true of the different elements in the national tradition. As France has been unified from the Ile de France, French history has been written from a Parisian angle. The history of the southern provinces, which lived their own life for centuries, is unknown to the average educated person, while every detail in the reigns of the most unimportant of the Capetian kings has been studied with minute care. The states that have failed to survive were not, however, the least important in their own days—as we see notably in the case of the Byzantine Empire. If we wish to see the European development as a whole we must discard not only nationalist prejudices but also a national approach and study it according to its own formal principles, in the same way that we study an oriental or a prehistoric culture.

Let us then try to look at the Europe of A.D. 1000 as it would have appeared to a disinterested observer from outside —to one of those wandering Jews, for example, like Ibrahim ibn Yakub, the African merchant who visited Germany in the tenth century, or Benjamin of Tudela, the Spanish scholar-pilgrim of the twelfth century. To such a one "Western civilization" would have had a very different meaning from what it has today. It would not have been specifically European, since Europe hardly existed as a historical or geographical concept. Western civilization in the tenth century was still, no less than in the days of the Roman Empire, practically identical with the Mediterranean world. Three great powers dominated and shared this world: the Byzantine Empire in the Balkans and Asia Minor, the Fatimid Khalifate in Africa and Syria, and the Spanish Khalifate in the far west; and their capitals—Constantinople, Fustat (Old Cairo) and Cordova—were the three foci of Western civilization.

At that date no one could have guessed that these great empires were on the eve of their decline and that the future lay with the barbarians of the North. On the contrary, they seemed at the moment stronger and more prosperous than ever. The Fatimid Empire was at the height of its power and wealth under the great Khalif al-'Aziz (975–96), whose wise and tolerant rule made Cairo one of the greatest and most splendid cities of the Islamic world.[1] The Byzantine Empire had recovered its power and was expanding its territory alike in the Danubian lands, in Syria and in South Italy under the leadership of Basil II, the conqueror of the Bulgarians, while in the West the Khalifate of Cordova had reached the climax of its development under the great vizir al-Mansur (977–1002), who had subjugated the Christian principalities of the North by a series of campaigns in which he had destroyed Barcelona and Coimbra and Leon and

---

[1] Maqdisi, writing at the close of the tenth century, says: "Cairo today is what Bagdad was in its prime and I know no more illustrious city in Islam."
In the following century the Persian Nasir-i-Khusrau estimates the population of Cairo as five times that of Nishapur, the capital of Khorasan, and at that time perhaps the greatest city in Persia.

carried off the bells of the cathedral of Compostella to adorn the mosque of Cordova.

This civilized Mediterranean world was no less rich and populous than it had been under the Roman Empire. Each of the three great capitals probably had a population of over half a million.[1] And these were but the metropolises of a world of cities, which, except in Africa, were hardly less numerous and prosperous than in ancient times. Seville, Saragossa and Almeria in Spain; Palermo in Sicily; Mahdiyya in Africa; Alexandria in Egypt, Antioch, Aleppo and Damascus in Syria; Thessalonica and Thebes in Greece; Trebizond, Nicaea, Smyrna and Tarsus in Asia Minor, were all of them rich and populous cities with flourishing trade and industries. In spite of the piracy which often rendered navigation unsafe, the whole of the Mediterranean world was bound together by a network of trade routes which connected the great world markets of Constantinople and Egypt with Central Asia and India on the one hand and with Spain and North Africa on the other. It was thus possible for private individuals to accumulate great fortunes, like the Christian merchants of Cairo, whose wealth astonished Nasir-i-Khusrau in 1046, and for the governments to draw vast revenues from shop rents and customs and market dues. In the twelfth century Benjamin of Tudela reckons the revenues from these sources at Constantinople as amounting to no less than 7,300,000 gold nomismata, while in 1046 Nasir-i-Khusrau estimated the Egyptian government drew upwards of 1,200,000 gold dinars from the shop rents at Cairo alone.[2]

---

[1] Diehl reckons the population of Constantinople at between 800,000 and 1,000,000, that of Cordova in the tenth century has been estimated at 500,000 (Lévi-Provençal, *L'Espagne Musulmane au Xe siècle*), while that of Fustat, together with the court city of Cairo, was certainly not smaller.

[2] In the middle of the tenth century the income of the Khalif of Cordova from his private estates and market rights amounted to 765,000 dinars. This is apart from the public revenue from tithe and land tax, custom dues and duties on sales. (Lévi-Provençal, *L'Espagne Musulmane au Xe siècle*, pp. 72–7.)

Thus the Mediterranean world possessed a relatively uniform type of cosmopolitan culture. From Constantinople to Cairo and from Aleppo to Cordova we find the same type of city with its palaces and bazaars and public baths, the same intensive type of garden-agriculture, the same industries and arts. Even the royal palaces, which were the centres of the different governments—the Sacred Palace of Constantinople, the Twin Palaces of Cairo and the palaces of Az Zahra and Az Zahira at Cordova—resembled one another not only in their pomp and ceremonial, in their guards of foreign mercenaries and their population of slaves and eunuchs, but also in their external appearance. The Spanish khalifs ornamented their palaces with Greek sculpture and works of art, while the Byzantine architects sometimes imitated Arabian and Persian models.[1] This cosmopolitanism was characteristic of society as a whole. Religion and not nationality was the dominant factor, and at least in the Moslem lands even religious barriers were less exclusive than one might have supposed. The favourite wife of the Fatimid Khalif al-'Aziz was a Christian, and her brothers were the patriarchs of Alexandria and Jerusalem, while another Christian, Isa ibn Nestorius, became chief minister. So, too, in Spain, the great khalif, 'Abd al-Rahman III was the grandson of a Christian princess, and another Christian lady, the daughter of the King of Navarre, became the wife of al-Mansur. Even more important were the Jews, who formed a considerable element of the Spanish population and often came to hold important offices in the government. Thus the great Jewish physician Hasday ben Shaprut (945–70) occupied an important position at the court of 'Abd al-Rahman III, while in the following century the kingdom of Grenada was governed for years by the famous Jewish vizir Samuel ibn Nagdela. Partly owing to the influence of these

[1] E.g. the Triconchus of Theophilus and the "Persian House" of the Comneni.

men Spanish Judaism enjoyed a period of extraordinary prosperity, and the eleventh century became the golden age of medieval Judaism.

The cosmopolitan character of the Mediterranean culture is to be seen at its best in the intellectual co-operation between Moslem, Jewish and Christian scholars which bore fruit during this period in a great flowering of Arabic science and philosophy. This was essentially an international movement which extended from central Asia to Spain and North Africa. Although it was nominally Arabic, it was based on the tradition of Greek culture transmitted by Syriac scholars and developed by the common activity of Moslems, Christians and Jews. A good example of this intellectual co-operation is to be seen in the story of the sumptuous manuscript of Dioscorides which was sent as a royal gift from the Byzantine emperor Constantine Porphyrogenitus to the Spanish khalif 'Abd al-Rahman III and translated by the Jew Hasday ibn Shaprut with the assistance of a Greek monk who was specially obtained from Constantinople for the purpose.

But although the Greek and Syrian Christians still contributed their share to the international culture of the age, the leadership in both philosophy and science had definitely passed from Eastern Christendom to Islam. It was the age of Avicenna (Ibn Sina) and al-Biruni (973–1048); of Alhazen (Ibn al-Haitham) (965–1039), the physicist, and Ibn Yunus, the astronomer (940–98); of Ibn Hazm (994–1064) the writer on comparative religion, and Avencebrol (Ibn Gabirol), the philosopher and poet. All these are among the greatest names in the history of medieval thought, and their influence dominated the world for centuries, as we see from the debt that Western scholasticism owes to Avicenna and Avencebrol, and Western science to Avicenna and Alhazen. All of them wrote in Arabic, and, with the exception of the Spanish Jew Ibn Gabirol, all of them were Moslems. But they were by no means all of them Arabs. The greatest of them, Avicenna and al-Biruni, were Persians from the far east and spent much of their time in the service of the Turkish Sultan, Mahmud, who conquered north-west India. Ibn Hazm and Ibn Gabirol were Spaniards, while the other two, Alhazen and Ibn Yunus, lived at Cairo in the service of the Fatimid khalif al-Hakim (990–1021). For by this time Moslem culture was no longer concentrated round the court of the Abbasid khalifs in Bagdad, and local centres of culture were developing alike in the far east in Turkestan and Afghanistan and in the far west in Spain and Morocco.

Nevertheless, the bonds of common religion, common language and common law still held Islam together as a vast cultural unity, in comparison with which Western Christendom seemed small and provincial. The Islamic west, though it far surpassed Western Christendom in wealth and population, was itself but the western province of a society which stretched from India and Turkestan to Portugal and Morocco. The resources of Moslem culture were increased rather than diminished by the development of new centres of culture which took place in the tenth and eleventh centuries. Scholars and theologians travelled from one end of Islam to another; Persian artists and musicians worked at the Spanish court, and scientific and artistic development was stimulated by the rivalry of so many different centres of learning and culture.

The most cosmopolitan of all these centres was to be found in the Fatimid capital at Cairo. It was here that the trade routes from all over the Islamic and Byzantine world converged, and whatever passed from east to west or *vice versa* had to pass through Egypt on its way. And in addition to this, the brilliance of the Fatimid court and the generous though erratic patronage of learning by the Fatimid khalifs also made Cairo a centre of attraction. Some of the greatest of the men of science who worked in Egypt during this period were not Egyptians by origin but natives of Mesopotamia, like Ibn al-Haitham, who was born at Basra, and the great Christian physician Masawayh al-Mardini,[1] who spent the earlier part of his life at Bagdad.

In Spain, on the other hand, we see the development of a centre of culture like that of eastern Persia, far removed from the old focus of Moslem civilization on the very borders of the Islamic world, but one which was richer than Egypt in promise and in its own native resources. Even the break-up of the Spanish Khalifate in the eleventh century, though it weakened the political power of Islam, still further enriched its cultural life by the creation of a number of new centres of intellectual activity. The petty kingdoms and city-states—Seville, Toledo, Badajoz, Almeria, Valencia, Murcia and Saragossa—rivalled one another in their patronage of literature and learning. Many of their rulers were themselves poets and men of letters, like al-Mu'tamid (1040–95), the famous poet-king of Seville, and al-Mu'tasim (1051–91) of Almeria, the head of a whole dynasty of poets. Yusuf al-Mu'tamin, King of Saragossa from 1081 to 1085, was the author of a celebrated mathematical treatise, and both under him and his father, al-Muqtadir, who reigned from 1046 to 1081, Saragossa was a centre of scientific and philosophical studies. Here al-Karmani (c. 976–1066), the disciple of Maslama and the man who was probably responsible for introducing the strange scientific theosophy of the Brethren of Purity into Spain, spent his later years. Here Ibn Gabirol (Avencebrol) (1021–58), the great Jewish neo-Platonist, wrote his famous work which was known to the Christian West as the *Fons Vitae*; and here in the last days of the dynasty, at the beginning of the twelfth century, Ibn Bajja (Avempace) inaugurated the study of Aristotelian philosophy in the West.

[1] He was the author of the standard medieval pharmacopœia and was known in the West as Mesue, "pharmacopœorum evangelista". Cf. Sarton, *Introduction to History of Science*, I, 725.

The other main centre of scientific studies was at Toledo, where al-Zarkali (Arzachel) (c. 1028–87), the greatest of the Western astronomers, prepared the famous Toledan Tables with the assistance of Ibn Sa'id of Almeria (1030–70), who was a historian as well as an astronomer.

Finally, Cordova still retained some of its old cultural supremacy. It was the home of Ibn Hazm (994–1064), the greatest writer of his age, of Ibn Hayyan, the historian (987–1076), who composed an immense history of Spain in sixty volumes, and of Ibn Zaydun (1003–70), one of the greatest of Andalusian poets.

The breadth and richness of Spanish culture during this period is to be seen, above all, in the work of Ibn Hazm, who was at once theologian and poet, philosopher, statesman and canonist. He occupies somewhat the same position in Western Islam as al-Ghazali did in the East in that he is the chief Western representative of the movement of orthodox reaction against the rationalism of the philosophers and the theosophy of the *Shi'ah*. Like al-Ghazali, he was no narrow reactionary; indeed he suffered much himself from the intolerance of the orthodox theologians, who prohibited him from teaching in the schools of Cordova and finally condemned his works to be burnt and forced him to live in retirement near Huelva.[1]

His scientific treatment of religious questions and the breadth of his knowledge is to be seen in his *Fisal,* a critical history of all the known types of religious sects and philosophical schools from absolute scepticism to strict Moslem orthodoxy. It is a remarkable work, which Don Miguel Asin, its translator, regards as one of the richest and most trustworthy documents for the history of medieval thought

[1] It was on this occasion that he composed the following lines:
"Trouble me not regarding this burning of books and of papers, but say rather 'Now we shall see what he knows'. If they have burnt the paper, they have not burned that which the paper contained. That is in my breast and I carry it whithersoever my horses take me. It stays where I halt, and it will only be buried in my tomb."

and as an outstanding witness to the continuity of the *philosophia perennis*.

This, however, is only one of the aspects of Ibn Hazm's many-sided genius. No less characteristic is his famous treatise on the philosophy of love—*The Ring of the Dove—Tawq al Hamana*[1]—which throws so much light on the romantic cult of love in medieval literature. For it was in the brilliant and artificial atmosphere of the Spanish Moslem courts in the tenth and eleventh centuries that there first arose that romantic idealization of love and that almost religious devotion of the lover to the beloved which afterwards found expression in the courtly literature of medieval Europe and most of all in the *dolce stil nuovo* of thirteenth-century Italy. The love of the poet Ibn Zaydun for the princess Wallada, and of the poet-prince al-Mu'tamid for the slave girl Romaica are historical examples from real life of the romantic attachments which were later to become the staple theme of the courtly literature of France and Western Christendom. And in the same way Moslem Spain led the way in the creation of the new lyrical poetry which has so much in common with the Romance lyric of the Troubadours that was later to arise in Languedoc and spread through western Europe with extraordinary rapidity.

All this brilliant intellectual life seemed to foreshadow the rise of a great national Spanish culture in Western Islam similar to that which was being developed at the same time in Persia. It is true that Spain had no Firdausi to restore the native language to honour and to give classical expression to the national tradition. Nevertheless, even in Spain the use of the vernacular was increasing and the khalifs themselves did not disdain to show their knowledge of it.[2] By the

[1] Ed. D. Petrof (Leyden, 1914). Trans. A. J. Arberry (Luzac, 1953).
[2] E.g. Ibn Idhari gives a story of how 'Abd al-Rahman III capped an Arabic poem by a vernacular verse in the same metre. Cf. Lévi-Provençal, *L'Espagne Musulmane au Xe siècle*, p. 51.

eleventh century the original distinction between the Arab conquerors and the native converts to Islam—the *muwallad* —had become entirely effaced, and even the native Spaniards who preserved their Christian faith had come to share the same culture as their Moslem neighbours. The inhabitants of Moslem Spain were no longer divided by the barriers of race; all of them, whether Arabs, Spaniards or Berbers by origin, were regarded indifferently as Andalusians or "Westerners", and the way seemed open for the development of an Andalusian national culture.

Unfortunately Moslem Spain, in spite of its high civilization, was based on insecure social foundations, and the very age which produced so brilliant a flowering of intellectual culture was also the age of its political decline and fall. The Moslem State in Spain no less than in Egypt and Mesopotamia was an artificial creation which had no organic relation to the life of the people and rested its power on mercenary troops and on the class of slaves and freedmen from which most of its servants and officials were drawn. The slaves were known as *sakaliba*—"the Slavs"—owing to the fact that they were originally imported from eastern Europe by the Jewish slave-dealers, who carried on their operations both in eastern Germany and south Russia, but by the tenth century the name had come to be applied indifferently to any slaves of European origin, whether imported from eastern Europe or captured by the Saracen pirates who raided all the coasts of the western Mediterranean. Their numbers and influence increased rapidly during the tenth century. By the end of the reign of 'Abd al-Rahman III in 961 the *sakaliba* of the palace of Az Zahra are said to have numbered 3,750, and under his successors they played a growing part in government and political intrigue. The later Khalifate was, in fact, a slave state, not in the modern sense of a state that treats its subjects as slaves, but because it was itself controlled by slaves or men of servile origin. Thus the decline of the Khalifate ended in a scramble for power between the Berber and Castilian mercenaries and the members of the slave guard. The ex-slaves became masters of the rich provinces of eastern Spain and founded the petty kingdoms of Almeria, Valencia, Denia and the Balearic Islands, while the Berbers held the south and established principalities at Malaga, Granada, Carmona, Algeciras and elsewhere.

This was, however, but a temporary regime, which gradually tended to give place to the rule of new native dynasties like the Beni Hud of Saragossa, the Beni Dhun Nun of Toledo and the Beni 'Abad of Seville. But the tradition of dependence on mercenaries and foreigners could not be shaken off. The new kingdoms became more and more dependent on the northern Christian states to which they paid subsidies for protection and military support, until each of the northern kingdoms had its allotted sphere of influence —Leon in Toledo, Galicia in Badajoz, Castile in Valencia and Aragon in Saragossa. This was the situation which was exploited by heroic adventurers like the Cid, Rodrigo Diaz, who alternately plundered and defended the Moslem princes with chivalrous impartiality and finally succeeded in establishing himself in 1094 at Valencia as an independent Christian ruler of a Moslem state.

Such a situation was inherently unstable, and the conquests of Alfonso VI of Castile forced the Moslem princes to call in the barbarians of the south to save them from the barbarians of the north. A new power had arisen out of the desert, or rather on the southern limits of the Sahara, where a religious reformer had founded a kind of military order on an island in the Senegal River. At Zalaca, in 1085, the armies of Castile and Leon were overwhelmed by the fierce veiled riders of the desert who followed the standards of the Almoravid fanatics from the Sahara, and that night the muezzins gave the call to prayer mounted on piles of

Christian heads. But though the cause of Islam was saved
for the moment, the cause of culture had little to gain. Ibn
Hazm had compared the Christian Spaniards to the Berbers
and the northern Europeans to the Sudanese, and now the
rich civilization of Andalusia was almost ruined in the
conflict of these rival barbarians.

Many of the leading Spanish men of letters were among
the victims of war and revolution. The historian Ibn Bassam
has described how the incessant invasions of the Christians
forced him to fly from Santarem in Portugal—"the last of
the cities of the West"—after seeing his lands ravaged and
his wealth destroyed, a ruined man with no possessions save
his battered sword. Many scholars, such as Abu Salt of
Denia and Abu Behr al-Tortuchi of Tortosa, left Spain
altogether to take refuge in Egypt. Others were still more
unfortunate, like the poet Ibn Wahbun, who was murdered
by Christian raiders on the road from Lorca to Murcia in
1087. The last decade of the eleventh century was especially
fatal to Spanish culture. While Valencia was enduring the
horrors of the great siege by the Cid, the puritanism of the
Almoravid conquerors was destroying the luxurious court
life of the kingdoms of the south. Al-Mu'tamid, the poet-
king of Seville, spent his last years in an African prison, and
the fair Romaica and her daughters were forced to earn their
bread by spinning.

Consequently it is not surprising that the prevailing note
in Spanish literature should be one of pessimism and dis-
illusionment. We see it not only in the lamentations of al-
Wakasi and Ibn Afasha on the fall of Valencia or in the
poems composed by al-Mu'tamid in the years of his captivity, but no less profoundly in the lines composed by Ibn
Hazm at a much earlier date: "Thou weepest for the dead.
Let him be. He is at peace. Weep rather for the living. He
is more worthy of your tears. The dead man rests in his
tomb: there is no need to mourn over his lot. But as for the

living, who perishes every day at the hands of injustice, there is none to comfort him."[1]

Spanish culture was overshadowed by the tragic contrast between its cultural superiority and its material impotence. It saw itself at the mercy of conquerors whom it despised, but whom it knew to be stronger and more vital than itself. And consequently its best and noblest representatives tended to turn away from political life and action and to take refuge in the world of the mind, like Ibn Hazm, the philosophic pessimist, or like the followers of the Sufi tradition of esoteric mysticism, the greatest representative of which was also the last great representative of Spanish Moslem culture, the Valencian Ibnu'l 'Arabi.

This premature blighting of the brilliant civilization of Moslem Spain is typical of the fate of this Mediterranean world as a whole. Everywhere we find the same wealth of material and intellectual culture and the same lack of social vitality or free political activity. Nowhere were these tendencies so marked as in Egypt, where the economic conditions have always been especially favourable to absolute government. Here the system of government by slaves and mercenaries was carried to its extreme conclusions, until in the later Middle Ages Egypt was governed by a picked corps of Circassian slave guards, who made and unmade sultans at their pleasure from among their own officers. Even in the eleventh century, when the Fatimid Khalifate was externally at the height of its power and prosperity, it was often at the mercy of its negro mercenaries and Turkish slave guards. Its greatest ruler was the terrible al-Hakim, who carried his despotism up to and beyond the borders of insanity, and who finally asserted his own divinity and was worshipped by his faithful under the singularly inappropriate titles of "The Compassionate", "The Merciful". The

---

[1] A. Gonzalez Palencia, *Historia de la Literatura Arabigo-Española*, p. 58 (1928).

whole story of al-Hakim has a fantastic and unreal quality which seems to belong to the world of the Arabian Nights rather than to the world of sober history. Yet, in spite of his cruelty and his insane caprice, he was a great patron of learning and founded the academy of science at Cairo and an observatory on the Mokattem hills. Yet no one in his dominions was too powerful or too humble to be safe from his tyranny, and such was the terror that his cold ferocity and his uncanny blue eyes inspired that none of his victims dared to attack him, even though he used to wander through the streets of his capital at night, riding alone and un-attended on a donkey. When at last in 1020 he failed to return from one of his solitary nocturnal excursions in the Mokattem hills many of his subjects refused to believe that he had been assassinated. Even today the Druse of the Lebanon worship him as the last and most perfect of the successive manifestations of the divinity and believe that he will one day emerge from his "occultation" to judge the world and inaugurate the reign of justice and truth.

Under the weak successors of al-Hakim, the Fatimid Empire, which had stretched from the Atlantic to the fron-tiers of Mesopotamia and the Byzantine Empire, gradually fell to pieces. Its fragments were divided among the Berbers in the west, the Seljuk Turks in the east and the Normans and the Franks in Sicily and Syria. But Egypt still remained the metropolis of Western Islam, and the cause of the Fati-mids still aroused the passionate devotion of the partisans of the Shiah all over the Moslem world. Even at the close of the eleventh century it was still strong enough to give rise to the new movement of Hasan i Sabbah and his sect of "Assassins", who carried on a campaign of propaganda and terrorism throughout Persia and the Near East; while for a short time in the years 1058–9 the claims of the Fatimid Khalif were acknowledged at Bagdad, the capital of the orthodox Sunni Khalifate. But meanwhile the dynasty itself was becoming a puppet in the hands of favourites and mercenaries, and the country was devastated by the rivalry of the black troops and the Turkish bodyguard. In the twelfth century, weakened by internal dissension and exposed to the attacks of the crusading armies from Palestine, it fell an easy prey to the rising power of the Atabegs of Mosul. As its Kurdish conqueror remarked, it was "a land without men and with a contemptible government". Nevertheless, there were still some who looked back with regret to the luxury and culture of the old Fatimid court. "O censurer of my love for the sons of Fatima," wrote an Arabic poet, "join in my tears over the desolate halls of the Twin Palaces."[1]

In comparison with Fatimid Egypt the situation in the Byzantine world seems relatively healthy and normal. The Roman traditions of law and civic responsibility had never entirely disappeared,[2] while the influence of classical literature and scholarship preserved the ideals of Hellenism and humane culture among the educated classes. The straightforward and plain-spoken Basil II, who was more at home in the camp than the palace, resembles the old Roman soldier-emperors rather than an oriental despot, and the scholarship of Michael Psellus links the tradition of the Greek rhetoricians with that of the Renaissance Humanists.

Nevertheless, the same seeds of decay were present in the Byzantine social organism as in that of the Moslem world. The army was full of barbarian mercenaries, and the life of the palace was dominated by eunuchs and slave officials, like the Slav Borilus who was the power behind the throne in the time of Nicephorus III. The empire possessed no genuine social or national unity; it was a patchwork of different

[1] S. Lane Poole, *History of Egypt in the Middle Ages*, pp. 179, 193.
[2] As Finlay writes: "A regular administration of justice which secured a high degree of security for life and property gave the people an immeasurable superiority over the subjects of all contemporary governments . . ." (*History of the Byzantine Empire*, Everyman Ed., p. 422).

races and nationalities who were only held together by the bureaucratic hierarchy of the State and by the ecclesiastical unity of the Orthodox Church, which provided the only available substitute for national unity. But the extreme other-worldliness of Byzantine religion counterbalanced its services to the cause of social unity, while the traditionalism of the Church combined with the conservatism of the bureaucracy to maintain the stationary character of Byzantine civilization.

Hence the revival of the Byzantine Empire in the tenth century was by no means an unmixed blessing for Eastern Christendom. It united the East against the West and imparted a political and quasi-national character to the schism between the Churches. Yet at the same time it destroyed the independent national life of the lesser Christian states by its policy of military expansion and political centralization. The new Christian kingdom of Bulgaria, which had already shown considerable cultural promise in the tenth century, was ruthlessly destroyed by the conquests of Basil II, while the ancient Christian civilization of Armenia, now at the height of its artistic development and its economic prosperity, was shamefully betrayed by Constantine IX, whose annexation of Armenia only helped to open the way for the conquest of Asia Minor by the Seljuk Turks. The Armenian capital of Ani, with its forty gates and its thousand and one churches, was captured and destroyed by Alp Arslan in 1064, and seven years later the Byzantine army under the Emperor Romanus Diogenes was overwhelmed by the Turks in the disastrous Battle of Manzikert, which left the whole of Asia Minor at the mercy of the invaders.

From this calamity the Byzantine Empire never recovered, for the Anatolian provinces were the backbone of the empire both from the military and the economic point of view, and their loss left it to face the growing menace of Western aggression with no resources save diplomacy and finance. The later Byzantine Empire was an Ægean empire, but it did not possess the sea power which alone could make such a situation tolerable. Nevertheless, it retained its cultural superiority; indeed, the loss of its continental provinces, by increasing the proportion of the Hellenic element in the population, did something to give the Byzantine culture a national character that it had not previously possessed. As in Moslem Spain, the intellectual and artistic vitality of Mediterranean culture survived its political decadence, but its activity was confined to the surface of society and had no depth of soil in which it could strike root, and consequently it was bound to wither prematurely without bearing fruit in a social revival of Eastern Christendom.

VIII

THE SCIENTIFIC DEVELOPMENT OF MEDIEVAL CULTURE

T HE ultimate criterion by which we must judge the value of a religion is not its cultural fruits but its spiritual truth. This, however, is not the criterion which the historian or the sociologist applies in his judgment of an age or a civilization. A false religion which produces a great art or a great literature, a religion which expresses itself in a brilliant civilization, will naturally be of greater interest to him than a true religion which produces only martyrs or mystics. But while the historian is justified in judging the cultural value of a religion by its cultural fruits, he has no right to treat his conclusions as final from the religious point of view. Actually, however, it is very difficult for an historian to preserve this distinction between religious and cultural values. If he believes a religion to be true, he will naturally tend to take a favourable view of the culture with which it is associated, and if he regards a culture as barbarous or unprogressive he will be apt to condemn or depreciate its religious standards and beliefs.

Now it was on this ground that the traditional humanistic criticism of medieval religion was based. Medieval literature, medieval philosophy and medieval science alike appeared beneath contempt in the eyes of the Renaissance scholar, and still more of the philosopher of the eighteenth-century Enlightenment, and consequently medieval religion either shared in their condemnation or, still more frequently, was regarded as primarily responsible for the cultural backwardness of medieval Europe—in Gibbon's famous phrase, the Middle Ages were "the triumph of barbarism and religion".

This wholesale condemnation of medieval culture has long since been abandoned by the educated world, and it was the rediscovery of the purely cultural values of the Middle Ages—of medieval literature and medieval art—which was the main factor in bringing about the change, and which contributed very materially to a wider appreciation of the value of medieval religion. The rediscovery of medieval thought came later and was far less general. It was mainly confined to those who were already convinced of the religious values of medieval culture, and it was slow to affect public opinion generally. Nevertheless, it has not been without its effect, and today there are few historians of philosophy who do not recognize the greatness of medieval intellectual achievement. It is true that so distinguished an historian as the late J. B. Bury could still describe medieval thought under the rubric *Reason in Prison,* but the book in question was written with a pronounced rationalistic bias, and as a rule even those who regard medieval metaphysics as of purely historical interest, nevertheless recognize, like Prof. Whitehead, that the European mind received from medieval scholasticism that fundamental training in rational thought on which all its later achievements are dependent.

But when we come to the question of natural science the old view still holds the field to a great extent, in spite of the work accomplished in recent years by writers such as the late Pierre Duhem and Dr. George Sarton. To the scientist the Middle Ages are still the Dark Ages, and medieval religion is still regarded as an obscurantist force which set back and retarded the development of scientific thought.

Now it must be admitted that the Middle Ages witnessed a great decline in scientific knowledge from the standards already attained in the Greek world, and that there is a good *prima facie* case for ascribing this decline to the advent of Christianity and to the consequent turning away of men's attention from this world to the next and from the facts of nature to the truths of faith. Does not St. Augustine, the patriarch of Western Christian thought, speak of science as a vain curiosity that distracts the mind from its true end, which is not to number the stars and to seek out the hidden things of nature, but to know and love God? Did not the monks murder Hypatia? And did not Justinian close the schools of Athens which still kept the sparks of Greek science and philosophy alive?

All this is true enough; nevertheless it is necessary to remember that the issue is not such a simple one as appears at first sight. The science of which St. Augustine speaks was the science of astrology, which in our eyes is no science at all, though to the men of that age it seemed inseparable from what we call astronomy; and in the same way the school of Athens, in spite of its genuine devotion to Hellenic science, was inspired by a belief in occultism and magic that is far more fatal to the scientific ideal than the theology and the theological philosophy of Augustine; while as to the murder of Hypatia, that had no more to do with her scientific accomplishments than the exile of Einstein from Germany had to do with Relativity. The fact is that the decline of ancient science is but one aspect of the vital decay of Hellenic culture, and when Christianity conquered ancient civilization, it occupied a house that was already empty. The life had gone out of it, and a new spirit was to take its place.

But if this is so, how are we to explain the backwardness of the Christian West in comparison with the Moslem East? It was the Arabs not the Christians who entered into the inheritance of Hellenic science and carried on its work, and throughout the early medieval centuries, while the West was completely barren of scientific achievement, the Moslem world, from Spain to Afghanistan, was the scene of an intense intellectual activity which showed itself not only in philosophy but in mathematics and astronomy and medicine.

The contrast is a very striking one, but it is impossible to explain it on religious grounds. For religion dominated Moslem culture no less than that of Christendom and Moslem theology was even more exclusive and universal in its claims than that of the Catholic Church. The causes of the difference were material rather than spiritual and are to be found primarily in the economic and social backwardness of the simple agrarian culture of western Europe in comparison with the rich urban civilization of the Moslem world.

But in addition to this, there is a further historical factor that is of prime importance. Moslem culture entered into direct relations with Hellenism and was able to draw on the rich resources of Greek literature. The new peoples of the West, on the other hand, were tributary to Latin culture, and only possessed an indirect and secondary contact with the Hellenic tradition. For while Latin culture had been schooled in the classical tradition of Hellenic literature, it had never fully assimilated the Greek scientific tradition. Consequently, where the Arabs could draw on the accumulated riches of the Aristotelian tradition, of Ptolemy and the earlier astronomers and the Greek mathematicians, the West had to content itself with the work of cultivated amateurs like Pliny, and the elementary notions of Greek philosophy transmitted by such writers as Boethius, Cassiodorus, Marius Victorinus, Macrobius and Apuleius. The responsibility for this state of things rests not on the Church nor on medieval culture but on the secular culture of the Roman Empire which had made no serious attempt to assimilate Greek scientific culture, or to use the golden opportunities afforded by the cosmopolitan conditions of the age for the transmission of Greek science to the Latin-speaking world.

But while there is no reason to suppose that the Dark Ages were dark because they were religious, it is none the less difficult to exaggerate their darkness, both as regards scientific knowledge and the completeness of the break between the science of antiquity and the science of modern times. Here the traditional view is justified, and it only becomes false when this judgment is extended from the early to the later Middle Ages so as to make the scientific development of western Europe begin with the Renaissance. In reality the recovery of Greek science and the restoration of contact with the main tradition of Greek thought was one of the most striking achievements of medieval culture. And it is even more than this: it is a turning point in the history of world civilization, for it marks the passing of the age-long supremacy of oriental and eastern Mediterranean culture and the beginning of the intellectual leadership of the West. It is, in fact, a far more important and original achievement than anything that the Renaissance itself accomplished. For the Renaissance scholars, in spite of their originality, were carrying on a tradition that had never been altogether lost: the tradition of humanism and classical scholarship that was founded on Cicero and Quintilian. But the rediscovery of Greek thought by the medieval scholars was a new fact in the history of the West: it was the conquest of a new world.

It is true that the scientific renaissance of the Middle Ages was far from being the unaided work of Western thinkers. It was not the result of a gradual process of experiment and discovery but rather of the importation into Christendom of a scientific tradition and a scientific literature that belonged to an alien culture. Thus it is a parallel phenomenon to the rise of the new lyric poetry and the new literary culture of which I speak in the following chapters. Like the latter, it had its origin in the mixed culture of the western Mediterranean, a world that is strangely neglected by the historian, but which is a key position for the understanding of later medieval culture. It was here, in Spain and Sicily, in the trading cities of the French and Italian Rivieras, and at the feudal courts of Provence and Catalonia, that the Christians first met the Arabs and the Jews on equal terms, and came under the influence of the brilliant civilization that had developed in Western Islam from the tenth to the twelfth centuries. It was here that the eyes of Western scholars were first opened to the riches of Greek and Arabic learning and to their own scientific backwardness; and it was here, at Toledo and Salerno and Barcelona and Montpellier and Palermo, that the Christians put themselves to school with the Arabs and the Jews and laid the foundations of the new scientific culture of the West.

The cosmopolitan character of the movement is shown by the names of the scholars to whom the introduction of the new knowledge was due. These include Italians like Plato of Tivoli, Gerard of Cremona, and Burgundio and Leonard of Pisa; Sicilian Greeks such as Henry Aristippus and Eugenius the Emir; Spaniards like Gundissalinus or Domingo Gonzalez, Hugh of Santalla, and Mark of Toledo; Englishmen, such as Adelard of Bath, Robert of Chester, Daniel of Morley and Alfred of Sereshel, a Scot, the famous Michael, a Slav, Hermann of Carinthia, and a Fleming, Rudolf of Bruges.

Apart from the Sicilians and from Burgundio of Pisa, who translated direct from the Greek, all these scholars owed much to the collaboration of men of Arabic speech. Some of them were Mozarabs—Spanish Christians of Arabic speech, like Galippus, the assistant of Gerard of Cremona, but the majority of them were Jews or converts from Judaism, such as John Hispanus (John Abendaud), who worked

with Gundissalinus, Savasorda, the assistant of Plato of
Tivoli, and Petrus Alfonsi, who visited England as the
physician of Henry I.

Nevertheless, the derivative character of the movement
and its lack of originality ought not to detract from the
achievement of these Western scholars who faced so many
difficulties and overcame so many obstacles in the disinterested pursuit of scientific knowledge. For, however
strange their scientific ideas may seem to us, there can be
no doubt that the ideal which inspired their activity was a
genuinely scientific one and that they are the humble and
half-forgotten founders of the long and glorious line of
Western scientists.

They were themselves by no means unconscious of the
greatness of the issues at stake or of the revolutionary
character of their work. One of the early translators, Plato
of Tivoli, prefaces his translation of al-Battani's treatise
on astronomy[1] with a remarkable indictment of the Western
attitude towards science. He attacks the ignorance and sloth
that have led the Latins to neglect scientific studies for easier
and less worthy pursuits. Rome, he says, has surpassed not
only the Greeks but every other people in warlike powers
and in the extent of its empire. But with regard to the
sciences, Rome has remained inferior by far, not only to
the Egyptians and the Greeks, the founders of all the liberal
arts, but also to the Arabs.

This holds good of all of the arts, for the Latins possess
them only in so far as they have received them from others,
but it is true, above all, of astronomy, which surpasses all
the other sciences in exactness of method, subtlety of reasoning, and completeness of proof. "In astronomy the Latin
world cannot show—I do not say a single author—but even
a single translator of whom it can boast. The Egyptians

---

[1] *De Motu Stellarum*, a work of great importance, not only for astro-
nomical science, but because it helped to introduce trigonometry into
western Europe.

have a multitude of masters in this art, of whom Hermes is the chief; the Greeks have Aristotle, Abrachis [Hipparchus], Ptolemy and innumerable others; the Arabs have Algorithm [al-Khwarizmi], Messehala, Albategni [al-Battani] and many more. But the Latins, on the contrary, have not a single author: for books they have only follies, dreams and old wives' fables. This is the reason that has moved me, Plato of Tivoli, to enrich our tongue with that which it lacked the most, by drawing on the treasures of an unknown language."[1]

But if the scholars of the West had a great deal of ground to make up, they lost no time in doing so. The activity of the translators and adaptors, above all of Gerard of Cremona, who worked at Toledo until his death in 1187, is almost incredible. In the space of little more than half a century the main tradition of Greek and Arabic learning, both philosophical and scientific, was transmitted to the Latin world—Euclid, Ptolemy, Galen, the Arabic mathematicians and astronomers, Avicenna, al-Farabi, Ibn Gabirol —but, above all, Aristotle, whose figure dominates the scientific tradition of both the Greeks and the Arabs, as it was also to dominate that of the medieval West.

The impact of this great mass of new knowledge on the Western mind could not but produce startling effects. It raised the whole question of the relations between religion and science, and between reason and faith, in a very sharp and accentuated way. The full realization of the issues at stake was indeed delayed until the strict Aristotelianism of Averroes was introduced into the West in the first half of the thirteenth century, but they were already implicit in the scientific doctrines that began to reach western Europe a century earlier with Adelard of Bath and Plato of Tivoli.

[1] P. Duhem, *Le Système du Monde de Platon à Copernic,* iii, pp. 199–200.

For the new scientific doctrines were not simply an addition to the common stock of knowledge which Western culture already possessed. They formed part of an organized system of thought which embraced every aspect of reality. The logical completeness and consistency of this system made it almost impossible to accept any part of it without assenting to the whole, to separate its physical from its metaphysical elements or to accept its explanation of natural phenomena while rejecting its theory of spiritual being. And hence, as the theologians of Islam had long ago realized, Hellenic science was not the obedient servant of revealed religion but an independent and rival power. It was a danger alike to Christianity, to Judaism and to Islam, since it challenged the fundamental dogmas that were common to the three religions: the doctrine of creation, the doctrine of personal immortality, and the belief in a personal Deity who governed the world by His providence and the free exercise of His omnipotent will.

Science always tends towards determinism, and Aristotelian science was perhaps the most thorough-going system of determinism that has ever been invented, since it embraced spirit as well as matter in the working of its mechanism. For this reason, the determinism of the Aristotelians was entirely different from that of modern science. The latter starts from the bottom, with physics and chemistry, and builds up its structure of reality from the atom and the electron. The Aristotelian starts at the top with the movements of the heavenly bodies and finds in them the principle that governs the laws of terrestrial change. Both systems are mechanical, but that of the moderns is a soulless and automatic mechanism, while that of the Greeks is animate and intelligent. In fact, so far from eliminating the idea of God as an unnecessary hypothesis, God is, for Aristotle, the mainspring of his whole system of physics, and the motor that drives the world machine.

Mind is the one principle of movement and order in the world. Without it the universe would be an inert mass, a shapeless chaos. And it is in the eternal and regular movements of the stars that the presence of divine intelligence is most indubitably manifested. They are "the radiant rejoicing, intelligent Sons of Heaven", "visible Gods", in Plato's words, whose ordered march governs the recurrent changes of the time process and the cycles of generation and corruption in the sublunary world.[1]

All this is very alien to modern ways of thought; for we are accustomed to regard regular movement as characteristic of blind natural forces, and our idea of an intelligent being is that of one which is always doing something different. But to the Greek mind the more regular a movement, the more intelligent must be the mover, and if the stars had not been guided by conscious intelligence they would stand still or fall blindly through space, like the atoms of Epicurus, without following any regular orbit. In fact one might say that the Greeks would have revered the man who planned the Inner Circle on the Underground Railway as a truly wise and good man, while they would regard the erratic and aimless course of the man who motors for pleasure and speed as evidence of an incurably weak and vicious mind.

[1] These views are very fully expounded by Adelard of Bath in his *Questiones Naturales,* c. 74–7: "If reason and foresight exist even in our dark and perturbed lower world, how much more must the stars employ intelligence in their determined and constant courses." "The man who contends that the stars are senseless must himself be without sense" (Thorndyke, *Magic and Experimental Science,* ii, 40–1). St. Thomas himself states that no wise man doubts that all natural motions of inferior bodies are caused by the motions of the celestial bodies since it is proved both by reason and experience (*Responsio ad J. de Vercellis,* cited Thorndyke, *op. cit.,* ii, 609 from *Opera* (Paris ed.), vol. XXVII, p. 249). So, too, Albertus Magnus admits that the whole world of terrestrial nature is governed by the movements of the stars. He tends, however, to minimize the importance of the celestial intelligences and concentrates the emphasis of his theory on the First Mover. *Sicut manus est instrumentum intellectus practici in artificialibus, ita totus caelestis circulus est instrumentum hujus intellectus ad totum materiam naturae quae ambit. Metaphysicorum* XI, ii, 12. Thorndyke, ii, 581.

Now the medieval mind was certainly nearer to that of the Greeks than is our own. But for all that they were on our side of the gulf that divides the ancient from the modern world. Spirit and matter no longer formed part of a single indivisible unity. God was not an abstract intelligence that acted as the magneto of the cosmic dynamo, but the Heavenly Father, the Creator and Saviour of Mankind. The cosmic process was no eternal cycle, but a spiritual drama with a beginning and an end, and the earth, instead of being the passive recipient of the planetary influences, the slave of fate and necessity, was a battleground on which supreme spiritual issues were decided.

To men who had been reared in this spiritual tradition the theories of Græco-Arabic science came as intruders from an alien world. They regarded them with the instinctive distrust and aversion with which the orthodox circles received the new geological and biological theories in the last century. William of Auvergne, the most representative figure among the schoolmen of the older tradition in the first half of the thirteenth century, sums up the orthodox view in the following sentences: "As for the Christian people, wholly dedicated to virtue and holiness and the service of the Creator, it has been occupied very little with philosophy, save when the perversity of heretics and the objections of fools have compelled it to defend its religion and its faith and to destroy the doctrines that are opposed to its salvation and contrary to the honour of God. The men of this religion have been concerned with their souls and have not troubled themselves about the souls of the heavens. It has seemed to them that, from the point of view of their religion and their eternal salvation, there was neither profit to be gained from knowing about these souls nor loss from ignoring them. Whether the world may be a single animate body or not, whether the entire heaven should be an animate being or the different heavens animate beings—these are questions that the Christian people have regarded with horror and treated as monstrous. It is plunged in astonishment by this discussion which has hitherto been entirely unknown to it, and in which it sees a novelty that does not concern it at all.'"[1]

But if orthodox thinkers like William of Auvergne could look with indifference on the cosmological theories of the neo-Aristotelians, it was a very different thing when the latter came to apply those theories to the world of men. For the Arabs, following the traditions of later Greek thought, taught that mankind no less than the celestial spheres derived its activity from a spiritual principle—the active intelligence. In other words, Reason was not a faculty of the human soul but a cosmic principle—the lowest in the hierarchy of spiritual substances—and man attained to rational activity only in so far as his passive and mortal intelligence became temporarily actuated by this immortal and impersonal power. This doctrine struck at the very heart of religious faith, since it involved the denial of personal immortality, and consequently William of Auvergne declared that it was no subject for philosophical discussion, but a deadly heresy which should be rooted out "with fire and sword and every kind of torture". It was, in fact, to remain a burning question for three hundred years and more, but even before it had become a living issue the authorities had already realized the danger to religious orthodoxy implicit in Aristotelian science, and a series of episcopal and Papal pronouncements, from 1210 onwards, were directed against the study of the physics and metaphysics of Aristotle at the University of Paris, which had now become the acknowledged centre of Western thought.

Nevertheless, ecclesiastical authority and theological traditionalism were alike powerless to check the advance of

---

[1] William of Paris, *Opera* (1516), *tom.* ii, cap. vii, 195, quoted in Duhem, *op. cit.*, iv, 318.

the new knowledge. In spite of the protests of conservative thinkers such as William of Auvergne and St. Bonaventure, in spite of successive attempts to forbid the study and teaching of Aristotelian science in the University of Paris, the new ideas proved irresistibly attractive and even the extreme conclusions of Averroistic rationalism found a hearing. There was a real danger that religion and science would declare war on one another and that Western thought would be sacrificed, like that of Islam, to the conflict between the orthodox fideism of the theologians and the scientific rationalism of the Aristotelians. Fortunately for Western culture, however, the issues were never narrowed to this dilemma. The vitality of medieval religion shows itself in the eagerness and intellectual courage with which the leaders of Christian thought, such as Robert Grosseteste, Albert the Great, Thomas of York, Thomas Aquinas and Roger Bacon, confronted the new situation and strove to assimilate the new knowledge. It is true that traditionalists like St. Bonaventure and Bishop Tempier attempted to resist the new movement of thought and to involve the Christian Aristotelianism of St. Thomas in the same condemnation as that of the Averroists. In 1277 Bishop Tempier, supported by John Peckham, the disciple of St. Bonaventure and the future Archbishop of Canterbury, issued a sweeping condemnation of modern errors which was aimed impartially at the three leading representatives of the new movement of thought: Siger of Brabant, Roger Bacon, and Thomas Aquinas. The result of this decree was the imprisonment of Siger and Roger Bacon, and the exclusion of Thomism from the schools of Paris and Oxford. Nevertheless, this was only a local and temporary reaction. The condemnation of Thomism was not confirmed by the Papacy, which recognized the importance of the new learning and which finally set the seal of its approval on St. Thomas's ideal of a reconciliation between Aristotelian science and the Christian faith.

The inaugurator of this work of reconciliation was the German, Albertus Magnus, the most learned man of the thirteenth century and the most complete embodiment of the different intellectual currents of his age. He is the master, on the one hand, of St. Thomas and the Christian Aristotelians, and, on the other, of Ulrich of Strasburg and the Christian neo-Platonists. His greatest achievement was to put the whole *corpus* of Græco-Arabic thought at the disposal of Western scholasticism through the encyclopædic series of commentaries and expositions by which, as he said, he made "all the parts of philosophy, physics, metaphysics and mathematics, intelligible to the Latins". Nor was he merely a passive intermediary between two intellectual traditions, like the translators of the previous century; he had a really original mind, and his scientific observations, above all in biology, botany and geology, were among the first independent achievements of western European science. It is indeed in science rather than in philosophy that his originality is to be found. As a philosopher he tended rather to syncretism than to synthesis, and his philosophical works form a kind of metaphysical museum in which theories of very diverse origin find themselves side by side.

The true creator of the Aristotelian-Christian synthesis was not the German encyclopædist but his Neapolitan pupil, St. Thomas, through whom the mind of Western Christendom finally succeeded in completely incorporating the intellectual heritage of the Aristotelian tradition. Nature had fitted him for his task. He was no child of the Gothic North, like Albert or Abelard, but a native of that strange borderland of Western civilization where feudal Europe mingled with the Greek and Saracen worlds. He sprang from a family of courtiers and troubadours whose fortunes were intimately bound up with the brilliant half-oriental, half-humanist court of the great Hohenstaufen emperor and his ill-fated successors—that court which was at once the cradle of Italian literature and one of the main channels through which Arabic science reached the Christian world. St. Thomas was born at the time when Michael Scot, under the patronage of the emperor, was making the first Latin translations of the great Aristotelian commentaries of Averroes. He was educated at the University of Naples, the first university to owe its foundation and organization to the State, and he received his philosophical initiation from Peter of Ireland, one of the first Western scholastics who came under the influence of Averroistic thought. Nevertheless, St. Thomas was never a pupil of the Arabs in the same sense as the majority of his contemporaries. With him the Western mind emancipates itself from its Arabic teachers and returns to the sources. Indeed, there is in St. Thomas a real intellectual affinity to the Greek genius. More than any other Western thinker, medieval or modern, he possessed the tranquil lucidity and the gift of abstract intelligence that mark the Hellenic mind.

Thus he was peculiarly fitted to interpret the thought of Aristotle to his age without either forcing it into the mould of an alien mentality or disregarding the autonomy and transcendence of the Christian faith. Unlike the many medieval thinkers, both Christian and oriental, who evolved a kind of theosophical syncretism that was irreconcilable alike with the ideal of religious faith and with that of a purely rational philosophy, St. Thomas was able to combine the peripatetic tradition in philosophy and the patristic tradition in theology without falsifying either of them. It is true that his thought was neo-Platonic rather than Aristotelian in its concentration on spiritual reality and its consecration to a religious ideal. Nevertheless, although the mind of St. Thomas was steeped in the thought of St. Augustine and the Pseudo-Dionysius, his philosophy marks a complete break with the old Augustinian neo-Platonic idealism that had hitherto dominated the intellectual development of the West. Not only did St. Thomas accept the cardinal principles of Aristotelian physics, but he applied them resolutely to the nature of man, teaching that matter is the principle of human individuation, and that the soul is the form of the body. Hence man is not, as the Platonists believed, a spiritual being temporarily confined in the prison of the flesh, a stranger in an alien world; he is a part of nature—that dynamic order which embraces the whole series of living beings from man to plant, as well as the things that are without life but not without their principle of form. And so the human intelligence is not that of a pure spirit which exists only for the contemplation of absolute reality. It is consubstantial with matter, subject to the conditions of space and time, and it can only construct an intelligible order out of the data of sensible experience, systematized by the scientific activity of reason. Thus while, on the one hand, human reason is distinctively animal, the lowest and most obscured form of intelligence, it is on the other hand the one principle of spiritual order in nature, and it is its essential function to reduce the unintelligible chaos of the material world to reason and order.

This theory of the human intelligence is the essential doctrine of Thomism and the keystone of the Christian Aristotelian synthesis. Hitherto both the Averroist and the Christian Platonist had regarded the spiritual principle of intelligence as something superhuman and divine. It was not *in* man as a part of his personality; it was a power which illuminated his mind from outside, whether it be regarded with the Christian Platonists as the ray of Divine Light that illuminates the immortal human soul, or whether, as Averroes taught, it was the power of a universal intelligence actuating the successive, transitory and mortal minds of men. To St. Thomas, on the other hand, the active intelligence is the very essence of the soul and the root of human responsibility and liberty. "For if," he writes, "the active intellect is a substance outside man, the whole of man's activity depends on an extrinsic principle. Man then will not be a free agent but will be acted upon by another, and so he will not be the master of his own acts nor deserve praise nor blame; and the whole of moral science and social intercourse will perish—*quod est inconveniens.*"[1]

This insistence on the rationality and freedom of the individual personality is a new note in medieval thought. It marks the end of the Oriental and Byzantine absorption of the human mind in the Absolute and the Transcendent, and the beginning of the distinctively Western ideal of a philosophy of man and of the human mind: a philosophy which recognizes the dependence of human knowledge on sensible experience without excluding it from the world of spiritual reality and religious truth. The intellectualism of St. Thomas is equally remote from an absolute idealism and a rationalist empiricism, from the metaphysical mysticism of the ancient East and from the scientific materialism of the modern West. It recognized the autonomous rights of the human reason and its scientific activity against the absolutism of a purely theological ideal of knowledge, and the rights of human nature and natural morality against the exclusive domination of the ascetic ideal; while in social life it substituted for the all-embracing unity of the Byzantine and Islamic theocracy the dual order of Church and State, each with its independent functions and its own principle of authority. Thus, though Thomism did far less for humane letters than the school of Chartres in the preceding century, it opened the way for humanism in the larger sense of the word, and though its scientific achievements were very inferior to those of the fourteenth-century Nominalists, it opened the way for an autonomous and disinterested scientific activity.

The comparative sterility of Thomism in natural science has a twofold cause. On the one hand it is due to its

[1] *Summa Contra Gentiles,* ii, c. 76 *ad fin.*

concentration on metaphysics and theology, and on the other to the very completeness of its synthesis with the Aristotelian tradition. The Aristotelian *corpus* supplied the Middle Ages with an organized body of scientific knowledge far in advance of anything that Western culture had hitherto known, and consequently it was accepted as the last word in human wisdom.

In this respect Aristotelian scholasticism tended towards the standpoint of Averroes, who regards Aristotle as the divinely appointed hierophant of the mysteries of nature. "It is he," wrote Averroes, "who has discovered the three sciences—Physics, Logic and Metaphysics, and who has completed them. He has discovered them, for what we find of this knowledge in the writings of the earlier authors is not worthy of being considered even as a part of this doctrine, and one can say without hesitation that it does not even contain the principles of it. He has completed them, for none of those that have come after him, even to the present day, has added anything to them; nor has anyone discovered in his words an error of any importance.

"Let us praise God Who in the domain of perfection has singled out this man from all others and has conferred on him in particular the dignity of humanity carried to its culminating point in such a measure as no other man in any age has been able to reach."[1]

This attitude to Aristotle is often regarded as typical of the authoritarianism and dogmatism of medieval Christian scholasticism. Actually, however, it has nothing to do with religion and is even more characteristic of the Aristotelian rationalism of the Averroists than of the Christian Aristotelianism of the Thomists. The influence of St. Thomas on

[1] From the preface to the Great Commentary on Aristotle, *De physico auditu,* and from the paraphase to the *De generatione animalium,* lib. i, cap. 20, quoted by Mandonnet, *Siger de Brabant,* 1st ed., p. 153, and by Duhem, *op. cit.,* iv, pp. 310–11.

modern Catholic thought is apt to make us exaggerate the completeness of his victory, so that he appears to us the philosophical dictator of the medieval world. We forget the immense prestige of Averroism, which maintained the tradition of a non-Christian Aristotelianism right through the later Middle Ages, and which, even in the later Renaissance, was still the most formidable opponent of the new European science. In fact, the rationalist orthodoxy of the Averroists proved a greater obstacle to scientific progress than the obscurantism of conservative theologians. If the new scientific and philosophical culture of the West had been purely Aristotelian it would probably have been no less sterile than the scientific culture of Islam in the later Middle Ages. But medieval Aristotelianism never possessed a monopoly in Western thought; it was counterbalanced by the existence of another intellectual tradition—that of Christian Platonism—which contributed no less to the new scientific development, and which is equally characteristic of medieval culture.

This tradition was no more independent of oriental influences than was that of Albertus Magnus and St. Thomas. It also incorporated considerable Aristotelian elements, just as Thomism preserved a large element of Platonism. But while the Aristotelian element in the Thomist synthesis represents a relatively pure Peripatetic tradition, the Aristotelianism of the Platonists was derived from the school of al-Farabi and Avicenna, and was already heavily charged with neo-Platonic elements: in other words, it was the synthesis of a synthesis.

The medieval Platonists, like their predecessors, differed from the disciples of Aristotle, above all, in their theory of knowledge. Sensible experience only gives a knowledge of sensible things, but the higher knowledge springs from the illumination of the mind by divine truth: it is intuitive and spiritual. Hence the true source of knowledge is not to be found in things, but in the divine ideas, the *rationes aeternae,* that are the ultimate foundation of reality. And this theory of knowledge naturally leads to the Platonic, as opposed to the Aristotelian theory of science. Though the Augustinians did not go so far as Plato and deny that any science of sensible things was possible, they did tend to exalt the deductive over the inductive method, to regard mathematics as the model science and to prefer the sciences that make use of mathematical methods, such as optics and astronomy, to the non-mathematical Aristotelian sciences of physics and biology. The most remarkable representative of this tendency was Robert Grosseteste, one of the most original and many-sided minds of the thirteenth century.[1] Influenced on the one hand by the neo-Platonic and Augustinian conception of Light as the type of spiritual reality and, on the other, by the Arabic works on optics and perspective of the great eleventh-century physicist Ibn al-Haitham (Alhazen), he attempted to deduce from the nature of light a complete cosmological theory. Light is not only the primary substance, it is the very cause of the extension of matter. It alone is auto-diffusive, for, given a luminous point, it at once creates for itself a sphere of illumination. Thus it is the infinite dynamic energy of light that generates the finite *quantum* and confers on matter its form and dimensions.[2]

This view of space as essentially the field of radiation of energy is curiously suggestive of modern physical theory, and no less modern is the scientific ideal of the mathematical explanation of nature which is associated with it in Grosseteste's philosophy. Since the laws of perspective—of optical geometry—are the foundation of physical reality, mathe-

---

[1] It is a remarkable fact that the only thirteenth-century philosophers who read Aristotle in the original and translated his works directly from the Greek were the two leading Platonists of the age—Robert Grosseteste and William of Moerbeke.

[2] Baur, *Die Philosophie des Robert Grosseteste* (1917), 76–84.

matics are the only path to the understanding of nature. "All causes of natural effects," he writes, "can be given by lines and angles and figures; without them it is impossible to understand natural philosophy. For they hold good in the whole universe and in its parts absolutely."[1]

These ideas are like the inspired guesses of the early Greek physicists. They were too far in advance of the contemporary state of science to bear immediate fruit, and it was not until the age of Galileo and Descartes that they were actually realizable. Nevertheless, the influence of Grosseteste on the thought of his age was far from being negligible. His scientific ideas, above all his faith in mathematical reasoning, influenced the direction of studies at the new University of Oxford which he did so much to organize and in the Franciscan Order of which he was the patron. Throughout the thirteenth century and the first half of the fourteenth Oxford maintained the tradition of Augustinian philosophy and of "mathematical" science, and it was from Oxford that the remarkable development of scientific thought in France during the fourteenth century derived its inspiration.

Moreover, it is difficult to overestimate the influence of Grosseteste's thought on the mind of one of the most remarkable figures of the thirteenth century, whose fame has indeed overshadowed that of his master—I mean Roger Bacon. It was from Grosseteste that Bacon derived not only his distinctive philosophical and scientific views, above all his conviction of the importance of mathematics, but also his interest in philology and in the study of Greek and the oriental languages, of which Grosseteste was one of the pioneers. But if Bacon owed far more to his predecessors than has usually been supposed, he was none the less a profoundly original mind. His originality is, however, to be found less in his scientific theories than in his personality

[1] Baur, *op. cit.*, 92–3.

and in his general attitude to contemporary thought. To a far greater extent than Grosseteste he stands apart from the main current of scholastic philosophical study; he belongs rather to the tradition of the men of science who were responsible for the introduction of Arabic science into the West, such as Adelard of Bath, Gerard of Cremona and Plato of Tivoli. It is true that he speaks with contempt of the translators, but this is owing to a somewhat exaggerated sense of their linguistic incompetence and not from any doubt as to the value of Arabic science, which he regards as the main channel by which Christendom could recover the wisdom of the ancient world. He resembles Adelard, above all, in his critical attitude to Western scholasticism; indeed, he quotes the actual words of Adelard with regard to the danger of a blind reliance on authority. In Bacon's view, the four fundamental obstacles to the progress of philosophy are dependence on authority, the influence of custom, the ignorance of the populace and the false pretensions of those who esteem themselves to be learned. He cannot find words strong enough to express his contempt for "these new theologians" of the teaching orders who become masters in theology and philosophy before they have studied, and who console themselves for their ignorance by belittling the sciences and display their emptiness before the eyes of the ignorant multitude.

Yet although Bacon includes the great Dominicans, Albert and Thomas, in his wholesale condemnation, he is far from hostile to the new learning. He dismisses Alexander of Hales, precisely because the latter had had no training in Aristotelian physics and metaphysics "which are the glory of our modern studies". The works of Aristotle are for him "the foundation of all wisdom", and he blames his contemporaries not for their cultivation of Aristotelian science but for their misunderstanding and corruption of it.

Still less can we regard his attitude to scholasticism and authority as an attempt to free science and reason from their dependence on theology. In this respect he is distinctly reactionary in comparison with St. Thomas. The unity of science in which he believes is a purely theological unity. To an even greater extent than the earlier Augustinians he is prepared to subordinate all human knowledge to the divine wisdom that is contained in the Scriptures. All knowledge springs ultimately from Revelation. The first and most perfect scientists were the patriarchs, and the philosophers of the Gentiles merely collected the crumbs that had fallen from the tables of Shem and Abraham and Solomon. He admits the possibility of scientific progress, for there is no finality in this life, and knowledge must continue to increase with the rise and fall of the world religions.[1] All the signs, he believed, pointed to the approaching end of the age and to the coming of Antichrist, and it was to arm Christendom for the struggle and to prepare the way for its renovation under the leadership of a great pope and a great king that he propounded his schemes for the reform of studies and the utilization of the power of science.

Thus Bacon was no devotee of knowledge for its own sake. His attitude is fundamentally far less rational and far less intellectualist than that of Aristotle or even that of St. Thomas. But though this detracts from the philosophic value of his work, it does nothing to diminish his personal originality and his historical significance. For the greatness of Roger Bacon consists not in his scientific achievement, which was small, nor in his scientific method, which was inferior to that of his master, Peter of Maricourt, the obscure *Magister Experimentorum*. His greatness is to be found in

---

[1] Thus the conjunction of Jupiter with Mars marks the rise of the religion of the Chaldeans, with the sun that of the Egyptians, with Venus that of the Saracens, with Mercury that of the Christians, and finally the conjunction of Jupiter with the Moon marks the coming of Antichrist. *De Viciis Cantractis in Studio Theologiae*, ed. Steele, pp. 43–50.

the scientific vision and imagination which made him the discoverer of a new scientific ideal and the prophet of the new world of modern science.

For the history of science is not that of a simple continuous development. It takes a different form in every culture, Babylonian, Greek, Moslem and Christian, and until a culture has created a scientific ideal that is in harmony with its own spirit, it cannot bear scientific fruit. In the thirteenth century Western Christendom had already acquired a considerable knowledge of both Greek and Arabic science, but it knew them as it were from outside, since neither the Greek nor the Arabic ideal of science answered to the needs of Western culture or could be fully assimilated by the Western mind.

The Greek ideal of science was essentially intellectualist. It was the contemplation of reality as an intelligible order. To the Greek mind the practical results of science were quite a secondary matter; indeed, in their eyes the application of science to mechanical ends seemed rather vulgar and childish. The end of science was not to do but to know: *felix qui potuit rerum cognoscere causas.* The reward of the scientist was to share the blessedness of the immortal gods who are eternally satisfied with the contemplation of the ordered course of the heavens and the vision of eternal law.

Now, this attitude of mind was as incomprehensible to the medieval Christian as it is to the modern Englishman. William of Auvergne, whom I have already quoted on the subject, treats the Hellenic cosmology with the rude common sense of a Philistine and irreverently compares the intelligences that move the heavenly spheres to a donkey turning a treadmill; the only difference, he says, being that the movement of the donkey serves some purpose, whereas the gyrations of the heavenly intelligences do no good to anybody. It is true that St. Thomas does not talk in this way. He at least could understand something of the Greek point of view, for he was an intellectualist himself and believed that man's highest good was to understand. Nevertheless, as a Christian he believed that this Good was to be found in the knowledge of God and spiritual things rather than in the science of nature. Moreover, his very intellectualism led him to despise the flux of material being—"those lower things which are subject to generation and corruption and are the least part of the universe and the furthest removed from intelligible order".[1] Hence the Hellenism of St. Thomas finds expression not in physical science but in his religious and metaphysical thought. He is the scientist of the spiritual world.

But it was only a few rare minds in the Middle Ages— men such as St. Thomas and Robert Grosseteste and Albert the Great—which attained any real contact with the Hellenic tradition. The living tradition of science was that of the Arabs, and the science of the Arabs was entirely different in its inner form and spirit from the science of the Greeks. No doubt the Arabic scientists were the heirs of the Greek tradition and were not unworthy of their inheritance. But while they preserved it, they unconsciously transformed it by infusing a different spirit into it. In spite of its achievements Arabic science belongs to the same world as the Arabian Nights—a world of magic and mystery—and the scientist was the man who could control these mysterious forces by the power of secret knowledge. What he sought was not knowledge, but Power: to discover the Elixir of Life, the Philosopher's Stone, the Talisman, the Word of Power, and the magic properties of plants and minerals. His astronomy was inseparable from astrology, and his chemistry from alchemy. In a word, Arabic science was magic.

Now when the tide of Arabic learning reached the West, it brought with it this conception of science. The first trans-

[1] *De Spiritualibus Creaturis*, 8.

lators and men of science, such as Adelard of Bath, Plato of Tivoli and Roger of Hereford, were primarily interested in astrology, and it is easy to understand how popular opinion came to regard men like Michael Scott and Roger Bacon as wizards and magicians. And Roger Bacon himself seems at first sight to belong entirely to the Arabic scientific tradition. Like the Arabs he believed that science was power and that the scientist was a wonder worker and a magician; and the very titles of his books on alchemy[1]—for example, *Of the Marvellous Power of Art and Nature, an Epistle of the secret works of Nature, Liber secretorum de spiritu occulto* and *The Book of the Green Lion*—are typical of the esoteric attitude to science which I have spoken of as characteristically oriental. Even his theory of experimental science, which has been regarded as an anticipation of modern scientific method, is by no means free from this magical element. For Bacon's experimental science is not the verification of hypothesis by experiment: it is not the inductive method that had already been so admirably described by Aristotle in the Posterior Analytics; it is essentially an esoteric science, the knowledge that teaches man to transmute metals, to read the future in the stars and to prolong human life for centuries.

All this is true; yet none the less Bacon is profoundly original and a genuine precursor and prophet of Western science. In spite of its fantastic claims, his experimental science is not magic but *applied science*, and his scientist is not a magician but an expert. For Bacon realized both the limitless possibilities of scientific knowledge, and also its potential dangers, and his desire to confine experimental science to a class of chosen initiates was due not to occultism, but to his fear of the new knowledge being perverted to anti-social ends. His scientific ideal was essentially a utilitarian one. Science existed not for its own sake, not for private

---

[1] Some of them, however, are probably not authentic.

ends, but for the service of divine wisdom and "the guidance of the whole world". His ideal was no less theocratic than that of his contemporaries; but whereas they conceived this ideal primarily as the subordination of the temporal to the spiritual power, Bacon believed that it could only be realized by the co-operation of science. As philosophy was the hand-maid of theology, so experimental science was the handmaid of philosophy, and it was the divinely ordained instrument by which the Church could fulfil its mission towards man-kind and bring about the kingdom of God on earth. If the Church made use of this instrument she could rule the whole world and subdue the infidel, as she failed to do by the bloody and wasteful method of the Crusades. Experi-mental science was inevitably an esoteric tradition confined to a small body of experts. If these experts were left to their own devices they might become an anti-social force, as was the case with magicians and the astrologers. It was, there-fore, necessary that the Papacy should take control and organize a select body of scientists which would be, as it were, the brain of Christendom.

This grandiose vision of a world ruled by a science dedicated to moral and spiritual ends has an importance that far transcends the half-scientific, half-magical forms in which Bacon embodied it, since it marks the emergence of the new ideal that was to dominate the development of Western science. For, after all, it is not the intellectualist ideal of pure science—the "theory" of an intelligible order —but Bacon's ideal of science as an instrument of world conquest, a means for the subjection of nature to the service of man, which is that of the modern world. The former looks backward to the classical perfection of the Hellenic world, the latter looks forward to the brilliant and disorderly progress of the Western mind. When Bacon sings the praises of the experimental science that can create automobiles and flying machines and devices that will destroy a whole army at once, he is the prophet of modern science, nor can we, in these days of mechanized warfare and mechanized production, afford altogether to despise his warnings of the danger of allowing these vast forces to escape moral direction and social control.

No doubt there is an immense gap between Bacon's prophetic vision and its realization by modern science. Nevertheless, it was not merely a fruit of the imagination of a pseudo-scientific charlatan. The seeds of the new Western scientific development were already being sown in the thirteenth century. At the very time when Roger Bacon was dreaming dreams and seeing visions of the future of experimental science, his master, Peter of Maricourt, was already giving a striking example of the genuine experimental method in his treatise on the Magnet, which was composed, significantly enough, in the camp of the crusading army before the Saracen city of Lucera in Apulia in 1269. For, in spite of the imposing appearance of Arabic science, the intellectual leadership was already passing to the younger culture of Western Christendom. Western mathematics were being reborn with Leonard of Pisa and Jordan Nemorarius and Robert Grosseteste, and there were already signs of the advent of the new science of mechanics which is, as it were, the scientific expression of the dynamic spirit of Western culture and through which Bacon's vision of the application of mathematics to practical ends was one day to be realized.

Moreover, Bacon's own teaching was not so lacking in influence as has usually been supposed. As Duhem has shown, the leading writers on astronomy in the next generation—Bernard of Verdun, William of St. Cloud, and John of Sicily, not to mention Peter d'Ailly at a later date—were among his followers. And apart from this direct or semi-direct influence, the spirit of his teaching, with its appeal from authority to experience and its exaltation of mathematical reasoning, survives in the tradition of critical and scientific nominalism which was the dominant force in the intellectual life of the fourteenth century. In the schoolmen of that age—William of Ockam, John Buridan, Albert of Saxony and Nicholas Oresme—we find not only a critical reaction against the authority of Aristotelian and Arabic tradition, but also an original movement of scientific research which prepares the way for the coming of Leonardo da Vinci and Copernicus and the science of the Renaissance.

Thus the strictly theological tradition of medieval thought —the tradition of St. Augustine and St. Bernard, which finds its complete thirteenth-century representative in St. Bonaventure—is not the only intellectual element in medieval culture. The latter widens out in the thirteenth century to include, on the one hand, the philosophic humanism of St. Thomas, which represents the birth of Western philosophy, and, on the other, the scientific idealism of Roger Bacon, which marks the emergence, if not of Western science, at least of a new scientific ideal. No doubt, in this, as in so many other respects, the later Middle Ages failed to realize the brilliant promise of their earlier development. The wide metaphysical vision of the thirteenth century degenerated into the sterile logomachy of the later Scotists, which St. Thomas More compared to the process of milking a he-goat into a sieve, while the spirit of scientific research which had been so active at Oxford in the thirteenth century and at Paris in the fourteenth, gave place to a blind reliance on authority and an arrogant disregard of new knowledge.

These tendencies in later scholasticism brought it into conflict with the living thought of the age and tended to throw discredit on the whole tradition of medieval thought. It was responsible for the belief that scholasticism was essentially anti-scientific and anti-humanist, and that the Middle Ages were a long period of mental degeneration— the night of the human spirit. It is easy to find excuses for the men who originated this view—for the Renaissance men of science and Francis Bacon and the Cartesians—for they were actually suffering under the incubus of an unintelligent traditionalism. But for all that it is a profoundly unhistorical attitude and one that is no less false than that of the humanist who thought that all the literary and artistic production of the Middle Ages could be dismissed as Gothic barbarism, or that of the Reformers who believed that medieval religion was nothing but superstition and apostasy.

IX

THE LITERARY DEVELOPMENT OF MEDIEVAL CULTURE

W E have seen how the medieval development consisted, above all, in a gradual process of inter-
penetration between the barbaric society of the
young peoples of western Europe and the Christian culture
of the later Roman Empire embodied in the Catholic
Church. The new peoples received Christianity, and in
doing so they acquired a new culture and a new soul.

And nowhere do we see this process so clearly as in the
history of medieval literature, for here we are not forced
to rely, as in social history, on partial and fragmentary
evidence which at best only throws light on the surface of
the social process; we have the living witness of the mind
of the age that we are studying. It is true that this evidence
also is by no means complete; there are whole classes and
societies that never attained to literary expression, but while
in the early part of the Middle Ages, at least, much that
must once have existed has perished, nevertheless enough
remains of medieval literature to make us realize the complexity of the medieval development and the multiplicity
of intellectual strands that have been woven into the pattern
of medieval culture.

For, as I pointed out in the first chapter, the Christian
culture of the later Roman Empire was by no means a
simple and uniform phenomenon. It represents itself a synthesis between two different traditions: that of the Classical
culture, and that of Christianity, a synthesis which was
achieved only with difficulty and on the very eve of the dissolution of the Empire. The great representatives of Latin-

Christian culture—Ambrose, Jerome, Augustine, Rufinus, Marius Victorinus, Prudentius—all flourished in the last days of the Western Empire and their work was only partially accomplished when the storm broke. Yet, incomplete as it was, it was strong enough not only to survive the downfall of the Empire and of Classical civilization but to impose itself on the conquering peoples and become the intellectual patrimony of the new world. What has perished, strange to say, has not been the literature of the conquered, but that of the conquerors. Nothing remains of the old heroic poetry of the Germans in which Charlemagne himself delighted, save a single fragment. Only in the outer lands, in the British Isles and in Iceland, did the tradition of vernacular literature survive unbroken. And consequently the literature of the Dark Ages is not, as we might expect it to be, the literature of warlike barbarians; it is a literature of schoolmasters and grammarians, of commentators and homilists. The children of the barbarians put themselves to school with the monks and the Fathers, with the result that they wrote the same language and thought the same thoughts. No one could guess from the study of his works that a man like Bede, for example, was hardly two generations removed from pagan barbarism. He belongs rather to the world of Jerome and Rufinus, and wrote better Latin than many an educated Roman of the later Empire.

But while the Dark Ages are by no means lacking in learning or literature, there is no literature that is less read or, it must be admitted, less readable. Of the hundred volumes or so into which Migne has compressed the literary remains of the period there are but three or four which still retain any literary vitality or human interest. Boethius, Bede, Adamnan, Einhard, Gregory the Great and Gregory of Tours, these, I think, are the only authors that are ever read for their own sake, together with the authors of a few hymns; above all, the two famous ones ascribed to Venantius

Fortunatus, the *Vexilla Regis* and the *Pange lingua,* which give their author the right to the title of the first medieval poet. For the rest it is a literature of schoolmasters whose very quotations are not original but have been borrowed from the writings of some grammarian or epitomist of the later Empire.

It is characteristic of the age that the most famous and popular work that it produced should have been the *Etymologies* of Isidore of Seville—that extraordinary collection of miscellaneous information which was the encyclopædia of the Dark Ages. Isidore was no doubt the most learned man of his age and thus deserved the praises lavished on him by his contemporaries. But he was by no means as learned as he seems at first sight. All those quotations from Pacuvius and Afranius and Ennius and Livius Andronicus, which suggest to the unwary readers that Isidore was deeply read in the works of early Roman poets and dramatists that we no longer possess, are in reality lifted bodily and without acknowledgement from the pages of Servius and Festus.

This lack of originality is the most striking feature of later Latin literature—above all, in its secular forms. It has nothing to do with the "monkish obscurantism" of eighteenth-century legend; it was due to the exhaustion of the classical tradition itself—the dying literature of a dying society. Secular literature perished not from neglect so much as from pedantry. It finds an inglorious end in the jungle of sham erudition in which the crazy genius of Virgilius Maro of Toulouse flourished so luxuriantly. It is only in the religious literature of the time that we find the seeds of life. The great Passion hymns of Fortunatus stand in an entirely different category from his secular poetry, though he himself probably would have rated the latter far higher. Consequently we have no right to blame Gregory the Great for his depreciation of secular culture and his refusal to allow the word of God to be fettered by the rules of the grammarians, for in this he is the champion of the rights of the new world, and he stands for the living culture of the Church and the religion of the people against the traditionalism of the rhetoricians and the dead world of classical culture.

But though the Church insisted on the primacy and the independence of the Christian tradition, she was by no means unwilling to accept the classical tradition as an instrument of Christian education and as the vehicle of Catholic culture. And it was, in fact, this adoption of the classical tradition by the Church which saved it from the sterility and emptiness that had destroyed its secular vitality, and which gave it a new spiritual purpose and a new social function that ensured its survival and its transmission to the new peoples. If the culture of the Dark Ages is a culture of schoolmasters, they were the schoolmasters of Europe, and all the subsequent achievement of Western culture rests on the foundation of their work. Hence the real interest of the period lies not so much in the literature that it produced as in the educational work that it accomplished by the transmission of classical and patristic literature to the new peoples and the consequent modification of their own cultures.

The most striking example of this process is to be found in Ireland and England, for here it was entirely religious in origin, being wholly due to the work of the monastic schools and missions, owing little or nothing to the social inheritance of the Roman tradition which was so important in Gaul and Italy and Spain. On the Continent the Church was Latin not only in its intellectual culture, but by its social traditions and its political associations. It remained in a sense the Church of the Empire, even when the Empire had fallen. But in the British Isles it was not so; above all, in Ireland, which had no traditional connection with the Roman Empire and which possessed an exceptionally strong and developed form of native culture. Consequently in Ireland alone the native culture met the Latin tradition of the Church on relatively equal terms and it was there that a synthesis of the two elements was achieved which resulted in the formation of a vernacular Christian literature and culture. Nor was the influence of this vernacular culture limited to the Celtic-speaking peoples; it was transmitted to Northumbria through the Irish missionaries and was the source and model of the brilliant development of vernacular Anglian culture in the seventh and eighth centuries which created Anglo-Saxon literature. And the Anglo-Saxons in turn transmitted it to Germany, where the earliest beginnings of vernacular literature are associated with the missionary activities of Boniface and his Anglo-Saxon foundations; above all, at Fulda, and later with the old Celtic foundation of St. Gall, which retained its contacts with Irish scholarship and culture down to the eleventh century.

It is a characteristic feature of this culture that, though it was essentially monastic, its interests were not confined to ecclesiastical literature. We owe to it the preservation of the heroic epic traditions, not only in Ireland, but also in England, with *Beowulf* and *Waldere,* and in Germany, where it was a monk of Fulda who saved for us the only remaining relic of the old German heroic poetry, the *Hildebrandslied.*

It is difficult to exaggerate the importance of this "insular" Celtic-Anglo-Saxon tradition of vernacular culture in the history of the Dark Ages. It marks the turn of the tide of barbarism in the seventh and eighth centuries. It infused new life into the continental Church and the decadent classical civilization and was one of the main formative influences in the development of Carolingian culture. Nevertheless, it was not destined to endure. It was gradually superseded by the Carolingian culture which it had done so much to create, and medieval culture as a whole is based not on the Christian-vernacular tradition of the Irish and the Anglo-Saxons but on the Carolingian-Latin tradition that replaced it.

In England the Anglo-Saxon culture gradually came under the sway of continental influences, until it was finally incorporated in the unity of western continental culture as a result of the Norman Conquest. In Ireland, on the other hand, the old tradition of vernacular culture was too strong to be forcibly uprooted and it preserved its identity and continuity unbroken through the Viking and Anglo-Norman invasions. But in consequence Celtic Ireland lost touch with the rest of Western Christendom and was isolated from the dominant current of medieval culture to such an extent that by the twelfth century St. Bernard can write of the old pioneer of Christian learning as an outer land of barbarism and semi-paganism.

No doubt the ravages of the Viking invasions were largely responsible for the decline of the insular cultures, but the fundamental cause of the change was the divergence between continental and insular civilization that followed the rise of the Carolingian Empire. Both of them were founded on the culture of the Church and the monasteries, both looked back to the patristic and classical tradition; but while in the British Isles these traditions were fused with those of the native vernacular culture, on the Continent they united with the tradition of the Christian Empire to form an international ecclesiastical Latin culture which was common to France and Germany and North Italy, and gradually extended its influence westwards to the British Isles, northwards to Scandinavia and eastwards to Bohemia and the Slavonic borderlands.

It was on the foundation of this Latin-Carolingian culture rather than on that of the old vernacular literary tradition that the new vernacular literature of medieval Europe was finally developed in the eleventh and twelfth centuries. It is true that this was not realized by nineteenth-century scholars, who looked for its origins in a lost epic tradition which would bridge the gap between the *chansons de geste* and the old Teutonic heroic poetry and the national epics of the Franks. But, as Prof. Bédier has shown, this is an *a priori* hypothesis that has no basis in fact. The *chansons de geste* have no links with the old Frankish national literature. They grew up in the age of the crusades around the shrines of the great abbeys, along the pilgrimage roads that led to Spain. Their models were not the old Germanic epic but the new vernacular versions of the Latin legends of the saints like the *Vie de Ste. Foy* and the *Vie de St. Alexis.*

Nevertheless, in spite of the errors of the nineteenth-century view, it contains, as is so often the case with mistaken theories, an important element of truth. For though the medieval epic is a new creation of the new culture of Latin Christendom and not the direct descendant of the Germanic national epic, there is a certain continuity, both spiritual and sociological, between these two traditions. The feudal noble was in a real sense the descendant of the barbarian warrior. He inherited his social traditions and spiritual ideals. His moral standards were those of the heroic age—of Beowulf and Hildebrand and the Nibelungs—the fidelity of the tribal warrior to his chieftain and his kin, the bloodstained law of private vengeance and family feud, the ideals of honour and contempt of death and boundless liberality. During the Dark Ages these standards and ideals stood in sharp contrast to those of the Christian tradition, as embodied in the Church and the monastic life. The virtues of the warrior were vices to the monk, and the virtues of the monk were the vices of the warrior. But in the new vernacular literature this dualism of tradition begins to disappear. The heroic type is partially Christianized, and the barbarian warrior becomes the medieval knight. The heroes of the *chansons de geste* are still bloodthirsty barbarians; they still hold to the law of vengeance and feud; but they are now conscious of a higher loyalty and a new religious conception of Christian heroism.

Thus in the *Song of Roland*, for example, we see the old heroic tradition in the process of transformation under the influence of new religious ideals. Turpin, the warrior archbishop, stands side by side with Roland and Oliver as one of the central figures in the poem, and his sermon to the Franks before the battle is a faithful expression of the union of heroic and Christian elements that went to make up the crusading ideal.

> *My lord barons, Charles left us here for this;*
> *He is our king, well may we die for him;*
> *To Christendom good service offering.*
> *Battle you'll have, you all are bound to it.*
> *For with your eyes you see the Sarrazins,*
> *Pray for God's grace, confessing Him your sins!*
> *For your souls' health, I'll absolution give,*
> *So though you die, blest martyrs shall you live,*
> *Thrones you shall win in the great Paradise.*[1]

Above all, as Prof. Faral has pointed out,[2] in the cycle of Doon of Mayence—the Song of Raoul of Cambrai, and the rest—we find a remarkable attempt to bring out the conflict and opposition between the two elements in the tradition of the feudal warrior, the law of fidelity and the law of vengeance, destructive barbarism and Christian heroism, pride and obedience. Each of the poems in this cycle centres in an act of rebellion and vengeance, followed by a long sequel of violence and outrage and ending in an act of

[1] The *Song of Roland*, trans. C. Scott-Moncrieff (1919), 1127–35.
[2] In Bédier et Hazard, *Histoire de la Littérature Française*, i, 14.

humility and repentance. Thus Ogier the Dane dies in the habit of a monk, Renaud of Montauban works as a labourer among the masons of the Church of St. Peter at Cologne, and Ybert of Ribemont in *Raoul of Cambrai* builds seven churches as monuments of his humility on the site of the seven castles that were the monuments of his pride.

Thus there is a genuine religious element in the medieval French epic which is all the more striking on account of the background of ferocity and barbarism against which it stands out. For the *chanson de geste,* to a far greater extent than either the old heroic epic of the type of *Beowulf* or the later medieval romance, is entirely devoid of all literary sophistication and gives a faithful reflection of the mind of feudal society. It is the literature of the camp as opposed to the literature of the school.

For we must not forget that the age of the *chansons de geste* was also the great age of medieval humanism and classical scholarship, when cultivated men of letters like Hildebert of Lavardin, Baudri of Bourgeuil, Marbod of Rennes and John of Salisbury modelled their style on Ovid and Cicero, and exchanged scholarly epigrams and epistles like the humanists of a later age. Such men seem to belong to a different tradition, and indeed to a different world from that of the jongleurs who sang of the bloody deeds of their barbarous heroes to men whose only interests were in war, and the contrast makes us realize the dualism which underlay early medieval culture and how great a gap had to be bridged before the churchman and the feudal warrior could meet on a common ground of Christian culture. It is true that the new social and economic conditions that began to develop in the eleventh century tended to raise the level of secular culture and to tame the barbarism of feudal society. But it does not necessarily follow that as society grew less barbarous it would grow more Christian. On the contrary, the new conditions favoured the development of new ideals that were to some extent incompatible with Christian standards, and it seemed possible that feudal society might pass direct from the paganism of barbarism to an even more pagan culture.

For, as a matter of fact, the literary development which was to transform the standards of feudal society and to create the new vernacular poetry and the new secular culture had its origins neither in the Latin Christian culture of the Church nor in the heroic tradition of Northern feudalism. It was an exotic growth which arose in southern France under the shadow of the brilliant and advanced Moslem culture of Spain and the western Mediterranean, to which it probably owed some of its most distinctive features. It shows itself not only in a new style of poetry but in new forms of social life and new ideals of moral conduct. It created the new attitude to woman, the new cult of romantic love and the new ideals of courtesy and chivalry that did so much to transform medieval culture that they now appear almost inseparable from it. Yet it has no roots in the older medieval past. It is neither Christian nor Germanic, and it has no contact with the heroic epic tradition which had hitherto been the inspiration of Western vernacular literature.

Nothing, in fact, could be more mistaken than the old view which derives the poetry of the troubadours and the new ideals that are associated with it from the influence of Christian idealism or Northern feudalism. We see that influence in the *chansons de geste,* but it finds expression not in the cult of woman and of romantic love but in the exaltation of the heroic virtues and of the ideals of the crusade. But even this modicum of Christian influence is lacking in the new poetry of the South. It is not without its own idealism and its moral code, but they are not those of Christianity. Its outlook is entirely this-worldly, and is equally opposed to the asceticism of medieval Christianity and to the barbaric simplicity of the Northern tradition. It finds expression, above all, in the cult of woman and the romantic ideal of love and in the elaborate code of courtesy and chivalrous behaviour, which is at once so rigid and so antinomian.

This new literary movement, and the culture of which it was the expression, spread with extraordinary rapidity through western Europe in the second half of the twelfth century. Its chief centre of diffusion was the Angevin court, where Eleanor of Aquitaine, the grand-daughter of the first of the troubadours, was its great patron; while her daughters, Marie of Champagne and Mathilda of Saxony, and her niece, Elizabeth of Vermandois, the Countess of Flanders, also took a leading part in the work of diffusion. It was in these circles that there arose the new courtly epic which grafted the ideas and motives of the courtly literature of the South on to the Northern legendary stock, thus producing the romances of Tristan and Lancelot and the rest of the Arthurian cycle, which gradually took the place of the *chansons de geste* as the standard literature of feudal society.

This was, in a sense, a victory for culture over barbarism, since it taught the feudal nobility of northern Europe new standards of social intercourse and civilized behaviour. The brutal violence of the barbarian warrior, which appears no less plainly in the heroes of the *chansons de geste* than in those of the Nordic Sagas, gradually yielded to the new ideals of honour and courtesy and the service of ladies. But from the religious point of view there was no such progress. The new spirit was not merely non-religious; it was potentially unorthodox and anti-clerical. It is no accident that the cradle of the courtly literature and culture should also have been the centre of the Albigensian heresy and the first country in western Europe to revolt against the religious unity of Christendom. Nothing, it is true, could seem more dissimilar at first sight from the "joyful wisdom" of the

troubadours than the world-refusing asceticism of the Catharists. Nevertheless, they are, in a sense, parallel phenomena.
Both of them were exotic growths which had no roots in
Christian culture, but which found a favourable soil in the
brilliant and precocious society of Languedoc. Moreover,
our knowledge of medieval Catharism is too scanty for us
to be able to trace its relations to contemporary literature,
and I do not think that we can entirely exclude the possibility of the existence of an esoteric and unorthodox tradition in courtly literature, such as the late Luigi Valli
maintained in his ingenious and often extravagant theories
on the secret language of Dante and the *Fedeli d'Amore*.[1]
Certainly the centres of the new poetry both in southern
France and southern Italy were also the centres of disaffection to the Church, and the philosophy that under-
lies the erotic mysticism of the *dolce stil nuovo* in Tuscany
owed more to the speculations of the Averroists and to
Islamic mysticism than to the orthodox tradition of Western
scholasticism.

It is a sign of the vitality and cultural influence of medieval religion that it succeeded in assimilating this new
literary tradition and making it the instrument of its own
spiritual ideals.

Instead of secularizing medieval culture, the courtly tradition itself became Christianized. We see this, above all, in
the development of the medieval tradition of chivalry. That
tradition had its origins in the military institutions and
ideals of the feudal warrior caste. It acquired from the
courtly tradition of the South a code of manners and a
common type of culture which transformed the knight from
a mere fighting man into a gentleman and a man of the
world. But medieval chivalry at its best was something

[1] Valli, *Il Linguaggio Segreto di Dante e dei Fedeli d'Amore*, Rome,
1928.

much more than this. It was a sacred institution consecrated by religious rites and dedicated to the service of God and the defence of Holy Church.

This religious conception of chivalry is already implicit in the crusading movement; it finds explicit expression in the new military orders, whose ideals were set forth by St. Bernard himself in his work *In Praise of the New Knighthood,* and finally in the thirteenth century it becomes organically united with the classical institutions of medieval knighthood as shown in the religious ceremonies by which a knight was created and the religious character of the engagements which he swore to observe.

Now this same process of development is reflected in the literature of feudal society and in the evolution of medieval epic. The *chansons de geste* represent, as we have seen, the barbaric heroism of Northern feudalism already coloured in some degree by Christian ideals. The development of the romantic epic by Chrétien de Troyes and the authors of *Tristan* marks the introduction of the new courtly literature into the North and the development of new forms of secular culture. But this new literature, whether in its epic or lyrical forms, lacks the religious inspiration which the *chansons de geste,* for all their rudeness, undoubtedly possess. It is an exotic and artificial development which has no contact with the deeper elements in the Western soul. Consequently we find in the thirteenth century a deliberate attempt to moralize the courtly tradition and to infuse an element of religious idealism into the secular romanticism of the courtly epic. The result of this is to be seen in the romantic mysticism of the Grail legend; above all, in the great prose cycle of *Lancelot del Lac,*[1] which was composed, probably under

---

[1] This is a trilogy, consisting of three parts: the Book of Lancelot, The Quest of the Holy Grail, and the Morte d'Arthur. I follow the view of Prof. F. Lot—*Étude sur le Lancelot en prose* (1918)—in ascribing the whole trilogy to a single author, but opinions differ on this subject, and many scholars regard it as a composite work.

Cistercian influence, in the first quarter of the thirteenth century, between 1220 and 1225. Here the whole material of Arthurian romance is remoulded in accordance with the religious conception of chivalry, and the courtly motive of romantic love is subordinated to the religious allegory of the quest for the Grail, the symbol of spiritual vision.

The same tendency to spiritualize the courtly epic by the infusion of a religious motive is to be found in Germany in the *Parsifal* of Wolfram von Eschenbach, while even the courtly lyric, which in France retained its secular character to the end, acquires in the work of Walter von de Vogel-weide a new depth of thought and religious feeling which raises it far above the formal artificiality of the great bulk of courtly poetry, whether Provençal or French. It is indeed a remarkable fact that this moralization of the courtly tra-dition by the introduction of religious motives represents in each of the cases we have mentioned a distinct gain from the literary point of view. In post-Renaissance literature this is rarely the case; the literature of edification is usually bad literature, and the attempt to give a good story a good moral is usually fatal to both. Yet in the case of the Arthurian legend we find the author of the prose *Lancelot* ruthlessly recasting a series of romantic tales of love and adventure in the interests of religion and morals and making a triumphant success of it, since the introduction of the religious motive gives the whole cycle an artistic unity and a spiritual significance that it had never before possessed.

Thus we see how the courtly tradition, in spite of its purely secular origins and its somewhat antinomian tendencies, was gradually brought into relation with religious thought and incorporated in the spiritual unity of medieval Christendom. It is true that the literature of chivalry is so remote from real life that it is difficult to draw definite conclusions from it with regard to medieval culture. Far more significant is the evidence of the new vernacular religious literature that makes its appearance in the thirteenth century, for this is perhaps the most vital and spontaneous expression of the medieval mind. And the characteristic feature of this literature is its use of the forms and ideas of the courtly tradition to express religious experience—the transformation of romanticism into mysticism and of chivalry into religious devotion.

The root of this development is to be found in St. Francis, who had an instinctive attraction to the romantic idealism of the courtly literature. Unlike the other great religious leaders of the Middle Ages, St. Francis was a stranger to the Latin traditions of ecclesiastical culture; he belonged to the new world of the Italian city-states, a world that was already outgrowing the semi-Byzantine traditions of the older Italy, but which had not yet begun to realize the new forms of social life and secular culture that were to find expression in the age of the Renaissance. We see from the vernacular literature of the following century—for example in the sonnets of Folgore of San Gemignano—how the aristocratic society of the new commercial cities adopted the fashions of the feudal courts and strove to outdo them in magnificence and display, and in the same way St. Francis himself in his youth was dazzled and attracted by the ideals of courtly chivalry that were then entering the Italian peninsula from across the Alps.

Now his conversion, so far from causing him to abandon these ideals for the traditional monastic asceticism, gave them a new significance which inspired his whole religious mission. The ideals of his fraternity were founded on those of romantic chivalry rather than on those of Benedictine monasticism. It was to be an order of spiritual knighthood, dedicated to the service of the Cross and the love of the Lady Poverty. The friars were his "Brethren of the Round Table", "jongleurs of God", and they were to set forth like

Knight Adventurers on the path of God, performing deeds of spiritual prowess, shrinking from no hardship or danger and finding their reward in the service of love. Thus the courtly ideals of courtesy, joy, generosity and romantic love found a new religious application of which the life of St. Francis himself was the perfect manifestation and which already appears in literary form in the writings of the early Franciscans; above all, in the *Sacrum Commercium,* which describes the wooing of the Lady Poverty by St. Francis in the form of a symbolic romance.

In the course of the thirteenth century this religious adaptation of courtly literature and chivalrous idealism spread —whether by Franciscan influence or by a spontaneous development—from one end of Christendom to the other. One of the earliest and most perfect examples is to be found in Flanders, in the writings of the obscure Béguine, Hadewych, who composed her vernacular mystical poems entirely in the form and spirit of the courtly lyric about the middle of the thirteenth century. Another example of the same period is the famous German mystic Mechtild of Magdeburg. In Italy we have the great Franciscan poet Jacopone da Todi who uses the passionate language of romantic poets to sing the praises of Divine Love. But above all the founder of Catalan literature, Ramon Lull, who was at once poet and philosopher and mystic, is the supreme example of this, and his elaborate mystical romance, *Blanquerna,* embodies every aspect of the new literary movement; its romanticism, its chivalry, its mysticism and its contacts with Moslem culture.[1] This literature is of exceptional interest to the student of medieval religion, since in it are to be found the beginnings of the great mystical movement which reached its full development in the fourteenth century and which we

[1] Nothing could be more explicit than Ramon Lull's reference to the Sufis as the model of the mystical *Book of the Lover and the Beloved* which is the culmination of the whole work. (*Blanquerna,* trans. E. Allison Peers, p. 410).

have discussed in a previous chapter. For while that movement was, on the one side, learned and speculative, based on
the metaphysics of the Dominican Schoolmen and on the
Christian neo-Platonism of the Pseudo-Dionysius, on the
other hand it was connected with the vernacular tradition
of secular culture and with the popular appeal of the Franciscan spirit. Both these elements already exist side by side
in the writings of Jacopone da Todi and Ramon Lull, and
we find them reappearing in the full tide of fourteenth-
century Dominican German mysticism with Henry Suso,
who embodied the tradition of Eckhart in the forms of the
courtly literature. Moreover, at the same time we find this
transformed courtly tradition, at once spiritualized and
popularized, as an important element in the formation of
the new vernacular poetry which was making its appearance
in England.

But the influence of medieval religion on the literary
tradition of the courtly culture does not only show itself in
the adaptation of this tradition to the service of vernacular
mysticism and popular piety; it also plays an essential part
in the formation of the greatest literary genius of the Middle
Ages. Dante's earlier poetry is the crown and consummation of the courtly tradition in its most mature and exquisite
form, and even in the *Divina Commedia* he still acknow-
ledges his debt to the masters of Provençal and Italian
courtly poetry, Arnaut Daniel and Guido Guinicelli. Nevertheless, as Dante's genius ripens, it transcends the limits of
the courtly tradition and becomes at once more classical
and more Christian. The Lady of the *Convivio*, and perhaps
also the Beatrice of the *Vita Nuova*, belong to the strange
twilight world in which the abstractions of Averroistic metaphysics are clothed in the forms of Provençal love poetry,
and the return of Dante from the strange lady of the *Convivio* to the heavenly Beatrice of the *Divina Commedia*

marks the progress of his thought back from the exotic half-oriental world of the courtly poets to the central tradition of Christian culture. It is Virgil, the representative of the classical tradition, who is Dante's leader in this spiritual pilgrimage, and it is in him, rather than in Guido Guinicelli or Arnaut Daniel, that Dante recognizes his true master.

> *Tu se' lo mio maestro e il mio autore,*
> *Tu se' solo colui, da cui io tolsi*
> *Lo bello stile che m'ha fatto honore.*

> *Thou art my master and my author thou,*
> *Thou art alone the one from whom I took*
> *The beautiful style that has done honour to me.*

Thus Dante's great poem represents the achievement of a final synthesis of the literary and the religious traditions of the Middle Ages, a synthesis that embodies all the vital elements of medieval culture. Christian theology and the science and philosophy of the Arabs, the courtly culture of the troubadours and the classical tradition of Virgil, the mysticism of Dionysius and the piety of St. Bernard, the Franciscan spirit of reform and the Roman order, Italian national feeling and Christian universalism—all find their place in the organic structure of the poet's thought and in the artistic unity of his work. Yet at the same time the *Divina Commedia* also faithfully reflects the crisis of the later Middle Ages and the failure of medieval Christendom to overcome the centrifugal forces that were about to destroy its unity. It is true that Dante still stands for the ideal of Catholic universalism against the territorial and ecclesiastical self-assertion of the new national monarchies. But he no longer looks to the Papacy as the representative of Christian universalism and the leader of the movement of Catholic reform. The Papacy had itself become compromised in his eyes by secularism and by its subservience to the French monarchy. And consequently it is to the Empire rather than to the Papacy that he looks for the realization of a universal Christian order and the delivery of the Church from its state of bondage.

But Dante's ideal of the Empire no longer has any relations with history and reality. His Emperor is not the real Henry VII but an apocalyptic figure, the Messianic DVX whose coming he foretells in a strain of prophetic inspiration in the great vision of the Earthly Paradise in the concluding cantos of the *Purgatorio*. But the Prince who was actually to come was a very different figure; it was the Prince of Macchiavelli, who was, after all, the lineal descendant of the Can Grandes and the Castruccio Castracanes in whom Dante had put his trust. Thus Dante's conception of a world state which should be the perfect embodiment of *humana civilitas*, and should actualize all the potentialities of human nature, had no relation to political reality or to the historical facts of his age. It is the last glimpse of that vision of spiritual unity which had inspired the medieval mind for nine hundred years, and had guided the development of medieval culture from its beginnings in the age of St. Augustine and Prudentius, through the age of Alcuin and Charles the Great, of Nicholas I and Otto III, to its fullest yet still incomplete realization in thirteenth-century Christendom.

An incomplete realization, I have said, for on the one hand no society or culture has ever realized the aspirations of its greatest minds, and, on the other, the Christian ideal most of all tends to transcend all cultural forms. Nevertheless, there has never been an age in which Christianity attained so complete a cultural expression as in the thirteenth century. Europe has seen no greater Christian hero than St. Francis, no greater Christian philosopher than St. Thomas, no greater Christian poet than Dante, perhaps even no greater Christian ruler than St. Louis.

I do not maintain that the general level of religious life was higher than at other times or that the state of the Church was healthier, still less that the scandals were rarer or moral evils less obvious. What one can assert is that in the Middle Ages more than at other periods in the life of our civilization the European culture and the Christian religion were in a state of communion: the highest expressions of medieval culture, whether in art, in literature or in philosophy, were religious, and the greatest representatives of medieval religion were also the leaders of medieval culture. This is not, of course, an inevitable state of things. It may even be argued that the dualism of religion and culture that existed under the Roman Empire, and more or less generally in modern times, is the normal condition of Christianity. Nevertheless, the other alternative, that of a co-operation and collaboration between religion and culture, is undoubtedly a more ideal system, and from this point of view the medieval achievement remains unsurpassed by any other age.

X

THE FEUDAL SOCIETY AND THE CHRISTIAN EPIC

IN THE tenth century the state of western Europe seemed not far removed from that state of universal war which Hobbes regarded as man's natural state. It was a time when every man was the enemy of every man, and men lived without other security than that which their own strength and cunning could give them. "In such condition there is no place for Industry, because the fruit thereof is uncertain . . . no commodious Building . . . no Knowledge of the face of the Earth . . . no Arts; no Letters; no Society; and what is worst of all, continual fear and danger of violent death; And the life of man, solitary, poor, nasty, brutish, and short."[1]

Yet, strange as it may appear, the birth of the new order came out of the very midst of this weakness and disorder. It was not the restored Christian Roman Empire of the Ottos and the Henrys, for all its imposing appearance, but the apparently anarchic society of the west Carolingian realm that was the real focus of the revival of cultural activity in the West. It was as though the breakdown of the State and the disappearance of public authority, legal rights and social order were the necessary conditions for the free expansion of the vital energies of the new men and the new classes who created a new society.

We are apt to think of feudalism as essentially aristocratic, surrounded with all the pageantry of chivalry and heraldry as it was in the later Middle Ages. But, as Guilhiermoz

---

[1] Hobbes, *Leviathan*, pt. i, ch. xiii. "Of the natural condition of Mankind as concerning their Felicity and Misery."

has shown, the new feudal class was not an hereditary caste like the old nobility of the barbarian world and the new nobility of later medieval times. It consisted to a great extent of self-made men—adventurers who had pushed themselves to the front by hard fighting, or local counts who were half local officials and half robber chiefs, and who had made a position for themselves by a judicious combination of intimidation and protection, like the bosses and racketeers of the American underworld. Indeed the ethos of early feudal society has, in some respects, more in common with that of the gangster and the gunman than with the later code of chivalry. Many of the founders of the great feudal dynasties were tough and sinister individuals, who owed their power to treachery and the complete disregard not only of moral but even of feudal obligations. Such was Thibaut le Tricheur, the founder of the house of Blois; such, above all, was Herbert II of Vermandois, "the most wicked of the wicked and the worst of infidels", who owed his power to the betrayal of his king, Charles the Simple, and to the skill with which he exploited his royal captive. Some of them, again, were men of humble origin, like the founders of the great house of Anjou, the ancestors of the English royal house. They were descended from a soldier of fortune from the marches of Brittany who had distinguished himself by his hard fighting against the Northmen. And in the same way the royal house of France goes back to an obscure soldier, Robert le Fort, who was the son of a Saxon stranger who had settled in Neustria in the ninth century.[1] Finally, Normandy, the greatest of all the feudal principalities, was not even Christian in its origin, but a purely Scandinavian settlement of Viking pirates.

In short, it was an age in which only the strong could survive but wherein a career was open to any man who

[1] Richer speaks of him as "Witichinum, advenam Germanum", and it has been suggested that this stranger was no other than Witikind, Charlemagne's great enemy, the last champion of Germanic paganism.

possessed the simple and barbarous talents of the chieftain and war leader. Western society seemed to be returning to a state of barbarism in which the fundamental institutions of civilized society—the State, the law, and private property —seemed to have practically disappeared. Nevertheless, we must remember that the political system which had collapsed was not a civilized state like the Roman Empire or the modern national state but a rickety and insecure super-structure which hid but did not change the fundamentally barbarous character of Western society. The true "state" of the Dark Ages was not the ambitious pseudo-Roman Empire of the Carolingians, which owed all its positive cultural achievements to the Church, but the semi-tribal society of barbarian Europe, as it existed in northern Germany and Scandinavia and in Anglo-Saxon England. This society differs alike from that of the Roman Empire and from that of feudal Europe in that it was based primarily not on slavery or serfdom but on the free tribesman—or, as we should say, "citizen"—who was at once a landowner and a warrior.

Nevertheless, it was not a democratic society, as writers like Green and Freeman tend to suggest with their theories of folkland and folkmoots, but an elaborate hierarchy of hereditary classes. Every man had his price—his *wergild*— and this price depended on his hereditary status. In Wessex, for example, the noble was worth six times as much as an ordinary freeman, and the freeman was worth twice as much as a member of one of the subject races, while the thrall represents, at it were, the minimum social value. This system was enforced by the barbaric law of the blood feud and private war, and consequently was based not on the authority of the State but on the power of the kindred to protect its members. The stranger or the freeman who had no powerful kindred behind him was forced to put himself under the protection—*munborh* or *mundium*—of a lord who would defend and aid him in return for homage and service. Thus a man's importance was measured not by his wealth but by the strength of his kindred and the number of followers who were pledged to support him in peace and war. And in the same way the power of the prince still depended, as in the days of Tacitus, on the number and quality of the personal retainers—*comites, antrustions,* thanes and vassals —who were supported by his bounty and formed his personal bodyguard in war.

These institutions obtained not only in the purely Germanic lands but also among the peoples, whether Franks, Lombards or Burgundians, who had established themselves in the Roman provinces. Here, however, they came into contact with Christian culture and Roman institutions. The barbarian chief stepped into the place of the Roman governor, and his followers into that of the old ruling class of senators and great landlords. Nevertheless, though the tribal tradition was limited and modified by the influence of the Church and Roman law and institutions, it still persisted and assumed new forms in its new environment. The old Germanic nobility—the god-descended race of heroes—disappeared almost entirely among the Franks[1] during the age of invasions, and its place was taken by the new aristocracy of service which incorporated considerable Gallo-Roman elements. On the other hand, the conquering race itself acquired some of the characteristics of a noble caste, as we see from the social and ethical prestige that attached itself to the name "Franc". At the same time, the vast increase in the numbers and proportion of the subject population led to a great extension of the custom of recommendation and of the client or vassal relation.

With the advent of the Carolingians the evolution of Frankish society entered on a new phase. While, on the one

---

[1] It still survived among the Bavarians in the eighth century and formed a relatively numerous and important class in Saxony.

hand, the restoration of the Western Empire, the reform of the Frankish Church and the renaissance of monastic learning show the strength of the Latin and Christian elements in Carolingian culture, there was, on the other hand, a no less strongly marked development of the feudal elements in Frankish society. The incessant wars of the Carolingian period and the growing importance of heavy armed cavalry made it necessary for Charles Martel and his successors to maintain a permanent force of professional soldiers in addition to the national levy of freemen which had hitherto been the basis of the Frankish military system; and the only way to achieve this end was to make grants of land—usually church land—to their followers on condition that they should provide and arm a certain number of soldiers for the king's service. Thus the old Germanic institution of the chief's military following developed into the feudal institution of a body of vassals provided with benefices or fiefs, and the greatest in the land were not ashamed to become the king's "men" and to enter into that relation of homage and personal dependence which had in earlier times been characteristic of the dependent class of freemen who put themselves under the personal protection of a powerful lord. Hence the bond of fidelity and personal loyalty to a leader began to take the place of the political relation of the official and the magistrate. It is true that the Carolingian count was still a public official, but his position became more and more assimilated to that of the vassal class to which he usually belonged. It was only necessary for his office to become hereditary and to be regarded as a feudal benefice in order to complete the disintegration of the State and to remove the last link with the Roman tradition of political authority.

This process was completed in the ninth and tenth centuries by the new wave of barbarian invasions which overwhelmed the Carolingian world. Not only the old order of the State and the royal administration but the social and economic bases of society were disintegrated and transformed into something new.

The same causes which produced the disintegration of the State also led to the disintegration of property and the disappearance of the class of independent freeholders who were the foundation of the old order. The age of the Viking invaders proved disastrous to the small landowner. He was obliged to forfeit his freedom by offering his land to a lord or to a church while continuing to cultivate it as a dependent tenant. This change in the position of the class of freemen is shown by the transformation of the word "pagensis" from its Carolingian meaning of a freeholder who was not a vassal into its medieval sense of a "peasant".[1] In this way private property in land as understood by the Romans and by our forefathers practically ceased to exist. It became, as it were, diffused among a number of lords and tenants, each of whom had rights in it, but none of whom was the absolute owner of it. The typical freeman remained, indeed, a warrior, but he was no longer necessarily a landowner. He was a professional soldier who lived for war and who might be supported either directly by the bounty of his lord or indirectly by the "benefice" which his lord gave him in return for his service.

As a result of these changes, the new feudal society represents a distinct reversion to barbarian and Germanic traditions.[2] The artificial structure of the Carolingian Empire had collapsed and had left no principle of social cohesion behind save the old barbaric relations of the serf to his lord and of the warrior to his leader. Even the old barbaric institutions of kin solidarity, blood feud and *wergild*, are preserved, and possibly owed a fresh lease of life

[1] Cf. Guilhiermoz, *Origine de la noblesse*, p. 455, note 19.
[2] It is significant that the technical terminology of feudalism—such words as *fief feuda, feud faida, ban, marshall, liege, truce and trève, seisin*—is mainly Germanic and shows little trace of Latin influence.

to feudalism, since it is in the cradle lands of feudalism—northern France and Belgium—that we find the clearest traces of their existence in the later Middle Ages, whereas in less feudalized regions, such as England, they are already replaced by the presence of royal power as early as the tenth century.[1]

In spite of the distance in time and the differences in religion and language, there is a strange resemblance between the relations of the feudal lord to his *mesnie* and those of the Northern war lord to his *hird*. There is the same bond of personal loyalty in place of the impersonal political relation of ruler and subject or of magistrate and citizen. There is the same economic motive arising from the dependence of the warrior on the favour and liberality of his lord, though this liberality now manifests itself by the distribution of fiefs rather than, as of old, by the gift of arms and gold rings. Above all, there is the same heroic ethical code with its ideals of honour and contempt of death, its pride of race and its spirit of implacable revenge.

But while the feudal vassal was thus the true descendant of the barbarian warrior, he was at the same time a Christian knight. He had become conscious of his membership of the Christian society and had acquired a new spiritual loyalty that transcended the narrow limits of the old tribal society. The very weakness of the feudal state as a political society and its failure to achieve national unity favoured the

[1] Cf. B. S. Philpotts, *Kindred and Clan*, pp. 184–202. "There are extraordinarily close resemblances between the Lex Salica and the capitularies on the one hand, and the actual practice of the thirteenth and fourteenth centuries on the other, and we cannot really attribute these resemblances to a critical study of the former on the part of medieval antiquarian lawyers." The accepted practice of the thirteenth century is given by Beaumanoir: "It used to be the custom that one could take revenge by right of feud as far as the 7th degree of kinship and this was not strange in the days of yore, for one could not make marriages within the 7th degree. But as the kindred has been narrowed so that one can make marriages after the 4th degree, so too one ought not to make war on anyone who is further removed [from the offender] than the 4th degree because the kindred stops there" (Philpotts, *op. cit.*, p. 193).

development of this wider loyalty which found its supreme expression in the universalism of the crusading movement.

It was in the feudal world that the traditions and ideals of the old Northern warrior society were translated into new Christian forms and incorporated in the traditions of Western culture. For the rise of chivalry meant not only the creation of new social institutions but also the birth of a new ethos and new ideals of behaviour which were destined to have a far-reaching influence on Western culture throughout the Middle Ages and even to some extent in modern times.

This creative activity of the feudal culture finds its literary expression in the new heroic epic which makes its appearance in northern France in the eleventh century. The problem of its origin has been fiercely debated by scholars of many nations for more than a hundred years, and though it seemed a generation ago that the researches of M. Bédier had at last provided a definitive solution, there are today once more signs of a renewal of the controversy. It was at one time the accepted view that the French epic was the culmination of the national Frankish epic which had had a continuous tradition from Germanic times. Siegfried, the great figure of the German epic tradition, was himself the national hero of the Franks. Charlemagne, who was to become the centre of the later epic, himself, according to Einhard, "wrote down the very ancient barbarous poems in which the achievements and wars of ancient kings used to be sung and transmitted them to posterity".[1] It was only necessary for this Germanic epic tradition to be taken up by the Frankish speakers of a Romance language for the Old French epic to arise, and this, it was believed, was what happened in the ninth and tenth centuries, when the great figures of the Carolingian age became the heroes of a national epic cycle centring, above all, in the wars with the

[1] Einhard, *Life of Charlemagne*, ch. xxix.

Saracens of the Spanish March. This theory, which gained the almost universal assent of scholars during the nineteenth century, was, however, completely undermined by the brilliant and subtle criticism of M. Bédier in his volumes on *Les légendes épiques*.[1] He argued that there were no solid grounds for the derivation of the French epic from the Teutonic heroic poetry and the old national epic of the Franks, but that it was a new creation of the eleventh century. The *chansons de geste* grew up in the age of the crusades round the shrines of the great abbeys and along the pilgrimage roads that led to Compostella and Rome. Their models are to be found neither in the lost Germanic epics nor in the *cantilenae* of Merovingian times, but in the new vernacular romance versions of the lives of the saints such as the *Vie de Ste. Foy*, the *Vie de St. Alexis* and the *Vie de St. Léger*.

It is impossible not to be convinced by the strength of the chain of evidence by which M. Bédier establishes his two main conclusions: first, that the *chansons de geste* are a new and original creation of the North French genius in the eleventh century; and, secondly, that the new epic has grown up in a Christian atmosphere and derives much of its material from monastic legends, especially those associated with the great pilgrimage routes which were in that age the chief channels of cultural influences.

But, on the other hand, there is no need to go to the other extreme, and to deny all relation or resemblance between the *chansons de geste* and the old heroic epic of the Northern peoples, or to declare, as M. Faral does, that they must be considered in their origin as an enlargement under the auspices of the Church of the most archaic type of the vernacular lives of the saints. It would be possible to go on composing lives of saints for a thousand years without ever

[1] J. Bédier, *Les légendes épiques, recherches sur la formation des chansons de gestes* (1908–12), 4 vols.

creating an epic, still less an epic of the characteristically heroic type of the *Song of Roland* or the *Song of
William*. The new literature is not the literature of monks
but of warriors—not the creation of the Church but of the
feudal society; and as that society itself represents a fusion
of Nordic and Latin-Christian elements, so it is with the
literature.

There is therefore a substantial element of truth in Uh-
land's famous saying that "the French epic is the Germanic
spirit in a romance form". The new French epic resembles
the old Germanic heroic poetry, not because it is directly
derived from it but because it is the result of similar social
conditions and the expression of a kindred spirit. As the
late W. P. Ker wrote: "Heroic poetry requires a court like
that of Alcinous in the *Odyssey* or that of Hrothgar the
Dane in *Beowulf*." It "requires a particular form of fighting, not too highly organized", one in which the personal
factor is all-important and where battles may still be decided
by the prowess of a single champion. Above all, it requires
an audience which is democratic in its community of taste
and interests but aristocratic in its standards and ideals, an
audience which possesses "something like the epic frame of
mind, a rudimentary heroic imagination which already gives
to mere historical events and situations a glimmering of
their epic magnificence. The 'multitude' in an heroic age
interprets life heroically; and it is this common vague
sentiment of heroism, not any bare uncoloured unaccom-
modated thing in itself, with which the epic poets made their
beginning".[1]

Thus the heroic epic is the creation of the social conditions of the age—of the common life of the great hall
where the warriors sit over their cups in the long winter
evenings, boasting of their prowess and listening to the
minstrels' songs of the great deeds of the heroes of old. The

[1] W. P. Ker, *The Dark Ages*, pp. 73–86.

demand created the supply, and the minstrel was as integral a part of the warrior society, as the rhetorician in the ancient city-state or as the journalist in modern society.

Unfortunately we are unable to follow the early stages of this epic development. The vast majority of the *chansons* date from the twelfth and thirteenth centuries, when the feudal society had already lost its primitive simplicity and when literary taste was being transformed by the influence of a new courtly literature. These influences are responsible for the transformation of the *chansons de geste* from an heroic epic into a romance of love and adventure, a transformation which is usually accompanied by a loss of poetical quality. It is significant that the three poems which seem to be the oldest of all—the *Song of Roland,* the *Song of William* and *Gormont and Isembart*—are the most warlike, the most heroic and also the greatest of the whole literature.

Nevertheless, it is impossible to say that they are the earliest in an absolute sense or that we can find in them the starting point of the whole development. It is only by chance that they have been preserved, since the most archaic versions have survived only in single manuscripts. *Gormont and Isembart* is a mutilated fragment that was discovered in Belgium a century ago, the *Song of Roland* in its primitive form exists only in the Oxford MS. discovered about the same time, while the *Song of William* was found only a few years ago in an English private library. This last discovery is of exceptional interest, for it gave us an entirely unexpected version of two of the most famous later *chansons, Les Aliscans* and the *Chevalerie Viviens,* while, as M. Bédier has shown, it points in turn to the existence of older versions that have entirely disappeared. Moreover, apart from the *Song of Roland,* it is the most powerful and heroic work which this literature produced, and certain passages are even superior to anything in *Roland* itself in pathos and tragic intensity. Such are the scenes of the death of Vivien and of the boy Guischard who denies his God in a moment of despair; such, above all, the scene of the return of Count William, wounded and alone, to meet his wife Guiburc:

> *"Sire," dist ele, "Qu'as tu fait de ta gent,*
> *Dunt tu menas quatre mi e .VII. cent"?*
> *"Par ma fei, dame, uencu les unt paens,*
> *Bouches sanglantes gisent en l'Archamps."*[1]

They sit in the hall with no one left to serve them, and when the count sees the empty benches and tables where the barons were wont to sit he laments them—*"cum gentil hom deit faire"*—as a gentleman should.

> *"Ohi, bone sale, cum estes lung e lée!*
> *De totes parz vus uei si aürnée,*
> *Beneït seit qui si t'ad conreiée.*
> *Ohi, haltes tables, cum estes leuées!*
> *Napes de lin vei desure getées . . .*
> *N'i mangerunt les fiz de franches meres,*
> *Qui en l'Archamp vut les testes colpées!"*[2]

And he vows to depart to St. Michel al Peril de la Mer and to become a hermit in the desert. But Guiburc, like the heroic women of the Germanic epic, dissuades him from abandoning the task of vengeance:

> *"Sire," dist ele, "ço ferum nus assez,*
> *Quant nus aurom nostre siecle mené."*[3]

For three-quarters of the poem this note of tragedy and

---

[1] *"Lord," said she, "what have you done with your people,*
Of whom you led four thousand and seven hundred?"
"By my faith, lady, the pagans have conquered them,
With bloody mouths they lie at Archamps."

[2] *Alas! good hall, so long and wide*
In every way I see you so arrayed
Blessings on her who has made you ready!
Alas! high tables that are so set out
And spread with table cloths of linen
Never more will the sons of free mothers eat there
The men who have lost their heads at Archamps.

[3] *"Sire," she said, "it will be enough to do that when we have finished our business."*

heroism is maintained unbroken, and then the tone changes and the conclusion of the poem is taken up with the grotesque exploits of an heroic clown, Reneward,[1] whom William finds in the kitchens of the emperor at Laon and who proves to be the long-lost brother of his wife Guiburc. How did this apparently incongruous element find its way into the epic? Is the Reneward episode an addition which has been added to the original poem by some later hand? Or is the explanation to be found in the jongleur's attempt to cater for the tastes of the lower end of the hall as well as the high table? Is Reneward, on the contrary, a traditional figure from ancient folklore who had become associated with the legend in its pre-literary form? One is tempted to see in it the growing influence of the new popular audience which the jongleurs found in the fairs and pilgrimage places rather than in the feudal hall, an influence which is certainly to be seen in the very early *Pélerinage de Charlemagne,* which was composed for the audience which resorted to the fair of Lendit at St. Denis and which reads like a comic travesty of the *chanson de geste.* It may be so, but we cannot tell. All we know is that the Reneward episode forms part of the earliest-known version of the story of William, and that this version is in all probability the result of a long process of literary development.

We cannot point to any existing poem, even to the *Song of Roland,* and say: "Here the *chanson de geste* begins." We know from Einhard that the Franks of the age of Charlemagne already had their heroic literature. We know from the anonymous Saxon poet, who wrote at Corvey about 888, that the Carolingians had already become the heroes of vernacular poetry.[2] We cannot deny with safety that this

---

[1] "Rainoart" in the later version.
[2] *Est quoque jam notum: vulgaria carmina magnis*
    Laudibus ejus et proavos celebrunt:
  Pippinos Carolos Hludovicos et Theodricos
    Et Carlomanos Hlothariosque canunt.

vernacular tradition was not carried on by the Romance-speaking Franks of the tenth and eleventh centuries. It is not enough to say with M. Bédier that Charlemagne was a German, and the evidence of Einhard and the Saxon poet only applies to German literature, for this is to carry our modern conceptions of nationality back to an age when they can hardly be said to have existed. The men of that age did not regard themselves as French or Germans, but as Franks and Saxons and Lombards. Linguistic divisions were fluid and inchoate, and there was a real sense of social tradition and continuity between the Romance-speaking Franks of Neustria and their Carolingian ancestors. When the Franks began to speak French they did not necessarily abandon their social habits and forget their national legends. We see the beginnings of a semi-popular heroic poetry even in the Latin language as early as the eighth and ninth centuries, as, for example, in the stirring rhythmic poems on the defeat of the Avars and on the Battle of Fontenoy.[1] And if this was possible in Latin, why not also in Romance? No doubt ecclesiastical influences were strong and the first vernacular poems to be written down may have been the lives of the saints, but there is no reason to suppose that the lives of the saints were the only intellectual recreation of the early feudal age or that the wandering jongleur did not from the first make some effort to satisfy the demand of a society of warriors for heroic poetry. All that we can say is that the full literary development of the new Romance heroic poetry corresponded with the full development of the new feudal society in northern France, and that the *chanson de geste* is the outcome of the same creative spirit which gave birth to feudal chivalry and the feudal state and the crusading movement.

But however obscure may be the origins of the new epic literature, there can be no question as to the light that it

[1] *Poet. Lat. Aev. Carol.*, ed. Traube: i, 435 *seq.*; ii, 138 *seq.*

throws on contemporary culture. For the *chansons de geste,* in contrast to the courtly literature of the following period, are concerned with the real world and not with the romantic fairyland of the Arthurian legend. No doubt the *chansons* interpret this real world in an heroic fashion and thus give us an idealized picture of the feudal warrior and his world. But they idealize reality only by exaggerating and simplifying it and not by altering it in the interests of some alien standard of values. The conduct and motives of the Arthurian hero have no relation to those of the real world. He wanders through an enchanted forest on some imaginary quest or in fulfilment of some impossible vow. He lives without visible means of support and has no thought for mundane cares. But the hero of the *chansons de geste* is a man of flesh and blood who does not despise a good dinner and always expects good payment for loyal service. Even in the height of the tragic section of the *Song of William* the hero finds time between two battles to sit down and devour an heroic meal, so that his wife swears by God that a man who can eat and drink like that is still capable of hard fighting.

> *Par Dev de glorie, quie conuertir me fist . . .*
> *Qui si manguë un grant pain a tamis,*
> *Pur ço ne laisse les dous gasteals rostiz,*
> *E tut manguë un grant braün porcin,*
> *E en aproef un grant poün rosti,*
> *E a dous traiz beit vn sester de vin,*
> *Ben dure guere deit rendre a sun veisin!*[1]

Yet in spite of this often brutal realism which distinguishes the feudal epic from other types of heroic poetry, it has its own heroic and even religious idealism which is not remote from historical reality as in the Arthurian romances but is inseparable from the moral values of feudal society—the bond of fidelity and loyalty and the ideal of Christendom

[1] *La Chançun de Willame,* 1423–31.

as a concrete reality for which the warrior no less than the monk must be ready to sacrifice his life.

In the earliest and the greatest *chansons* the dominant motive is not revenge or private feud but the nobler theme of the war of the Franks against the infidel—*gesta Dei per Francos*. Hence the story of the wars of Charlemagne and his peers against the Saracens in Aquitaine and Spain holds as central a place in the feudal epic tradition as the war of Troy in that of ancient Greece. There was, indeed, no breach in continuity between the tradition of these earlier wars when Barcelona and the Spanish March had been recovered for Christendom by the historical Charlemagne and the historical William of Toulouse and the later Spanish crusades in which the French crusaders played an important part in the reconquest.

It was in these wars far more than in the local dynastic conflicts of northern France that feudal society transcended its local particularism and acquired that wider sense of Christian patriotism which is characteristic of the feudal epic. In the *Song of Roland,* above all, the love of "dulce France" inspires the heroism of the action no less than the prowess of the warrior and the bonds of feudal loyalty and of kinship, and the motives are combined in the great passage of Roland's death scene:

> *Li quens Rollanz se jut desuz un pin:*
> *Envers Espaigne en ad turnet sun vis.*
> *De plusurs choses a remembrer li prist:*
> *De tantes teres cun li ber cunquist,*
> *De dulce France, des humes de sun lign,*
> *De Carlemagne, sun seignur, ki l' nurrit.*[1]

[1] *The Count Rollanz, beneath a pine he sits;*
Turning his eyes towards Spain, he begins
Remembering so many divers things:
The many lands where he went conquering,
And France the Douce, the heroes of his kin,
And Charlemagne, his lord, who nourished him.
Lines 2375–80; trans. C. K. Scott–Moncrieff.

It is, however, in a passage of *Le Charroi de Nîmes*, recorded by M. Bédier, that this spirit of patriotism finds its noblest and most complete expression. As William leaves Auvergne and enters the Marches of the Saracens he turns his face for the last time towards "France".

> *Vers douce France a son vis retorné*
> *Uns vans de France lou fiert an mi lou neis:*
> *Ovre son sain, si l'an laist plain antrer.*
> *Ancontre l'ore se prist a guarmenter:*
> *"Hei! Ore dolce, qui de France venés,*
> *Tu ne viens pas de vers la Rouge mer,*
> *Ains viens de France, qui tant fait a loer;*
> *Orliens et Chartres et Beauvaisz la cité.*
> *La sont mi dru et mi ami charné!*
> *A Dameldeu soiez tuit commendé!*
> *En telle terre m'en cuit ge ore aler*
> *Ne vos cuit mais veoir ne esgarder."* [1]

This patriotic sentiment, however, has a religious rather than a political character. France is Christendom and Christendom is France. And here, at least, the epic tradition is faithful to history, since it still retains memories of a time when the realm of the Franks was identical with Western Christendom. This spirit of religious patriotism gives the

---

[1] Quoted by Bédier, *Les légendes épiques*, i, 77, from the MS. B.N. 1448. The passage is not found in the other MSS. or in Perrier's edition of *Le Charroi de Nîmes*.

> *Unto fair France he turned once more his face,*
> *A wind from France blows full upon his face:*
> *Baring his breast he lets it enter free,*
> *And to the wind he utters his lament:*
> *"Hey! gentle breeze which blows to me from France,*
> *Thou comest not from off the southern sea,*
> *But from fair France that is so praiseworthy;*
> *From Orleans and Chartres and Beauvais town.*
> *There are my friends and my beloved kin.*
> *May the Lord God have you in his keeping!*
> *For to such lands methinks I now must go,*
> *I shall not look upon your face again."*

French epic and the feudal society a new spiritual ideal which is not to be found in the older type of heroic poetry. The warlike deeds of the champions are not an end in themselves, they are performed in the service of Christendom,

> *Et la loi Deu essaucier et monter,*

and the knight who dies in battle for the faith is not only a hero but a martyr.

> *Pes ne demandent ne trimes nen unt pris*
> *Car Saint Estephne ne les altres martirs*
> *Ne furent mieldres que serrunt tut icil*
> *Qui en Larchamps serrunt per Dei ocis.*[1]

> *They ask not peace nor have accepted truce*
> *For St. Stephen and the other martyrs*
> *Were not better than all of those*
> *Who for God's sake will be slain at Archamps.*

In such passages as this, and still more in that of the *Song of William*, where the dying Vivien remembers the death of Christ and refuses to pray that his own life may be spared,[2] we see the birth of a new ideal of Christian heroism which transcends the barbaric ethos of the old Northern heroic tradition. But for the most part it must be admitted that the religion of the *chansons de geste* is of a very barbaric and rudimentary kind and consists, above all, in the killing of Saracens. The beliefs of the feudal society in this respect are well expressed by William's reply to his Saracen brother-in-law, who taxes him with the wanton slaughter of his kin.

> *Respont Guillaumes: "Vos dites niceté.*
> *Puis que li hom n'aime chrestienté*

---

[1] *La Chançun de Willame*, lines 543–6.
[2] *La Chançun de Willame*, lines 799–836.

Et qu'il het Dieu et guerpist charité,
N'a droit en vie, je le di par verté
Et ki l'ocist s'a destruit un malfé;
Dieu ai vengié, si m'en set molt bon gré." [1]

No doubt the *chansons* contain no lack of references to contemporary religious practice and belief. But apart from the religious consecration of the heroic ideal, religion does not enter very deeply into the spirit of the *chansons* which remains, on the whole, that of the unregenerate Northern warrior. The relation between the two is a genuine one, but it is external and often incongruous, like the relics in Roland's sword.

> *"Ah Durendal, most holy, fair indeed,*
> *Relics enough thy golden hilt conceals!*
> *St. Peter's tooth, the blood of Basile,*
> *Some of the Hairs of my lord Saint Denise,*
> *Some of the Robe, was worn by Saint Mary."* [2]

Although the heroes of the *chansons de geste* are ready enough to shed their blood for the Faith, their moral code is by no means over-strict, as we see in the passage of the *Couronnement de Louis*, where the Pope promises William in return for his championship that he may eat meat all the days of his life and take a wife whenever he wants to! [3] Moreover, the darker aspects of feudal society are by no means concealed. Raoul de Cambrai threatens to sack the

---

[1] *William replied: "You speak folly,*
Since the man who loves not Christendom
And who hates God and loses charity
Has no right to life, I say in truth,
And the man who kills him has destroyed a miscreant.
I have avenged God and He is well pleased with me."
　　　　　　　　　　　　　　　　　　Aliscans, 1059 ff.

[2] *Song of Roland,* trans. C. Scott-Moncrieff, 2344–8 (Cf. the relics which William of Normandy carried round his neck at the Battle of Hastings).

[3] *Couronnement de Louis.* Ed. Langlois, 388–94.

abbey of Origny, to stable his horses before the altar and to share out the nuns among his men-at-arms, though when the abbey has been burnt and the nuns inside he is shocked to find he has forgotten it is a fast day.

Thus we cannot look in the *chansons de geste* for that idealized and spiritualized chivalry which is to be found in the Grail romances and the Arthurian cycle. What they do give us is an insight into the authentic spirit of feudal society as it existed in the eleventh and twelfth centuries— the world of the warriors who conquered Palermo and Antioch and Saragossa, seen not by the historian or the ecclesiastic but through their own eyes. And what distinguishes this literature from the other traditional forms of heroic literature, like the *Iliad* or *Beowulf,* is that the heroic society that it describes does not belong to a remote legendary past but has already emerged into the full light of history so that we can see it simultaneously from several completely different angles. The First Crusade, for example, still belongs to the feudal heroic age and had its own heroic myths which find expression in one of the latest cycles of the Old French epic. But we can read of the same events in the monastic chronicles and in the work of a highly educated literary historian like William of Tyre. Better still, we can see them through the eyes of a Byzantine princess, who views them with the disdainful aloofness of an older civilization, just as though we had a contemporary description of the Siege of Troy and the personalities of Achilles and Odysseus written by a cultivated Egyptian princess. All the features which impressed her in these formidable barbarians—their headstrong valour and pride, their greed and generosity, their indiscipline and their flow of language —are the same features which we find in a more heroic setting in the *chansons de geste.*

"The Frankish Counts," she writes, "are naturally shameless and violent, naturally greedy, too, and immoderate in everything they wish, and they possess a flow of language greater than any other human race."¹ Above all, when Anna Commena describes Bohemund, who is at once the villain and hero of her story, we seem to see William or Vivien as he might have appeared to one of the Saracen princesses of the epic. "For the man was such as had never before been seen in the land of the Romans, for he was a marvel for the eyes to behold and his reputation was terrifying." "He was so tall in stature that he overtopped the tallest by nearly one cubit, narrow in the waist and loins, with broad shoulders and a deep chest and powerful arms. And in the whole build of the body he was neither too slender nor overweighted with flesh, but, one might say, built in conformity with the canon of Polyclitus." "A certain charm hung about this man, but was partly spoilt by a general air of the horrible. For in the whole of his body the entire man showed implacable and savage both in his size and glance, and even his laughter sounded to others like snorting. He was so made in mind and body that both courage and passion reared their crest within him and both inclined to war. His wit was manifold and crafty and able to find a handle in any emergency. In conversation he was well informed, and the answers he gave were quite irrefutable. This man, who was of such greatness and such a character, was inferior to the emperor alone in fortune and eloquence and other gifts of nature."²

The whole story of Bohemund is more like a *chanson de geste* than sober history—his life-long feud with the Byzantine emperor, his conquest of Antioch, his years of captivity in a remote fastness of Asia Minor, his unexpected liberation and his return to the West to gather new armies for the conquest of the East, and his final defeat in Albania. The opening episode of *Les Narbonais* in which Count

¹ *The Alexiad of Anna Commena*, trans. A. S. Davies, p. 372.
² *Ibid.*, p. 347.

Aymeri makes his youngest son his heir and sends out William and his brothers to win kingdoms for themselves from the Saracens finds a complete historical parallel in the behaviour of Robert Guiscard, who bequeathes the Apulian kingdom he had conquered to his younger and weaker son and leaves to his first-born Bohemund nothing less than the task of conquering the Byzantine Empire.

> *J'a n'en avrom vaillant une chastaigne*
> *Ainz conquirom a dolor e a paine*
> *Ce dont vivrom a joie.*[1]

In the same way the historical scene in which Bohemund, after his return to the West in 1106, stands before the altar of Our Lady at Chartres and appeals to the knighthood of France to follow him to the conquest of the East, promising them castles and rich fiefs and great deeds of arms, has its literary counterpart in the passage in *Le Charroi de Nîmes* in which William calls for recruits for the conquest of Spain.

> *Seur une table est Guillaume montez:*
> *A son voiz clere commença a crier:*
> *"Entendez moi, de France le barné.*
> *Se Deus m'aïst, de ce me puis vanter,*
> *Plus ai de terre que trente de mes pers,*
> *Encore n'en ai un jornel aquité.*
> *Ici di je as povres bachelers*
> *As roncins clops et as dras despanez,*
> *Quant ont servi por neant conquester,*
> *S'o moi vueulent de bataille esprover,*
> *Ge lor dorrai deniers et heritez,*
> *Chasteaux et marches, donjons et fermetez,*

---

[1] *Now we have nothing worth a chestnut.*
So we will conquer in pain and grief
That with which we shall live in joy.

Si le païs m'aident a conquester
Et la loi Deu essaucier et monter."[1]

But it is not only in such details that the *chansons de geste* reflect realities. Even the *gestes*, that seem to the modern reader to belong to the world of fantasy—the battles against impossible odds, the lack of discipline, the incredible achievements of single champions, the combination of ferocity and honour—are all the commonplaces of twelfth-century history. There was nothing fantastic about the heroism of Roncesvalles and Archamps to a generation which had seen the flower of Western chivalry destroyed in hopeless battles in the interior of Asia Minor, in Syria and beyond the Euphrates.

Morz sont franceis et pris a males pertes
Ne remaint cheval ne home en sele.[2]

It is impossible to judge this heroic ethos either by Christian or by secular standards. For the modern Christian and the modern secularist will agree in asking: "To what purpose is this waste?" It can only be understood as a spontaneous attempt to find a Christian outlet for the unlimited aggressiveness of a primitive warrior ethos which could not be expended internally without tearing society to pieces. One has only to read contemporary chroniclers,

[1] *On a table William has mounted.*
In his clear voice he began to cry
"Hearken to me, barons of France.
If God help me, this I can boast,
I have more land than thirty of my peers
Though I have not yet won an acre.
So I say to the poor bachelors
With lame horses and shabby clothes,
When they have served for nothing in the conquest
If they will prove themselves in war for me,
I will give them money and possessions,
Castles and marches, keeps and strongholds;
If they help me to conquer the land
And to exalt and set up the law of God."
Le Charroi de Nîmes, ed. J. L. Perrier, lines 635–648.
[2] *The French are dead and taken with sore loss,*
Not a horse is left nor a man in the saddle.

like the Anglo-Norman Ordericus Vitalis, to see that feudal society was not unconscious of the conflict between its cult of war and its religious principles. Indeed, the biographer of no less a man than Tancred, the nephew and partner of Bohemund, relates at some length how his hero found in the crusade a solution for his conscientious scruples about the legitimacy of war between Christians.[1]

Yet though the *chansons de geste* are a faithful reflection of the spirit of feudal society at its best and its worst, in its crusading idealism and in its lawless ferocity they do not give us the whole picture. Their view of life is already an archaic one, which disregards the new elements in medieval society. They show us the world of the feudal baron and the knights who fought in the crusade, but not that of the law-givers and administrators who compiled Domesday Book and organized the Exchequer, or of the rulers who thought less of conquering new kingdoms in the East than of husbanding their resources and protecting their subjects from war and famine. These were the men who made medieval civilization possible, but there is no place for them either in the heroic tradition of the *chansons de geste* or in the more sophisticated tradition of the troubadours and court poets. Almost the only literary expression of their point of view occurs, strangely enough, in the work of a writer who more than any other represents the heroic tradition of the North in its purest and most archaic form. In the *Heimskringla*, Snorre Sturlason contrasts the two rival ways of life and conception of kingship in a boasting match of the traditional epic type between two Norwegian kings.

When King Sigurd the Crusader returns to Norway from his Mediterranean journey, which was at once one of the first of the Scandinavian crusades and the last of the Viking

---

[1] The author of the *Vita Tancredi*, Raoul of Caen, knew Tancred personally, and his work is based on information supplied by Tancred himself.

raids, he taunts his stay-at-home brother for sitting at home and loving the home fires best while he had won renown by his heroic exploits. And King Eystein replies:

"There is not much that I can speak of compared to what thou hast achieved. I have heard that thou hast won many battles in foreign lands, but what I did at home might have been more useful to this land. North at Vagar I built booths for the fishing folk, so that poor people could get help and earn their living. There I founded a priest's garth and endowed the Church. Before this the place was almost heathen. These men will remember that Eystein was King of Norway.

"The road from Trondheim went once over Dovre-fell where people were lost in bad weather or had to sleep out of doors and suffer hardships. There I built a mountain inn and gave it an income. These men will know that Eystein has been King of Norway. . . .

"I have also, my brother, shaped the laws so that the people can now obtain justice, and when the laws are kept the country will be better ruled. I have set a warping pole with iron rings in Sinholm Sound. The Jämtland people are again under the Norse king's rule, and this was brought about by fair words and wise persuasion and not by force or fighting. Now these matters are of small importance, yet I do not know whether the people in the land are not better served by them than because thou hast killed black men in Saracen land and sent their souls to hell."[1]

Here Snorre's sympathy is evidently with the common-sense critic of the heroic ideal, and this is the more remarkable when we remember that the writer was not only the greatest exponent of heroic ideals in Northern literature, but was himself one of the leading actors in the events which led to the final downfall of the great families of Iceland.

[1] *Heimskringla. The History of Sigurd the Crusader and his Brother Eystein,* based on E. Monsen's translation.

The story of that period has been recorded by Snorre's nephew, Sturla Thordsson, who gives a realistic picture of an heroic society in a state of decay. But in the French epic and the feudal society of the West it is impossible to find any such criticism of the heroic tradition from within. Here the changes in feudal society were accompanied by a parallel change in literary style and ideas. The heroic chivalry of the *chansons de geste* was transformed into the courtly chivalry of the romances, and Lancelot and Gawain took the place of Roland and William. But this literary evolution was not the spontaneous product of Northern feudal society. As we shall see, it was the result of a complex process due to the coming of exotic influences which had their origin outside the feudal society in the more advanced cultures of the western Mediterranean.

XI

THE ORIGINS OF THE ROMANTIC TRADITION

THE quarrel between Romanticism and Classicism has caused more ink to be spilt than any other literary controversy, even that of the Ancients and the Moderns, and after more than a century of warfare matters stand very much where they were at the beginning. Goethe's famous definition "Classicism is health, Romanticism is disease" is typical of the sweeping generalizations on which the controversy has thriven. For each party has identified its enemy with anything that it despised in literature, and there has been little attempt to arrive at a common basis of definition. Moreover, the controversy has been embittered by the introduction of religious and political issues, and in our days it has become not so much a literary controversy as a heresy hunt conducted with inquisitorial rigour by Ernest Seillière or, with Prof. Babbitt, a crusade for the moral regeneration of society.

The fact is that Romanticism has become a label for half a dozen different things that have only an accidental connection with one another. We may perhaps be justified in giving the name to that great change in taste and feeling that passed over Europe at the beginning of the nineteenth century; but, strictly speaking, Romanticism is only one element in that change. The term originally possessed a perfectly simple and objective meaning, and though it may be pedantic to confine it to that meaning, it is at least desirable not to lose sight of it altogether. That meaning is very clearly defined by Mme. de Staël, who, I believe, was the first to introduce the word into French literature.

"The term 'Romantic'," she writes, "has recently been introduced in Germany to designate the poetry that had its origin in the songs of the Troubadours, that which was born of Christianity and Chivalry. . . . The word 'Classic' is sometimes taken as synonymous with perfection. I use it here in another sense, regarding Classical poetry as that of the ancients, and Romantic poetry as that which is in some way connected with the institutions of chivalry."

This, in fact, is a perfectly logical and satisfactory definition. Romanticism is the literary imitation of the medieval romances, as classicism is the imitation of the Latin Classics; and just as the Renaissance meant the return to classical antiquity and the revival of classical literature, so the Romantic Revival had its origin in the return to the Middle Ages and the revival of medieval literature. No doubt the Romantic movement met and mingled with that other movement of return to nature and sentiment that has its origin with Rousseau. But the two are no more to be identified with one another than the Renaissance is to be identified with the Reformation. Indeed, the relation between Humanism and Protestantism affords a very fair parallel to that between Romanticism and Rousseauism. The rediscovery of the Middle Ages by the Romantics is an event of no less importance in the history of European thought than the rediscovery of Hellenism by the Humanists. It meant an immense widening of our intellectual horizon. To Boileau and Pope and their contemporaries the Middle Ages were simply a gap in the history of culture. They had no eyes for the beauty of medieval art and no ears for the melody of medieval verse. All this was restored to us by the Romantics. They went to the Middle Ages not in order to prove a case or to justify their political or religious beliefs, but because they found in them something utterly different from the world that they knew—the revelation of a new kind of beauty. Was this but another example of the romantic fallacy that what is far away must be finer and more beautiful than what is near at hand and that human nature was different in the past to what it is in the present? I do not think so. I believe that the discovery of the Romantics was a genuine discovery and that there really is something in medieval culture essentially different from anything that is to be found either in the ancient or the modern world, and that we can never understand medieval history unless we discover what it is.

And if we wish to find this mysterious element which is the quintessence of the medieval spirit we cannot do better than to follow the example of the Romantics and look for it in the age and the country of the Troubadours, for it is there that we shall find it purest and least alloyed. Elsewhere medieval life differs from our own mainly by its more primitive character; it is, in fact, the ancestral form of our own culture. The predominance of the religious element may at first sight seem strange to us, but, after all, religion is always with us, and the emotions and thoughts of a religious man in the Middle Ages do not differ essentially from those of a religious man today. But in the world of the Troubadours it is the whole pattern of life and thought that is different. They differ from ourselves not so much because they are less civilized but because they are civilized in a different way, and there is no standard of comparison by which the two cultures can be judged.

The men of Provence and Languedoc were warriors and politicians, but they do not live by their political achievements, nor yet by their economic achievements, though they were also great merchant adventurers. Their supreme title to fame is their art of life, whether it be *el gay saber*—the joyful science of poetry and love in the technical sense— or the general standard of aristocratic behaviour which inspired their social life.

For it was the Provençal culture which created those

new ideals and conventions of courtesy and chivalry and romantic love that were gradually transmitted to the other countries of western Europe and that transformed the whole life and thought of aristocratic society. The significance of this element in medieval culture is missed alike by those who regard the Middle Ages as a time when life was darkened and narrowed by superstition and asceticism, and by those who idealize them as an age of mystical enthusiasm and high moral endeavour when all social life was inspired by the ideals of the Christian faith. To the latter, chivalry and courtly love seem to show the refining influence of Christian ideas on manners and morals, while the pessimists for their part are quick to seize on the moral weaknesses of courtly society as a proof of the shortcomings of medieval Catholicism.

In reality the ideals of the new culture had nothing to do with religion, and its practice was immoral not because it violated accepted standards, but because of the very nature of the standards themselves. Or rather one may say that Provençal society possessed an elaborate moral code, but it was not that of Christianity. Its ideal was a frankly pagan one—the glorification of life, the assertion of the individual personality and the cultivation of the pleasures of the senses. The supreme ends of life were "joy and honour", and they were embodied in the cult of woman and the ideal of courtly love which form the stock themes of Provençal literature. The contrast between this ideal and the Christian view of life finds open expression in the following famous passage from *Aucassin and Nicolette,* a work which in spite of its North French form belongs in spirit entirely to the southern society in which the scene is laid.

"In Paradise what have I to do? I seek not to enter there, but only to have Nicolette my most sweet friend, whom I so love: For into Paradise go none but such folk as I shall tell you. There go these old priests and the old cripples and the maimed, who all day and all night crouch in front of the altars and in the old crypts, and those who are clad in old worn-out coats and tattered rags, who go naked and barefoot and full of sores, who die of hunger and hardship and cold and wretchedness. All these go into Paradise, with these I have nothing to do. But into Hell I am willing to go; for to Hell go the fine clerks and the fair knights who have fallen in jousts and in ripe wars, and the skilled warriors and the brave men. With them I am fain to go. There also go the fair and courteous ladies who have two lovers or three and their lords beside. And there go the gold and the silver and the ermines and the grey furs; there too the harpers and the rhymers and the kings of the world. With these will I go too, so that I may have with me Nicolette, my most sweet friend."[1]

But perhaps this open disavowal of Christian ideals is less characteristic than the complete ignoring of them which we find in a Provençal romance like *Flamenca,* where the hero uses the most sacred rites of religion in order to gain the love of a married woman, without the slightest scruple or sense of moral incongruity.

These examples may perhaps be ascribed to the naïve immoralism of the medieval romantic tradition, but there is certainly nothing naïve about the Provençal literature as a whole. It has its roots not in the traditions of the folk-song and the life of the people but in a highly refined and sophisticated literary tradition.

The art of the Troubadours is, in fact, the starting point of modern European literature. As W. P. Ker wrote: "Everything that is commonly called poetry in the modern tongues may in some way or other trace its pedigree back to William count of Poitou, 'the first of a school that includes every modern poet'. It is a different thing with the verse of the old Teutonic school. It is possible to understand it but

[1] Trans. Laurence Housman, John Murray (1902), p. 13.

in spite of blood relationship its character is strange . . . the form is not that of the modern world. But the relations of the Provençal school are everywhere and they can be proved by historical evidence without any hazardous speculation on poetical affinities. They include all sorts and degrees of poets. By contrast with what precedes 1100, the whole of modern poetry since then appears one community."[1]

How are we to explain the abrupt appearance of this new literary art and the new secular culture that produced it? The accepted explanation has been that they are the natural flowering of the Northern chivalrous spirit—the Gothic genius—which developed precociously in the forcing-house of the Mediterranean lands. Thus, according to Karl Vossler, "the first who espoused the cause of the fair sex and set rolling, as it were, the emancipation of women were knights. The noble lords north of the Alps had remained true to the old German feeling of the frank acceptance and enjoyment of the good things of life".[2]

In reality, however, the new ideals of love and courtesy make their first appearance in northern Europe only in consequence of and in proportion to the reception of Provençal influences. Even in French literature, which is nearest to that of Languedoc, there is no trace of an independent development of the ideals of courtesy and romantic love. The behaviour of the heroes of the *chansons de geste* towards women is very much that of the cave man and their language is often as frank as a bargee's. Their idealism is to be found not in their attitude to women but in their religious patriotism—that spirit of crusading energy which is so nobly expressed in the *Song of Roland*. But as soon as we turn to the poetry of the Troubadours we find ourselves in a completely different world. Instead of the magnificent simplicity of the *chansons* with the clanging assonance like

[1] W. P. Ker, *The Dark Ages*, pp. 6 and 8–9.
[2] K. Vossler, *Mediaeval Culture*, trans. W. C. Lawton, i, 299.

the tramp of armed men, we have the delicate and difficult music of the Provençal lyric which aims at the same ideal of civilized perfection as the Petrarchan sonnet.

And the change in spirit and feeling is even more striking. In contrast to the objective and anonymous simplicity of the French epic poet, the Troubadour is absorbed in the study of his own emotions and has already acquired a passion for psychological analysis. But this does not lead them to romantic sentimentality as we might expect. The greatest of them, men such as Peire d'Auvergne and Arnaut Daniel, express the morbid intensity of their passion with an austere reticence which gives their poetry an almost classical character, as in the lines of the former:

> *Why doth she ask me naught? That grieveth me,*
> *Yet fear lest I not better fare but worse;*
> *The more the pain I say "So let it be".*

They pride themselves not so much on the obvious appeal of thought and expression as on an obscure and difficult beauty—*chantar ab motz serratz e clus*—and when there were two ways of saying a thing they always preferred the most difficult. It is the spirit of Arnaut Daniel's famous boast:

> *I am Arnaut who gathers air*
> *And with the oxen chase the hare*
> *And ever swim against the stream.*

Compare, on the one hand, a passage from the *Song of Roland*:

> *The count Rolanz has never loved cowards*
> *Nor arrogant nor men of evil heart*
> *Nor chevalier that was not good vassal.*
> *That Archbishop, Turpins, he calls apart:*

"Sir, you're afoot and I my charger have;
For love of you here will I take my stand,
Together we'll endure things good and bad,
I'll leave you not for no incarnate man:
We'll give again these pagans their attack;
The better blows are those from Durendal." [1]

And, on the other hand, these lines of Arnaut Daniel:

Only I know what over-anguish falls
Upon the love-worn heart from over-love,
Because of my desire so firm and whole
Toward her I loved on sight and since alway,
Which turneth not aside nor wavereth;
So far from her I speak for her mad speech
Who near her, for o'er much to speak, am dumb. [2]

In the one case the warlike simplicity of the thought is
matched by the ringing monotony of the assonance. In the
other there is no rhyme within the stanza, but the seven
several rhymes are carried over and repeated in the same
order six times with a concluding refrain of the last three.
As Ezra Pound says, it is one of the most musical arrange-
ments of words in sequence whereof we know, for it satisfies
"not only the modern ear gluttonous of rhyme but also the
ear trained to Roman and Hellenic music to which rhyme
seemed and seems a vulgarity". [3]

The two styles are practically contemporary, and both
of them developed on French or rather Gallic soil, yet in
spite of this they are as different from one another in form
and content as any two literatures well can be. There is
nothing save the name in common between the rude Christian chivalry of the North and the refined secular courtly

[1] Trans. C. S. Scott-Moncrieff, lines 2134–43.
[2] Trans. E. Pound in *The Spirit of Romance*, p. 18.
[3] *Op. cit.*, p. 13.

chivalry of the South. And if the French epic expresses, as it surely does, the Northern "Gothic" spirit of the Christianized barbarian warrior, then we must look elsewhere for the sources of the Provençal literature. One might have supposed that the persistence of the classical tradition in the old Roman *provincia,* the most Latinized region north of the Alps, might provide an explanation. But though some of the Troubadours, such as Arnaut Daniel, were not without the rudiments of Latin culture, there is obviously no direct connection between Provençal and Latin poetry. It was actually in the North, in the valleys of the Loire and the Meuse and the Rhine, that the influence of the classical tradition asserted itself most strongly and that the medieval revival of Latin literature took place. There were no Latin scholars in Provence to compare with those of Chartres and Tours and Liège in the eleventh and twelfth centuries, and while the schools of the North were returning to Cicero and Ovid, the chief centre of studies in Languedoc—Montpellier—was chiefly renowned for the study of the oriental sciences of medicine and astronomy.

And this fact, unimportant as it is for Provençal literature, does actually suggest an answer to the problem. For Provence was not then, as at the present day, in the middle of the European culture area, it was a border territory on the frontier of the oriental world. We are so accustomed to regarding our culture as essentially Western, that it is difficult to remember that there was a time when the most civilized regions of western Europe belonged to an alien oriental culture, and the Mediterranean, the cradle of Latin civilization, was in danger of becoming Arabic.

The eighth century had already seen the Moslem conquest of Spain and the invasion of Aquitaine, but it was not until the ninth that the expansion of the Moslem maritime states drove Christian shipping off the seas and converted the basin of the western Mediterranean into a Saracen lake.

The Arabs occupied all the western islands and even established themselves on the mainland of Italy and Provence, where Fraxinetum was for nearly a century (from 888–975) one of the greatest of their pirate strongholds. Finally, the tenth century saw the rise of the Spanish Khalifate and the development of a brilliant culture and literature in southern and eastern Spain, which I have described in an earlier chapter. Thus at a time when the rest of western Europe was just emerging from the depths of barbarism, the culture of Moslem Spain had attained complete maturity, and surpassed even the civilizations of the East in genius and originality of thought. Southern and eastern Spain was the richest and most populous country in the West. Its cities, with their palaces and libraries and public baths, were more like those of the Roman Empire than the miserable groups of wooden hovels which were growing up in medieval Europe under the shelter of an abbey or a feudal stronghold. In the tenth century Cordova boasted its 200,000 houses, its 900 bath-houses and its workshops which employed 13,000 weavers, as well as its armourers and leather-workers whose work was famous throughout the civilized world.

All this brilliant development of culture is completely ignored by the ordinary student of medieval European history. It is as though it were a lost world which had no more to do with the history of our past than the vanished kingdom of Atlantis. And yet, not only did it lie at the very doors of the Christian world; it was actually mingled with it. The frontiers of Christendom and Islam in the early Middle Ages were constantly shifting. The Moslem princes exacted tribute from their Christian neighbours or paid it to them, took them into their service as mercenaries, and married their daughters. There was a large subject population of Moslems in the Christian states of Spain and of Christians in the Moslem ones, and there was far more tolerance and mutual intercourse between the two elements than during the later Middle Ages. The Aragonese court in the eleventh century was largely Arabic in culture, and it is said Pedro I was unable to sign his name except in Arabic. Even the crusading movement which began in the eleventh century did not stop these relations; indeed, it widened the range of Southern influence, since it first brought the nobles of France and Burgundy and Normandy into contact with Arabic culture. In spite of their barbarism the Northern invaders often adapted themselves to the higher culture of the peoples they had conquered, as we see, above all, in Sicily, where the Norman kings surrounded themselves with all the luxury of an oriental court and patronized Moslem scholars and poets.

Nowhere was the contact between the two cultures closer than on the shores of the Gulf of Lyons. The County of Barcelona was a kind of bridge between the two worlds. On the one hand, it had suzerainty over some of the Moslem communities of eastern Spain, such as Tarragona and Saragossa; and, on the other hand, its rulers were allied by marriage with the great houses of Languedoc and Provence and aimed at building up a powerful state which should extend from Valencia to the frontier of Italy. The ports of this region—above all, Barcelona, Montpellier, Narbonne and Marseilles—were in relation with the Moslem trading states of the Balearic Islands and Spain as well as with Africa and the Levant. Indeed, during the twelfth century they were hardly inferior to the Italian cities in the wealth and extent of their trade. Nor were these relations solely commercial; for it was through this region, no less than Sicily and Toledo, that Western Christendom first established contact with Arabic thought. As Duhem has written, "Marseilles and Montpelier were gates wide open to Oriental science", and some of the earliest Latin translations of Arabic scientific works were made at Marseilles, Toulouse, Béziers and Narbonne, as well as at Barcelona and Tarragona. The numerous Jewish colonies of Provence were renowned for their learning as well as for their wealth, and Jewish scholars acted as intermediaries between the Christian and the Islamic worlds. They were equally at home in France and Spain and Africa, as we see from the activity of Samuel ibn Tibbon of Lunel, who produced his (Hebrew) translations at Arles, Marseilles, Toledo, Barcelona and Alexandria.[1]

Under these circumstances there seems no inherent improbability in the view that the rise of the new Provençal culture was affected by the older and more advanced civilization of Western Islam which already embraced the greater part of the western Mediterranean area. In fact, this was the solution which first suggested itself to the scholars of the Romantic period more than a century ago, and its abandonment was due less to scientific reasons than to the nationalist tendency to insist on the independent and native origin of Provençal culture.[2]

Of course, if we assume that the ideals of chivalry and courtesy which ultimately became so characteristic of medieval society were of purely native growth, then there is no difficulty in ascribing a similar origin to the rise of the new Provençal literature. But it is just this assumption which is open to criticism. In the tenth century the higher culture of Christian Europe was Latin and ecclesiastical, while the feudal society was still almost barbarian. In

[1] His son, Moses of Montpellier, was also a famous translator and so was his son-in-law, Jacob Anatoli of Marseilles, who collaborated with Michael Scott at Palermo in the translation of Averroes.

[2] This view was current throughout the eighteenth century. Its chief advocate was the Spanish Jesuit, J. Andres, in his *Origine, progressi e stato attuale d' ogni letteratura*, 1782–99. I have not seen Andres' work, but I believe that he bases his argument not only on the chivalrous character of the Moorish culture but also on specific literary resemblances, such as the occurrence of the refrain and the monorhyme and the existence of the *tenson* or poetical debate in Arabic literature. The theory was popularized by Ginguené and Sismondi, who derived their views from Andres. In the last decade of the eighteenth century the Moorish origin of the new poetry was also maintained by Herder, but I do not know whether he reached his conclusions independently of Andres. The opposite theory of Northern and Germanic origin was first clearly stated by Bouterwek in 1801.

Moslem Spain, on the other hand, there existed a rich and brilliant society which had already developed a characteristic type of chivalry. Fighting was not merely the hard and brutal trade of the professional soldiers; it was surrounded by a halo of romance and possessed an elaborate code of conventional etiquette. Horsemanship and the use of arms were fine arts which became the subject of learned treatises and of technical discussion. The exploits of the famous champions were famous throughout Spain and were the theme of poetry and romance.

Moreover, conditions in Spain in the tenth and eleventh centuries were far more favourable than those of northern Europe to the development of courtly society. It was a land of rich cities whose princes strove to outdo one another in the brilliance of their court life and in their munificence towards poets and men of letters.

While the nobility of feudal Europe was almost illiterate and the profession of the jongleur or minstrel was a despised and plebeian occupation, in Islam poetry was a noble art which even princes were not ashamed to cultivate. And thus it is in Moslem Spain rather than in northern Europe that we must look for the prototype of the knightly Troubadour whose art was thoroughly aristocratic and who could enter into the spirit of al-Mutanabbi's famous lines:

I am known to the horse troop, the night and the
    desert's expanse;
Not more to the paper and pen than the sword and
    the lance.

For the most distinctive feature of Spanish culture was its passion for poetry and music, and this passion extended through every rank and class from theologians like Ibn Hazm, philosophers like Ibn Bajja and statesmen like al-Mu'tamid, to the wandering minstrels who sang at tournaments or at street corners. An Arab writer of this age has left a curious description of how he suffered during an illness at Malaga in 1015 from the musical propensities of the Spaniards. "All round my house there was an incessant jangle of singing and of lutes, tomburs and lyres which disturbed me intensely and added to the restlessness and suffering caused by my illness. These toccatas and songs nailed themselves to my mind without hope of respite, so that I was filled with aversion for them and would have liked to find a house away from all the noise, but this was difficult in Malaga for the people are absolutely dominated by their passion for music."[1]

The development of Arabic music in Moslem Spain has recently been studied in detail by Professor Ribera, who maintains that it affords the key to the interpretation of the new secular music of medieval Europe that makes its first appearance with the Troubadours. If this is so, it goes a long way towards proving the wider thesis of the debt of Provençal culture to the Moslem world. In any case, it is generally acknowledged that the lute, the most popular medieval instrument, reached Europe through Spain, and this alone suggests the possibility that the music and prosody of the Troubadours may be derived from the same source.

There is certainly little resemblance between the classical Arabic poetry with its long metres and its sustained monorhyme, and the dancing measures and complex rhyme scheme of the Provençal verse. But in the eleventh century Spanish poetry was no longer confined to the traditional Arabic forms. As in Persia, at the other extremity of the Moslem world, the blending of Arabic and native traditions had produced new literary forms. But while in Persia the typical creation of the period is the *Mathnawi*—the epic, rhymed in couplets—the new development in Spain was essentially lyrical. It produced the new strophic form of verse, the

[1] J. Ribera, *Music in Ancient Arabia and Spain* (1929), p. 115.

Zajal and the *Muwashshah* or "girdled" poem—which became extraordinarily popular and spread from Spain to the other parts of the Islamic world. In these new types of verse each stanza consists of a number of short lines and has its own rhymes, but the Arabic tradition of the monorhyme is preserved in so far that each stanza ends in the same rhyme, which also appears in the refrain. In its simplest form the *Zajal* consists of a number of quatrains with two rhymes to the stanza (a a a b, c c c b, etc.) but it soon developed an elaborate metrical pattern with multiple internal rhymes. The resemblance between this new type of Arabic poetry and the Provençal lyric is unmistakable. Nor is it easy to explain this resemblance by the theory of a spontaneous parallel evolution, for the Provençal lyric also possesses the monorhyme in the last line of each stanza and in the refrain. This feature is not preserved by the majority of the French and Italian imitators of the Provençal poetry, and it is difficult to explain its origin except as a direct inheritance from Arabic tradition.

And, apart from this point, there is a remarkable resemblance in the general character of the two literatures. Both of them show the same tendency to an elaborate formalism of style which often degenerates into frigid artificiality. Both of them delight in verbal conceits and plays upon words, such as the "equivocal rhymes" of Arnaut Daniel, where the same words are used in each stanza in a different sense. Moreover, there is considerable resemblance in the main forms of poetry, the love song, the *planh* or lament, the *sirvente* or strife poem, and the *tenzon* or poetical debate.

Of these, however, only the last two are at all unusual types and even these may have arisen independently in Provence. But there remains one form which is so completely artificial and unnatural that it can hardly have arisen independently in two cultures during the same period. This is the *descort*, of which the alternate lines are each written in a different language. This curious device is well known in Islamic literature, especially in Persia, where it is known as the *mulamma* or "patchwork". The best-known example in medieval Christian literature is the *canzone* of Dante, *Ai fals ris! per qua traitz avetz*, in which the lines are alternately Provençal, Latin and Italian, but here Dante was only following an established Provençal convention, and the most elaborate example of the type is a *descort* in five different languages composed by Raimbaut de Vaqueiras in the twelfth century.

But it is not only the external form of Provençal literature which points to Arabic influence. There is an even more remarkable resemblance in the content of the two literatures. As we have seen, the poetry of the Troubadours was based upon the cult of woman and the service of the beloved, and it was in Provence that there first arose that ideal of romantic love which inspired the French romances of chivalry, on the one hand, and the *dolce stil nuovo* of Dante and the Italian poets of the Dugento, on the other. Now, there is nothing in the earlier history of medieval society to explain this development. The attitude of feudal society towards women, as we see it in the *chansons de geste* and in history, was completely unromantic. Woman was regarded either as a chattel or as the partner of her lord in the management of his fief. Christian morality, especially in its ascetic monastic form, was naturally hostile to and contemptuous of sexual love. Latin erotic poetry certainly existed even in the Dark Ages, but it was based on the tradition of Ovid and was frankly sensual and hedonistic in its conception of love.

But the position in the Islamic world was totally different. The idea of romantic love had existed in Arabic literature from the earliest times and had reached its full development in the tenth century. The misfortunes of lovers and the sorrows of unrequited love are the stock theme of the poet and the story-teller and were treated in every imaginable detail. We need look no further than the *Arabian Nights* to realize how widespread and how strong was this romantic tendency. And even in this popular and plebeian form we cannot but recognize that the attitude to love is not only more romantic but even in a sense more spiritual than anything to be found in Latin literature. Take, for example, the following verses which I quote almost at random:

> *I see you with my heart from distant tracts. Do you also see me with your heart from afar?*
> *My heart and my eye are sorrowing for you, my soul is with you and you are ever in mind.*
> *I should not delight in life without seeing you, even were I in Paradise or the Garden of Eternity!*[1]

And if this was to the taste of the street audiences of medieval Cairo, what must the attitude of the chivalrous and courtly society of Spain have been in the eleventh century? For in that society woman enjoyed a much higher position than either in modern Islam or in Western Christendom during the Dark Ages. Women were highly educated, especially in calligraphy, music and poetry. There was a considerable number of poetesses, including several of the queens and princesses of the Spanish dynasties. The most famous of these was Wallada, the Ummayyad princess of Cordova, to whom Ibn Zaydun, the greatest of the Spanish poets of the eleventh century, devoted his life. His poems express the same spirit of romantic passion and disinterested service which inspired the Troubadours and the poets of the *dolce stil nuovo*. Indeed, von Schack, who rather neglects the Provençal development, declares that it is only in

[1] From the Story of 'Otbeh and Reyya. Night 680 (Lane's trans.).

Petrarch that he finds a worthy successor, and that his poetry is the earliest expression of the romantic attitude to love and the feeling for nature which characterizes modern literature.[1]

It is, in fact, a great mistake to suppose that there is anything peculiarly Christian or European in the ideal or "Platonic" conception of love. The love of Beni 'Odhra, the "children of Chastity" who "die when they love", had been celebrated by Arab poets from a very early period, and in the tenth century Platonic love had become the subject of elaborate treatises by scholars and theologians.[2] Ibn Hazm, the great Spanish scholar, had written on the subject in the eleventh century and his *Ring of the Dove* abounds in authentic stories of Spanish Moslems, drawn from all ranks of society, whose love is Platonic and who render silent homage to their beloved and worship her with an almost mystical adoration.[3] At a still later period, at the beginning of the thirteenth century, Ibn u'l-'Arabi, the great Spanish mystic, uses the symbolism of love to express his deepest religious ideas, and his book of mystical odes is dedicated to a real lady whom he met at Mecca in 1201 and who occupied somewhat the same position in his life as Beatrice did in the life of Dante.[4]

This mystical doctrine of love does not appear in early Provençal literature. In fact, it could not do so, until poetry had come into contact with metaphysical thought, which first occurred in Italy in the thirteenth century. But already in the poems of Arnaut Daniel and the other great troubadours we find the same idealization of the beloved and the same morbid insistence on the frustration of desire which

[1] von Schack, *Poesie und Kunst der Araber in Spanien und Sicilien*, i, 280.
[2] Cf. Massignon's description of Ibn Da'ud of Ispahan in his great work on Hallaj the mystic (Paris, 1922).
[3] M. Asin, *Islam and the Divine Comedy*, p. 273.
[4] His book of mystical odes—*Tarjuman al-Ashwaq*—has been translated by R. A. Nicholson. London (1911).

characterized the Arab cult of love in the tenth and eleventh centuries. Moreover, in their treatment of these themes the Provençal poets tend to recur to the same stock motives that we find in the Arabic poetry. For example, one of the stock figures of the Arabic love song, who appears in almost every poem from the earliest times of classical Arabic literature, is the "slanderer" or "the talker", and the same figure— "lauzenger", "lusingatore"—reappears with monotonous regularity in the poetry of the Provençal Troubadours and their Italian and German pupils, though it has become a purely formal and often meaningless convention.[1]

Thus there seem to be sufficient grounds not only for admitting an Oriental element in Provençal culture but even for regarding the whole movement as due to the spread of the higher civilization of Spain and the western Mediterranean into southern and south-western France. And there is nothing surprising in this, for the whole tendency of modern archæology and culture-history, quite apart from the theories of the extreme diffusionist school, goes to show that the higher culture naturally influences the less advanced ones with which it comes into contact.

Owing to the lack of documentary evidence, it is impossible to say how the process of diffusion took place, though there was, as we have seen, no lack of opportunities for contact between the two cultures. The most obvious channel of communication was through the mixed and often bilingual population of north-eastern Spain, and it is quite possible that the jongleurs and minstrels who wandered from court to court in Catalonia and France may have transmitted to the North the music and popular songs of Moslem Spain, since, according to Ribera, the use of the Romance language

[1] Jeanroy draws attention to the recurrence of these mysterious "slanderers" (*merkaere, lügenaere*) in the poetry of the German Minnesingers, and uses it as a proof of their dependence on Provençal and French models (Jeanroy, *Les Origines de la Poésie lyrique en France*, pp. 283, 289). And the same argument can be applied to its occurrence in Provençal and Arabic poetry.

was not unknown even among the poets of Andalusia.[1] But this does not explain the origin of the thoroughly aristocratic poetry of the Troubadours which seems to have first developed not in Catalonia or Provence, but in Limousin. Even there, however, there was some contact with Spanish culture through the crusades of the eleventh century in which the nobles of that region played a considerable part. Not only did the crusaders become acquainted with the wealth and luxury of Spanish culture; they brought back with them to France Moorish slaves and captives, and in some cases they actually married Moorish women of high position.

When the French crusaders captured Barbastro in northeast Spain in 1064 each of the principal knights received a house with all that it contained, women, children and furniture. Ibn Bassam has preserved the report of a Jewish envoy who was sent to the town to ransom the daughters of one of the leading citizens. He found the crusader in Moorish dress seated on a divan surrounded by Moslem girls who were waiting on him. He refused all the offers of the Jew on the ground that he had married the daughter of the former owner and hoped that she would give him descendants. "Her Moslem ancestors did the same with our women when they possessed themselves of this country. Now we do likewise. Thus do we succeed." He then turned to the girl and in broken Arabic said: "Take your lute and sing some songs for this gentleman." The Jew adds: "I was surprised and pleased to see the count show great enthusiasm as if he understood the words, though he continued drinking."[2]

One can well imagine that the French count may have retained his taste for Arabic music, and that his children by the Moorish lady might have learned to compose songs in the Spanish fashion. Actually the leader of the expedition

[1] Ribera, *op. cit.*, pp. 120 ff.
[2] Ribera, *op. cit.*, pp. 113–14; and Lavisse, *Histoire de France*, II, ii, 86. Ibn Bassam copied the story from Ibn Hayyan the Spanish historian.

which captured Barbastro was the father of the first of the Troubadours, William VII of Poitou, who himself, like so many other Troubadours, took part in the Spanish wars, so that this passage is one of the very few pieces of direct evidence that we possess as to the cultural environment in which the new literature first developed.

In the twelfth century the contact of the Troubadours with the Spanish culture is well known. Some of them, like Ot de Moncada, were themselves of Spanish origin; others, like Marcabru, spent much of their lives in Spain; while almost all of them had relations with the court of Aragon. Moreover, Provence was also brought into relation with Moslem culture through the eastern crusades in which so many of the Troubadours took part and which resulted in the establishment of a Provençal dynasty on the Phœnicean coast.

In the twelfth century Languedoc, particularly the coastal region from Marseilles to Barcelona, possessed wider international contacts and a more cosmopolitan type of culture than any region in western Europe, apart from Spain and the Norman Kingdom of Sicily. This is especially evident in its religious development, in the wealth and culture of its Jewish colonies, which rivalled those of Moslem Spain, and above all, in the prevalence of the heresy of the Catharists which ultimately proved the downfall of the Provençal culture.

For the Albigensian crusade not only uprooted heresy, it also ruined the courtly society in which the art of the Troubadours had flourished, in the same way that the French invasions of Italy overwhelmed the brilliant culture of the Italian states in the age of the Renaissance.[1] The literature of the thirteenth century is full of lamentations over the

[1] The destructive effects of the Albigensian crusade have, however, been absurdly exaggerated. For example, in the *Testament of Beauty* (iii, 727–30), Robert Bridges writes as though the whole population was destroyed "and their language wiped out, so that a man today reading Provençal song studieth in a dead tongue". Yet the late Poet Laureate can hardly have been ignorant of the existence of Mistral and the *Félibrige*, even if he had never heard of the Consistory of the Gay Saber and the Leys d'Amors.

passing of Nobility and Honour and Joy—*Paratges, Pretz e Joi*—and the humiliation of "the courteous folk" before the clerics and the Frenchmen.

There is little evidence that the Troubadours showed any active sympathy with the doctrines of the Albigenses. The anticlericalism of poets like Peire Cardenal and Guilhem Figueira has no theological foundation, and the remarkable *Sirvente* of Guilhem Montanhagol against the Inquisition expresses the views not of a Manichæan but of a humanist in revolt against the puritan spirit which condemned the extravagance and display of the courtly society.

> The man who despises honour and generosity comes of no good stock, so I hold.
> For God wills honour and praise, and I know that God made himself true man.
> And the man who goes against the designs of God, when God has done him the honour to make him in his own image,
> noble and powerful and nearer to himself than any creature,
> such a one is mad if he does not hold himself dear,
> and behave in this world so that he should have reward hereafter.[1]

But although the culture of the Troubadours had no essential connection with the Albigensian heresy, it also had no organic relation to Catholicism. Its roots were in another culture and another spiritual tradition, and when these perished the sources of its own vitality were destroyed. The decline of the Provençal culture was but one episode in the general change that passed over the western Mediterranean in the thirteenth century with the fall of the Spanish Moslem culture—a change which was completed by the Angevin

[1] Audiau and Lavaud, *Nouvelle Anthologie des Troubadours*, pp. 165–7.

conquest of Sicily and the fall of the mixed Siculo-Arab culture of the court of Manfred.

The individualism, the moral laxity and the secular spirit of the Troubadours were abhorrent to the religious earnestness and the rigid theological orthodoxy of the new regime, and the poets were forced either to migrate to Aragon and to Italy or to adapt their art to the new conditions. When *el gay saber* was revived in the fourteenth century under the patronage of the University of Toulouse, the Grand Inquisitor, and Master Philip "surnamed the Elephant", it was a very pale reflection of what it had been in the twelfth century.

Nevertheless, the decay of the Provençal culture did not put an end either to its social or to its literary influence. Its real importance is to be found not so much in its own local and temporary achievement as in the abiding influence that it exercised on European culture. Already in the twelfth century the courtly culture and the new ideal of romantic love had spread to northern France and thence they gradually penetrated and transformed the spirit of feudal society throughout Europe. Not only did they inspire the new French and German and Iberian poetry which closely follows the forms of Provençal verse; they also blended with the tradition of Northern epic and with the Celtic legendary traditions to produce the new cycle of Arthurian romance which had such a vast influence on European literature and sentiment.

Here the Provençal ideals of love and courtesy have been brought into relation with the ethical and mystical tradition of medieval Catholicism. Nevertheless, the union of the two elements did not amount to an organic unity. It retained a certain unreality and moral inconsistency which was afterwards to provoke the pious indignation of Ascham and the profounder criticism of Cervantes. And yet it is just this pursuit of an unattainable unity, this mingling of idealism and sensuality, of chivalry and violence, which constitutes the romantic appeal of the Middle Ages. Where the Christian tradition is completely victorious, as in the case of St. Louis, chivalry ceases to be romantic and becomes spiritual; and where the other element becomes supreme, as in the court of Burgundy in the fifteenth century, romanticism passes away into gallantry. It is the middle region, the world of Lancelot and Tristan and Thibaut of Champagne, which is the region of Romanticism.

It is, however, in Italy that the Provençal tradition attained its highest expression, for there it was not transplanted into an alien culture but developed under similar conditions to those of its native land. In fact, northern Italy, like Catalonia, was so completely dependent on the Provençal culture that its native poets, such as Sordello and Lanfranco Cigalla, used the Provençal language and are practically indistinguishable from the Troubadours of Languedoc, while the culture of Sicily and Apulia, in which the earliest vernacular poetry originated, was even more coloured by oriental influences than that of Provence itself.

Moreover, the new school of Tuscan poetry which arose in the second half of the thirteenth century, was equally indebted to the Provençal tradition and owes its peculiar character to its union of the art of the Troubadours with the thought of Arabic philosophy. The poetry of Guido Cavalcanti and the other poets of the *dolce stil nuovo*— above all, the youthful Dante—attains a deeper and more spiritual beauty than anything in the literature of Northern chivalry or in that of Provence itself. It is metaphysical poetry in the true sense of the word and it appeals to the intellect no less than to the emotions. Nevertheless, it does not altogether overcome the inconsistency which is inherent in the romantic ideal. Its obscurity is due to confusion as well as to profundity of thought. It is an attempt to combine fundamentally dissimilar things, the ideal of the Troubadour, the ideal of the Moslem philosopher and the ideal of the Christian mystic.

The Moslems had, indeed, already succeeded in achieving a synthesis between the first two of these. This synthesis finds its expression in the erotic mysticism of the Sufi poets of Persia and of Arabic writers such as Ibnu'l 'Arabi and Omar Ibnu'l Farid.

The latter, for instance, writes:

> Declare the absoluteness of Beauty and be not moved to
> deem it finite by thy longing for a tinselled jewel,
> For the charm of every fair youth or lovely woman is lent
> to them from Her beauty.
> 'Twas She that crazed Qays the lover of Lubna, ay and
> every enamoured man like Layla's Majnun or 'Azzar's
> Kutbayyir.
> Every one of them passionately desired Her attributes
> which She clothed in the form of a beauty which shone
> forth in a beauty of form.[1]

This Platonic idealism received a still more elaborate treatment at the hands of the writers of the Spanish school, such as Ibnu'l 'Arabi. They combined it with the metaphysical theory of a series of emanations through which Being and Intelligence descend from God through the celestial spheres and intelligences to the sublunary world, a doctrine which is common to all the Arabic philosophers from Avicenna to Averroes. In accordance with this theory, the Beloved is conceived as the symbol or embodiment of a metaphysical idea. She represents the 'aql—the Universal Intelligence—which is the intermediary between the Divine Unity and the phenomenal world, and the light which illuminates the human mind.

Now it is this idea which was taken over by the Italian

[1] Trans. R. A. Nicholson in *Studies in Islamic Mysticism*, p. 222.

poets of the *dolce stil nuovo* and finds typical expression in the *canzoni* of Guido Cavalcanti and Dante.[1]

The lady of the *Convivio* on whom "every supernal intelligence gazes" and whose "beauty rains down flames of fire, made living by a gentle spirit which is the creator of every good thought", is neither the Christian Logos nor a woman of flesh or blood. She is the Averroistic Intelligence that actualizes and illuminates the human mind. Such an idea is quite in harmony with the doctrines of Moslem theology, but it is fundamentally inconsistent alike with the Christian tradition and with the realities of human love. Dante himself was conscious of this when he wrote the sonnet, *Parole Mie*: "Stay not with her for love is not found there." And consequently in the great synthesis into which he poured all the wealth of his personal experience and his intellectual inheritance, Christian, Classical and Romantic, this inconsistency is finally transcended. The lady of the *Convivio* is replaced by Virgil, and Beatrice herself becomes a completely Christian figure. And in this synthesis the Provençal element also finds a place. Though Paolo and Francesca, the lovers of romance, are left in Hell, the art of the Troubadours, purified and transformed, is admitted into new life. The beautiful and peaceful words of Arnaut Daniel with their echo of his own verse mark the final reconciliation of the art of the Troubadours with the classical and the Christian ideals.

[1] The point of contact no doubt is to be found in the Averroistic philosophy which was widely diffused in the West from the time of Michael Scott, but it is possible that the mystical poetry of the type of Ibnu'l 'Arabi may also have had some direct influence. This is the view of Professor Asin and Professor Ribera, and the latter has given as an example the resemblance between the opening stanza of Dante's great canzone, *Tre donne intorno al cor me son venute,* and the well-known Arabic verses about Harun al-Rashid and the three slave girls recorded in the *Kitab ul Agani* of *al-Isfahani* (tenth century). The parallelism is certainly very striking, but there is not a trace of mysticism in the Arabic original. Still, as Ribera shows, the "three ladies" became a standard theme of Arabic poetry, and they may well have been used by Spanish poets of the mystical school whose works have not reached us. Cf. Ribera, *op. cit.,* pp. 162-7.

Ieu sui Arnaut, que plor e vau cantan,
consiros vei la passada folor,
e vei jausen lo jorn, qu'esper, denan.

I am Arnaut, who weeps and sings
    as he goes,
Contrite I see the folly of the past,
And see with joy the day I hope,
    beyond.

It is one of the greatest of Dante's achievements that he succeeded in reconciling the two great currents of European literature before they had even attained to self-consciousness. Unfortunately he found no successors capable of carrying on his achievement, with the partial exception of Petrarch and Chaucer. Otherwise we might have been saved alike from the narrow rationalism of eighteenth-century Classicism and from the emotional debauches of nineteenth-century Romanticism.

Nevertheless, the age of Dante did not see the end of the Provençal influence in Italy. The Troubadours and Arnaut Daniel, in particular, found a new disciple in Petrarch, and through Petrarch, who was canonized by Bembo (himself a student of Provençal) as a pillar of classical orthodoxy, the Provençal tradition entered the full stream of the Renaissance. It would need another essay to show how much the literature and culture of the Renaissance owed to this element. It is enough to say that the influence of Provençal Romanticism survived the age of Aristotelian dictatorship and reappears in that last and most artificial manifestation of the courtly culture—the Italian Arcadia.[1] And before that movement had come to an end, the writings

[1] The subsequent revival of interest in Provençal literature actually owed much to the writings of the first president of the Arcadia, Crescimbeni. It is to him that Bodmer, for example, owes his knowledge of the Troubadours.

of La Curne de Sainte Palaye, Dom Vaissète and Millot were preparing the way for the awakening of interest in Provençal literature and culture which played so important a part in the Romantic Revival from the time of Herder onwards.

XII

THE VISION OF PIERS PLOWMAN

I T would be strange to write of medieval religion without
some mention of one who is not only one of the greatest
of English religious poets but also the most remarkable
and the most authentic representative of the religious sentiment of the common people of medieval England.

And yet for some reason William Langland has never
received the attention that he deserves. He is little read,
and those who read him seldom realize his true greatness.
It is a reproach to modern England that when every minor
poet has been edited and re-edited to satiety, and when the
classics of foreign literature are to be found on every book-
stall, this great classic, which is one of the landmarks of
English literature and English religion, should be inac-
cessible to the ordinary man except in abridged or incomplete forms[1] and that the only standard work on the subject
should have been written by a foreigner.[2] And this reproach

---

[1] The standard edition edited by Prof. Skeat (Oxford, 1886, 2 vols., and
E.E.T.S., 4 vols.) is too expensive to be in general use. Wright's edition
is both out of date and out of print. Skeat's popular edition of the text
(Oxford) and his modern version (Dent), both somewhat expurgated,
only contain the Prologue and the first seven *passus* (out of twenty) of
the B text. Perhaps the most handy and accessible version is that by
Arthur Burrell in Everyman's Library, but this is both translated and
abridged. An excellent school text of the Prologue and Passus V to
VII of the B text, edited by C. D. Pamely, was published by Messrs.
Sidgwick and Jackson in 1928. In this essay I have thought it best to
give my own versions of the passages that I quote, though I do not pretend
to have found a satisfactory *via media* between a literal translation and
a modern paraphrase. In 1935 Sheed & Ward published a version in
modern English by Henry W. Wells.

Since this note was written, a new version has been made by Mr. Nevill
Coghill, which is admirably faithful to the original style and sense and
spirit. But it is most drastically abridged and reduces the 7,000-odd lines
of the B text to some 100 pages.

See *Visions from Piers Plowman*, translated into modern English by
Nevill Coghill. Phœnix House (1949).

[2] *L' épopée mystique de William Langland*, by J. J. Jusserand, 1893.

239

ought to be felt by Catholics before all others, since for them Langland's poem is a part of their special heritage. Here is the Catholic Englishman *par excellence,* at once the most English of Catholic poets and the most Catholic of English poets: a man in whom Catholic faith and national feeling are fused in a single flame. He saw Christ walking in English fields in the dress of an English labourer, and to understand his work is to know English religion in its most autochthonous and yet most Catholic form.

It is true that there is much in Langland that is likely to prove shocking to Catholics who know their Middle Ages only in a modern bowdlerized form. His England is not the idealized Catholic England of the apologist, nor the Merry England of the medievalist myth. It is a grim enough land where oppression and misgovernment are rife, and famine and pestilence are never far away. For Langland, with all his Christian idealism, is also a realist who does not shrink from describing in pitiless detail the corruptions of the Church, the wrongs of the poor and the vices of the rich. He belongs to his age—the fourteenth century—which, in spite of Boccaccio and Chaucer, was not a cheerful one, but which, none the less, was a time of immense spiritual vitality and of momentous consequences for the future of Western civilization.

The fourteenth century was an age of profound social and spiritual change: an age of ruin and rebirth, of apocalyptic fears and mystical hopes. It was the age of the Great Schism and the Black Death and the Hundred Years War, but it was also the age of Dante and Petrarch, of St. Catherine and St. Bridget, of Tauler and Suso and Ruysbroeck, an age of poets and mystics and saints. It saw the breakdown of the universal theocratic order of medieval Christendom and the rise of political nationalism and religious division, and at the same time it witnessed the passing of the old agrarian feudal society and the rise of capitalism and urban industrial-

ism. Western Europe was stirred from end to end by a wave
of social unrest which showed itself in revolutionary movements and bitter class warfare. At no other time in European
history has the common people asserted itself more vigor-
ously or found more remarkable leaders. It was the age
of the Jacquerie and the Peasants' Revolt, of the wars of
the Swiss peasants and the German towns against the princes,
and the still more heroic struggle of the Flemish proletariat
against their own ruling classes and the power of the French
monarchy.

It was in the midst of this turmoil of change that the
English people first attained maturity and self-consciousness.
Three centuries earlier it had been submerged by a wave
of foreign invasion, and the Norman conquest had made
England for a time a province of continental culture. Its
churchmen belonged to the international unity of Latin
Christendom and its nobles to the hardly less international
society of French chivalry. Latin was the language of learning, and French the language of society. English became
the speech of peasants, the mark of the simple and the
uneducated. As the first English chronicler, Robert of
Gloucester, writes as late as the beginning of the fourteenth
century: "If a man does not know French he is little
esteemed, but low-born people hold still to English and their
own tongue." The fourteenth century changed all that, and
before its close English was not only the language of the
people but was making its way into court and parliament,
until in the last year of the century the first English-speaking
king opened his first parliament in English words. Trevisa
dates the change, at least in education, from the time of the
Black Death, and no doubt the great pestilence and the great
war with France mark a dividing line in the history of
English culture. But the vital factor in the new development
was not so much the decay of the artificial Norman-French
culture as the spiritual rebirth of the national consciousness.

The English genius found simultaneous expression in the work of Chaucer and Langland, the poet of the *Canterbury Tales* and the poet of *Piers Plowman*.

These two great voices of England expressed the two aspects of English character and English culture. Chaucer represents all that England had learnt from its three centuries of incorporation in continental culture. He is a courtier and a scholar who looks at the English scene with the humorous detachment of a man of the great world. He clothed the courtly tradition in an English dress and gave the common Englishman a right of entry into the cultivated society which had hitherto been the monopoly of clerks and knights.

This achievement is reflected in his style, which is so characteristically English and his own, and yet owes so much to the cultivation and imitation of French and Italian models. It is essentially classical in spirit, far more classical indeed than that of his French masters, such as Guillaume Machaut, since it is the result of a long process of experiment and elaborate artifice, which bears fruit not in the wooden rhetoric of Lydgate and Occleve or the empty grace of fifteenth-century French verse but in a simplicity and strength that make it not incomparable with that of the great Italian classics of the Trecento.

Nothing could be more different from this than the other great work of the new age, for it is as formless and as lacking in conscious literary artifice as any great work can be. It is a voice from another world—the submerged world of the common English—a voice that is by turns harsh and pitiful and comic, but always the authentic voice of the English people. Where Chaucer took the world as he found it, and found it good, the author of *Piers Plowman* judged the world and found it wanting. He represents the English view of life as it had been formed by nearly a thousand years of Christian faith, not the official view of the theologian and the scholar, but the spiritual vision of a prophet chosen among his fellows by his inspiration alone.

And this contrast is not simply a matter of temperament or class: it has its basis in a profound difference of cultural tradition. Chaucer belongs, as I have said, to the international tradition of the courtly culture, and already has his eyes open to the dawn of the Italian Renaissance; but Langland owes nothing to the courtly tradition with its gay rhymed measures and its cult of love and romance. He looks back to the forgotten Nordic world and to the grave Christian poetry of Saxon England. He uses the old alliterative accentual measure which was the native speech of English and Teutonic poetry and which now suddenly arose, as it were from the dead, as a sign of the renaissance of the English spirit. This return to the old alliterative metre was not peculiar to Langland—we find it also in the work of Huchown of the *Awle Ryale* and of the poet of the *Pearl* and *Gawain*. But Langland inherited the spirit as well as the form of the old Northern poetry. He has the same attitude to life—that profound and gloomy meditation on the world and the fate of man that distinguishes the old Teutonic poetry from the light-hearted courtly literature that had its origin in Provence.

There is a striking example of this in Langland's vision of "The Mountain called Middelerde":

> *And I bowed my body . beholding all about,*
> *And saw the sun and the sea . and the sand after,*
> *Where that birds and beasts . wander with their mates,*
> *Wild worms in the woods . and wonderful fowls*
> *With flecked feathers . of full many a colour.*
> *Man and his mate . both might I see,*
> *Poverty and plenty . peace and war,*
> *Bliss and bitter bale . both saw I at once;*
> *And how that men took meed . and mercy refused.*

In sooth I saw Reason . ruling all beasts
Save man and his mate . and thereof I wondered.[1]

Poetry such as this stands entirely outside contemporary literary tradition. Nevertheless, it has its tradition which is that of the old Teutonic literature. It has far more in common with the melancholy of Anglo-Saxon elegiac poetry or with the oracular solemnity of *Muspili* than with the smooth technical dexterity of Machaut or Froissart. And it is characteristic of the Nordic strain in Langland's poetry that his Christian epic should end, like the *Volospa* and the epics of the heathen North, on a note of defeat and despair—with the vision of a final battle for a lost cause against the unloosed hosts of hell.

On the other hand, Langland's style has none of the stately and artificial rhetoric of ancient Teutonic poetry. His language is the everyday speech of his time—at least of the friars and the popular preachers. It is full of racy vernacular turns of expression, as well as of latinisms and gallicisms borrowed from the mixed language of lawyers and clerks. Moreover, he belongs to his own age—the century of Boccaccio and Chaucer—by his interest in the spectacle of human life and his keen eye for realistic detail. And this union of profound melancholy and vivid realism shows itself in all that he wrote and imparts an extremely personal character to his poetry. There are, I know, learned men who deny the traditional authorship and the unity of the poem, and would make it the work of a whole platoon of poets. But it would be little short of a miracle if a single age had produced a succession of poets, or even two of them, with the same general attitude to the social and spiritual problems of their age and the same highly individual blend of realism and mysticism. It is true that there are considerable differences between the successive versions of the poem

[1] C, xiv, 134–43 and 153.

that have been classified by Professor Skeat as the A, B and C texts. But these are no greater than might be expected if the different versions reflect the changes of thirty years' experience; in fact, they seem to show a continuous development of thought and purpose which is entirely consistent with the author's character as he draws it himself.

Consequently, I see no reason to doubt either the unity of authorship or the traditional ascription to William Langland. Langland was born about the year 1333 in the heart of that West Country that has been so rich in poets, either at Cleobury Mortimer, or, as has been recently suggested by Mr. A. H. Bright, at Longlands, near Ledbury, just beneath the Malvern Hills, the scene of the opening vision of his poem.[1] Acording to the tradition recorded in a fifteenth-century MS. of the poem, he was the son of one Stacy de Rokayle, of Shipton-under-Wychwood, a tenant of the Despensers who held the lordship of Malvern Chase at this period. But if so, it is probable that he was a bastard, for the circumstances of his life as recorded in the autobiographical passages that occur in the later versions of his poem are irreconcilable with his being the lawful son of a noble and wealthy house. It is very hard to reject the evidence of these passages, for they bear an unmistakable note of sincerity; and though medieval authors often put their views into the mouth of a fictitious or pseudonymous character, so far as I know, they never created a purely imaginary character of this type. Internal evidence shows that the second version of the poem—the B text—was written about the year 1377-8, when the author was forty-five years of age. The first version—the A text—has been assigned to the year 1362 on the strength of a reference to the great storm that occurred on 15th January of that year,[2] while

---

[1] *New Light on Piers Plowman*, by A. H. Bright, Oxford, 1928.
[2] On the other hand, it is difficult not to see in the description of Lady Meed and her trial before the king an allusion to Alice Perrers, the mistress of Edward III, and to the events of 1376, when she was banished

the final version of the poem belongs to the last decade of the fourteenth century. It seems that Langland did not survive the year 1399, for a conclusion that has been added to one MS. of the A text by a certain John Bull before the close of the reign of Richard II writes of him as already deceased. Consequently he cannot be the author of the poem on the fall of Richard II—*Richard the Redeless*—which was ascribed to him by Skeat, but which is a purely political poem that bears little or no trace of Langland's characteristic mentality.

The greater part of his life seems to have been spent in London, for the autobiographical passages of the poem describe the author as living "in a cot on Cornhill" with his wife and his daughter, a member of that proletariat of clerks in minor orders who earned a bare livelihood by singing office in the chantries and saying prayers for the souls of their well-to-do patrons.

> *I live in London, and on London too*
> *The looms that I labour with . my livelihood to earn*
> *Are my paternoster and primer . placebo and dirige*
> *And my psalter sometimes . and my seven psalms.*
> *Thus I sing for the souls . of such as do me help,*
> *And those that find me my food . vouchsafe, I trow,*
> *To welcome me when I come . otherwhiles in a month,*
> *Now with him and now with her . and in this way I beg*
> *Without bag or bottle . but my belly only.*[1]

He pictures himself as a long, lean, eccentric figure wandering through the streets of London, paying little heed to those about him, "loath to reverence lords or ladies" or to bow before men in fur coats and silver chains, and

---

from court at the instance of the Good Parliament. If this were so, however, it would make the first version almost contemporary with the second, which is difficult to believe.

[1] C, vi, 44–52.

regarded by his neighbours as no better than a fool.[1] His
married life seems to have been unhappy, and he was always
pursued by poverty and ill-health. Thus he lived in bitterness
of spirit, in failure and suffering, always feeling the contempt
of men and the emptiness of his wasted life. And yet he was
continually spurred on by his power of spiritual vision and
by a sense that somewhere, just out of his reach, was the
prize that would make up for everything, the Pearl for which
a man will sell all he has. He saw himself as the unlucky
speculator who has always lost but who, some day, some-
how, will light on the bargain that will make him rich for
ever.

That is sooth I said . and so I beknow
That I have tynt [lost] time . and time mispended;
And yet I hope as he . that oft hath chaffered,
That aye hath lost and lost . and at last him happed
He bought such a bargain . he was ever the better,
And set his loss at a leaf . at the last end.

.   .   .   .   .   .

So hope I to have . of Him that is almighty
A gobbet of his grace . and begin a time
That all times of my time . to profit shall turn.[2]

Thus his poem is not a work of art like the poems of
Chaucer; it is the vessel into which the poet poured his
doubts, his hopes, his criticism of life and his prophetic
message. There is no other work of medieval literature,
not even the *Testaments* of Villon, which has such a direct
contact with life and which gives us such an insight into
the heart of medieval humanity. It is true that though his

[1] B, xv, 1–11.
[2] C, Passus vi, 92–101. The autobiographical passage of which this is
the conclusion is of itself, to my mind, a sufficient refutation of Professor
Manly's view that the author of the C text was an unimaginative pedant,
and that the picture of the poet himself is merely a rhetorical device.

style owes nothing to the medieval romance tradition, he borrowed from that tradition the external machinery of vision and allegory. All these cumbrous personifications of virtues and vices are the lay figures that had been the stock-in-trade of medieval didactic literature for centuries. And yet nowhere is the irrepressible originality and realism of the English poet more apparent. These abstractions are apt suddenly to become more personal and nearer to life than even the human characters of a great poet like Chaucer. As Blake showed, the classicism of the latter makes the Canterbury Pilgrims themselves universal human types, while Langland's realism transforms his allegorical abstractions into individual men and women. Gluttony goes into the alehouse and sits on the bench with

> *Watt the warner . and his wife both,*
> *Tim the tinker . and twain of his prentices,*
> *Hick the hackneyman . and Hugh the needeler,*
> *Clarice of Cockslane . and the clerk of the church,*
> *Dawe the diker . and a dozen other;*
> *A ribibor, a ratoner . a raker of Chepe,*[1]
> *A roper, a retainer . and Rose the disher,*
> *Godfrey of Garlickhythe . and Gryffin the Welsh,*
> *And a heap of upholsterers.*[2]

And he drinks with the best of them as though he were an honest drunkard instead of a moral abstraction.

In the same way Sloth appears as a lazy priest who knows the rhymes of Robin Hood better than his *Paternoster,* and who

> *can find in a field . or in a furrow a hare*
> *Better than in* Beatus vir . *or* Beati omnes
> *Construe one clause well . and ken it to my parishioners,*

[1] A musician (rebab-player), a rat-catcher and a Cheapside scavenger.
[2] B, v, 316–25.

while Avarice is a merchant who recounts his rogueries
with naïve relish and apologizes for himself as a plain man
who knows no French but that of the far end of Norfolk.

All this is characteristic of Langland's strength and weakness. He has no control over his pen. He is hardly launched
on his sermon before reality bursts in tumultuously and
turns his moral allegory into a vivid portrayal of the vulgar
humanity of a fourteenth-century English crowd.

Yet this realism is not always present. He is often content
to leave his allegory on a plane of frigid abstraction, and
there are occasions in which Langland surpasses the Puritans
themselves in the grotesqueness of his nomenclature. He
tells us of a croft called "Covet-not-men's-cattle-nor-wives-
nor-none-of-their-servants-that-might-annoy-them", and the
children of Piers Plowman have names that are longer and
odder than those of the Barebones family. Nevertheless, at
any moment the flame of pure poetry may blaze out and
silence the creaking machinery of didactic allegorism, and
the artificial vision of medieval literary tradition may pass
into the spiritual vision of the seer. His art is more like that
of the Hebrew prophets than that of the modern poet, since
it is not literature but the utterance of the word that God has
put into his mouth. It is the common speech, which human
folly has spoiled, brought back to its true function. For
speech, he says

> *is a shoot of grace,*
> *And God's gleeman . and a game of heaven.*
> *Would never the faithful Father . [that] his fiddle were*
>   *untempered,*
> *Nor his gleeman a gadabout . a goer to taverns.*[1]

The one poet with whom one may compare him is his
greater predecessor, Dante, though they represent in many
respects the opposite poles of fourteenth-century literature.

[1] B, ix, 100–03.

For Dante, no less than Langland, conceived his task in a prophetic spirit and used the convention of the vision to convey his criticism of life and his religious ideal. Both of them felt that the world had gone astray, and themselves with it: both had an intense faith in the Catholic way and yet were profoundly dissatisfied with the state of the Church and convinced of the need for a drastic reform. Both looked for a deliverer who should set priests and people on the right way. But Dante brought to his task all the wisdom of the schools and the art of a highly conscious literary culture. His way was the highway of classical tradition—the royal road of imperial Rome—and he found his guide in Virgil and his saviour in the Messianic Emperor, the *Messo di Dio*, who will slay the harlot and the giant with whom she sins.

Langland, on the other hand, had the scanty learning of a poor clerk, a knowledge of the liturgy and the Bible and the common faith of Christendom.[1] His way was the muddy highroad of common life, and he found his guide and saviour in the common man, Piers Plowman, who is the type of Labour and Christian charity and at last of Christ Himself.

In *Piers Plowman* the social crisis of the age attains clear and direct expression. It is not only the first authentic voice of the English people; it is the first and almost the only utterance in literature of the cry of the poor:

> *Old men and hoar . that be helpless and needy,*
> *And women with child . that cannot work,*
> *Blind men and bed ridden . and broken in their members,*
> *And all poor sufferers . patient under God's sending,*
> *As lepers and mendicants . men fallen into mischief,*
> *Prisoners and pilgrims . and men robbed perchance,*
> *Or brought low by liars . and their goods lost,*

[1] The limitation of his learning is shown by the fact that on one occasion he translates *ne moechaberis* as "thou shalt not kill"!

Or through fire or through flood . fallen to poverty,
That take their mischiefs meekly . and mildly at heart.[1]

With all its talk of class consciousness modern socialism has failed to produce any work of "proletarian" literature that is comparable to this in depth and poignancy. The bitter cry of the socially disinherited against the injustice of their lot breaks out again and again in Langland's poem, piercing through the cumbrous superstructure of theological exhortation and moral allegory:

There the poor dare plead
To have allowance of his lord . by the law he it claimeth,
Joy that never Joy had . of rightful Judge he asketh
And saith "Lo, birds and beasts . that no bliss knoweth,
And wild worms in the wood . through winter Thou
     grievest them,
And makest them well-nigh meek . and mild for default,
But after Thou sendest them summer . that is their sovereign
     joy,
And bliss to all that be . both wild and tame.
Then may beggars like beasts . ask after bliss,
That all their life have lived . in languor and in dearth."
But God send them some time . some manner joy,
Either here or elsewhere . else were it ruth;
For amiss he were made . who was made not for joy.[2]

Or again in a passage which I do not wish to weaken by translation:

Ac pore peple, thi prisoneres . lorde in the put of myschief,
Conforte tho creatures . that moche care suffren
Thorw derth, thorw drouth . alle her dayes here,
Wo in wynter tymes . for wantyng of clothes,
And in somer tyme selde . soupen to the fulle;

[1] C, x, 175-83.
[2] C, xvi, 289-301 (B, xiv, 108-20).

Comforte thi careful . Chryst, in thi ryche,
For how Thow confortest alle creatures . clerkes bereth
  witnesse.[1]

But Langland is not merely alive to the sufferings of the
poor, he is also intensely conscious of the social changes
that accompanied the introduction of the new economic
order and the evils that they brought in their wake. He
was loyal to the old hierarchical ideal of a society based
on custom and loyal service, and looked askance at the
new power of money that was transforming the world. In
his vision of Lady Meed, which occupies the first part of
his poem, he draws a picture of a society intoxicated by the
power of wealth and governed by purely economic motives.
The Lady Meed is nothing more or less than the power of
the purse.

Trust in her treasure . betrayeth full many,
She hath poisoned Popes . and impaired Holy Church.
Monks and minstrels . are among her lovers,
Both learned men . and lepers in hedges.
Summoners and jurymen . are such as prize her,
She is with the sheriffs . who rule the shires;
For she robs men of their lands . and their life as well,
And giveth the gaoler . gold and silver
To unfetter the false . to fly where he will.
And taketh true men by the top . and tieth them fast,
And hangeth them for hatred . that never did harm.
To be cursed in consistory . she counteth not a straw;
For she gives a cope to the commissioner . and coats to
  his clerks;
She is assoiled of sin . as soon as she will.
In a single month . she can do as much
As the privy seal . can do in six score days,
For she is privy with the Pope . provisors know it,

[1] B, xiv, 174-9.

Simony and she . seal their bulls.
She blesseth these bishops . though they be unlearned,
Promoteth parsons . and giveth protection to priests,
To keep lemans and lotebies . all their life days,
And to bring forth bairns . against the law's biddings.
Where she is well with the king . woe is the realm.[1]

In reply to this arraignment Lady Meed defends herself
by an appeal to the universality and sovereignty of the
economic motive:

It becometh a king . that keepeth a realm,
To give Meed to men . who serve him meekly,
To aliens, and to all men . to honour them with gifts,
Meed maketh him beloved, . and esteemed as a man.
Emperors and earls . all manner of lords,
By Meed get yeomen . to run and ride.
The Pope and all prelates . take gifts and presents,
And give Meed to men . to maintain their laws.
Servants for their service . take Meed of their masters:
Beggars for their prayers . beg for Meed in return;
Minstrels for their mirth . Meed they ask.
The king hath Meed of his men . to make peace in the
  land;
Men that teach children . crave of them Meed.
Priests that preach good words to the people
Ask Meed and mass pence . and their meat at meal times.
All kinds of craftsmen . crave Meed for their prentices;
Merchants and Meed . must needs go together,
No wight as I ween . without Meed may live.[2]

Against all this Langland sets his vision of a new age,
when Truth shall return and "Love shall be leader in the
land".

[1] B, iii, 123, 127, 132–52.
[2] B, iii, 208–26.

No more shall Meed . be the mistress as now,
But love and lowliness . and loyalty together,
These shall be lords in the land . truth to save.

.   .   .   .   .   .

And kind-love shall come yet . and conscience together,
And make law a labourer . such love shall arise,
And such a peace among the people . and so perfect a
*   truth,*
That Jews shall ween in their wits . and wax wondrous
*   glad,*
That Moses or Messias . be come into this earth,
And have wonder in their hearts . that men be so true.[1]

This apocalyptic hope of a spiritual renewal of Christendom was characteristic of the central period of the Middle Ages. It attained peculiarly clear expression with Joachim of Flora and with the Spiritual Franciscans, but it is also found in almost every quarter of the medieval world—among mystics like Mechtild of Magdeburg and Rulman Merswin and also among men of letters like Dante and Petrarch and even among politicians such as Cola di Rienzo, as well as among countless obscure visionaries and reformers of whom Langland is the spokesman. But Langland expresses this current of ideas in a new spirit of ethical realism that is characteristically English. His interests are more social than those of the mystics, while they are less political than those of Dante or Rienzo. He saw the need of his time primarily as a social need for a spiritual remedy. Society was diseased, and the only cure for its sickness was to be found in Christianity. The tragedy of the age was that although Christianity was nominally supreme and was surrounded by all the pomp and external recognition that society could give it, it seemed powerless to change human life. Christ had been proclaimed king, but He was king in

[1] B, iii, 288–90, 297–302.

name only; the real sovereign was Lady Meed, who was honoured by clergy and nobles, while Christ stood without in the dress of the poor.

> *And now is ruth to rede . how the red noble*
> *Is reverenced before the rood . and received for the*
> *   worthier*
> *Than Christ's cross, that o'ercame . death and deadly sin.*
> *Both rich and religious . reverence that rood*
> *That is graven on groats . and on golden nobles.*[1] . . .

> *It seemeth now soothly . to the world's sight*
> *That God's word worketh not . on learned or on lewd*
> *But in such manner as Mark . meaneth in the gospel:*
> *"If the blind lead the blind . both shall fall into the*
> *   ditch."*[2]

That is why Langland's anger is so hot against the new Scribes and Pharisees, the men who sit in Moses' seat and bind burdens on the people which they will not touch themselves. He describes the fat theologian who has just preached before the Dean of St. Paul's on the sufferings of the apostle "*in fame et frigore* and flappe of scourges", sitting down himself at the high table and gorging on wild boar and tripe and pies and puddings, while the poor man sups below on a sour loaf.[3] He describes the rich men arguing on religious matters "at meat in their mirth when minstrels are still".

> *Thus they drivel on their dais . the Deity to know*
> *And gnaw God in their gullet . when their guts are full.*
> *But the careful may cry . and complain at the gate*
> *Both a-hungered and athirst . quaking with cold*

---

[1] B, xv, 501–3, 506–8.
[2] B, x, 274–6.
[3] B, xiii, 60–110.

Is none to call him near . to help his need.
But they hue him away like a hound . and order him off.

.   .   .   .   .   .

God is much in the mouths . of these great masters,
But among mean men . His mercy and works.[1]

In Langland's eyes the only true religion is a religion of
works, and the only works that avail are works of charity.

For though you be true of your tongue . and earn truly,
And as chaste as a child . that weepeth in church,
But save you love loyally . and lend to the poor,
And such goods as God sends you . give in goodly fashion.
You have no more merit . in Mass nor in Hours
Than hath Malkyn of her maidenhood . that no man
    desireth.
For James the gentle . judged in his book
That Faith without Fact[2] *. is right nothing worth*
And as dead as a doornail . except deeds follow.
Therefore Chastity without charity . will be chained in
    Hell,
It is lacking as a lamp . with no light in it.[3]

Langland's aim is to bring religion out of the palace and
the pulpit into direct contact with common humanity. He
wants to strip it of its rich vestments, its pious knick-knacks
and its load of useless learning, and set it to work in the
slums and the highways, clearing up the mess that had been
accumulated by generations of neglect. This ideal is embodied in the symbolic figure that has given its name to the
whole poem. While Dante, a type of the political idealist,
puts his faith in the coming of a prince

[1] B, x, 51–70.
[2] i.e. works, deeds.
[3] B, i, 177–87.

Who may far off behold
Of the True City the eternal towers,

Langland finds the man who will put the world right in
the shape of an English farmer, ploughing his half-acre by
the wayside. Piers Plowman is at first simply the type of
honest husbandry, a medieval John Bull who does his duty
by Church and State and has no use for beggars or lazy
workmen. But he is John Bull spiritualized, "Truth's pilgrim
at the plough for poor men's sake", whose mission it is to
bring Christendom back into the way of salvation.

Thus the conception of Piers Plowman is a composite
one which includes both a sociological and a theological
element. Piers is primarily the peasant who works for all
and toils to win the harvest that the idle waste. He is the
true economic foundation of society, as opposed to Meed,
which is the false economic motive. But also since the poor
stand nearest to God,

And in the apparel of a poor man . and a pilgrim's likeness
Many times God has been met . among needy people,

Piers Plowman stands for none other than Christ Himself,
the pattern of divine charity.

Therefore not by looks nor by learning . shalt thou know
*   charity,*
Neither by words nor by works . but by one will only,
And that knoweth no clerk . nor creature on earth,
But Piers the Plowman . Petrus, id est, Christus.
For he is not in lollers[1] . or land leaping hermits
Nor at anchorholds with an alms box . all such are
*   deceivers.*
For charity is God's champion . and gentle as a good
*   child,*

[1] Literally *idlers*, but also used as equivalent to the Latin *Lollardus*.

And the merriest of mouth . where he sitteth at meat.
The love that lieth in his heart . maketh him light of
  speech,
And he is companionable and comfortable . as Christ
  Himself.
I have seen him in silk . and sometimes in russet,
Both in grey and in fur . and in gilt armour,
And gladly he gave . to all men that needed.
Edmund and Edward . each was a king,
And set as saints . for following of charity.
I have seen charity also . singing and preaching,
Running and riding . in ragged weeds,
But bidding as a beggar . behold I him never,
But in rich robes . rather he walks,
Both capped and chrisomed . with shaven crown
And cleanly clothed . in cipress and silk.
And in a friar's frock . once was he found,
But it is far ago . in St. Francis' time.[1]

Here the conception definitely transcends all class limitations and becomes as wide and universal as charity itself.
Nevertheless, Langland does not entirely abandon the
sociological aspect of his figure. The last section of the
poem, the vision of Dobest, opens with the passage in
which he dreams

That Piers the Plowman . was painted all bloody,
And came in with a cross . before the common people,
Like in all limbs . to our Lord Jesus,

and goes on to treat of Piers as the symbol of St. Peter
and the Church. But presently there is an approximation
to the Piers Plowman of the earlier visions in the speech
of the "ignorant curate" who wishes that conscience should
be the keeper of the king's court and grace the guide of
the clergy:

[1] B, xv, 203–26.

And Piers with his new plough . and eke with his old,
Emperor of all the world . so that all men should be
  Christian,
Imperfect is the Pope . that should help all people,
Yet sendeth men to slay . such as he should save.[1]

.   .   .   .   .   .

But blessed be Piers Plowman . who toileth to till
As well for the wastrel . and the wench of the stews,
As for himself and his servants . save that he is first
  served.
And travailleth and tilleth . for a traitor as sore
As for a true tidy man . all times alike.[2]

Thus the figure of Piers Plowman has both theological and economic implications and stands for an ideal of social and spiritual renewal—a drastic reformation of both Church and State. It is obvious that such an ideal is not devoid of revolutionary potentialities, and it seems at first sight easy enough to connect it with the two revolutionary movements that were making themselves felt in England in Church and State at the very time when the poem was being written; I mean the Revolt of the Peasants and the Wyclifite movement.

Now there can be no question but that Langland's allegory made a strong appeal to the minds of the discontented peasants. Not only was the poem in itself an expression of the new social consciousness that also inspired the revolt, but we have direct evidence of its use for propagandist purposes by the leaders of the movement. The famous manifesto of John Ball to the commons of Essex calls on

[1] This probably refers to "The War of the Eight Saints" between Gregory XI and the Florentines in 1376–8, especially to the massacre perpetrated at Cesena in 1377 by Cardinal Robert of Geneva, the future Pope Clement VII, in which the English mercenaries were concerned and which aroused much indignation at the time.
[2] C, xxii, 428–31, 436–41.

Piers Plowman to go to his work and chastise Hob the Robber, and it concludes with yet another reference to the poem:

> *And* Do Well *and* Better *and flee sin*
> *And seek peace and hold therein.*
> *And so bid John Trueman and all his fellows.*[1]

Nevertheless, there is no reason to suppose that Langland was himself a revolutionary or in sympathy with the aims of the insurgents. In the first version of the poem, written long before the rising, there is a curious passage dealing with the exorbitant demands of the working classes:

> *Labourers that have no land . to live on but their hands,*
> *Deign not to dine any day . on yesterday's cabbage.*
> *No penny-ale pleases him . nor no piece of bacon,*
> *But he must feed on fresh meat . or fish that is fried,*
> *Both* chaud *and* plus-chaud *. for the chill of his maw.*
> *Save he have high wages . else will he chide,*
> *Woe on the time . that he was born a workman,*
> *And curse against the king . and all his council,*
> *For allowing such laws . labourers to grieve.*[2]

While in the later versions of the poem he writes against the propagation of communist ideas by the Friars, who

> *Preach men of Plato . and prove it by Seneca*
> *That all things under heaven . ought to be in common.*
> *And yet he lieth, as I believe . that to the lewd so*
>   *preacheth,*
> *For God made men a law . and Moses it taught:*
> Thou shalt not covet thy neighbour's goods.[3]

[1] Thomas Walsingham, *Hist. Angl.*, ii, 33 (Rolls series).
[2] A, vii, 295–303.
[3] B, xx, 273–6.

Langland is, in fact, thoroughly English in the way in which he combines an intense class-consciousness and a hatred of social injustice with a strong conservatism and a respect for the established order. He has the traditional conservative prejudice against the middle classes—against the lawyers and officials, above all, "who would do more for a dozen chickens or a sack of oats than for the love of Our Lord or all his dear saints",[1] but also against the merchants, who get little pardon, and against the shopkeepers,

> *The men who do most harm in the world*
> *To the poor people . who purchase piecemeal,*
> *For they grow rich by retail . and buy rents*
> *With that which the poor . should put in their belly.*[2]

On the other hand, he is no leveller. He holds kingship and knighthood in high honour, and accepts the traditional Christian ideal of society as a hierarchical order that has its pattern in heaven.

> *When God began heaven . in that great bliss*
> *He made knights in His court . creatures ten*
> *Cherubim and seraphim . seven such and another.*[3]

> *Kings and knights . should keep the truth,*
> *Riding and roaming . the realm around,*
> *And take transgressors . and tie them fast,*
> *Till truth has determined . their trespass to the end.*
> *That is the proper profession . that pertaineth to knights,*
> *And not to fast on Fridays . for fivescore winters,*
> *But to help him and her . that hold by the truth*
> *And never leave them for love . or for lacking of silver.*[4]

[1] A, iii, 71–5.
[2] C, ii, 104–6.
[3] B, iv, 37–9.
[4] B, i, 94–101 (C, ii, 90–101).

Such an ideal had indeed little in common with the practice of the fourteenth century, and Langland laments the degeneracy of his own post-war period, when gentle blood is of little account in comparison with money, when "soapmakers and their sons are made knights for silver" and lord it over the sons of the old families that have mortgaged their estates in the national cause during the Great War in France.[1]

But though Langland is no democrat in the modern sense, he remains a great exponent of the ideals of Christian democracy in the sense in which it has been defined by Leo XIII.[2] Indeed, nowhere else in English literature, nor even perhaps anywhere in the literature of Catholic Europe, do we find these ideals so clearly and passionately expressed. For Langland's social consciousness is rooted in his religious faith and finds its ultimate ground in the doctrine of Christian brotherhood:

> *For all we are Christ's creatures . and of his coffers rich,*
> *And brethren as of one blood . as well beggars as earls.*
> *For on Calvary of Christ's blood . Christendom gan*
>   *spring,*
> *And blood brethren we became there . of one body won,*
> *As quasimodo geniti . and gentlemen each one,*
> *No beggar or serving-boy among us . save sin made us*
>   *so.*[3]

Thus Langland's social teaching is not based on revolutionary class hatred nor on a sentimental pity for the unfortunate. It transcends all purely social and economic categories, since it is nothing else but a logical development of the central doctrine of the Christian faith in its social

[1] C, vi, 72–5 (not in A and B).
[2] In his Encyclical *Graves de Communi* (1901).
[3] B, xi, 192–7, cf. B, xix, 38–40: "Those that became Christians—Are franklins and freemen, and gentlemen with Jesus."

implications. Langland's hope of salvation for society rests on his faith in the redemption of humanity in the Incarnation, and his work finds its true culmination in the great vision of the Harrowing of Hell which is justly regarded as the finest passage in the whole poem:

> *For I that am Lord of Life . love is my drink,*
> *And for that drink to-day . I died upon earth.*
> *But I will drink of no ditch . nor of no deep learning,*
> *But of the common cup . of all Christian souls;*
> *Though the drink was death . and Hell the deep bowl.*
> *I fought so that yet I thirst . for man's soul's sake;*
>   Sitio.*[1]*

Here Langland is at one with the great tradition of medieval mysticism and with the spirit of the universal Church. His social ideal is not limited to his own age and country: it is the same as that of the New Testament and that of the social encyclicals of Leo XIII and his successors—the realisation of the Kingdom of God on earth and the restoration of all things in Christ.

But if his social teaching is thoroughly Catholic, what of his attitude to the Church and the Papacy? Are his bitter complaints against the corruption of the clergy and his demand for drastic reforms reconcilable with orthodoxy? Or should they be regarded as part of the same movement of religious disaffection and revolt which culminated in England during Langland's lifetime in the heresy of Wyclif and the Lollards? It is easy enough to understand how later Protestant ages should have taken this view, as, for example, when Thomas Fuller hails the poet as the morning star of the Reformation, belonging rather to the day than to the night. Langland's criticism of the degeneracy of the religious orders is alone sufficient to explain this, above all the

[1] C, xxi, 406–11; B, xviii, 363–6.

famous prophecy which enjoyed such popularity in Tudor times:

> *But yet shall come a king . and confess you all,*
> *And beat you, as the Bible telleth . for breaking of your*
> *rule.*
> *And amend you monks . moniales and canons,*
> *And put you to your penance .* ad pristinum statum ire.
>
> .   .   .   .   .
>
> *For the abbot of England . and the abbess his niece*
> *Shall have a knock on their crowns . and incurable the*
> *wound,*
> *But ere that king come . as chronicler me told,*
> *Clerks and Holy Church . shall be clothed anew.*[1]

But it is not difficult to find parallels to this passage in medieval writers of the most unblemished orthodoxy, notably in the no less famous prophecy of St. Hildegard two centuries before.[2]

But the resemblances between Langland and Wyclif go much further than this. Not only do we find in both of them the same attitude of hostility to the religious orders—above all, the Friars; the same contempt for pardoners and pilgrimages; the same attacks on the financial corruption of the papacy and the Curia; and the same belief in the evil effects on the Church of excessive wealth and the desirability of a measure of disendowment by the secular power; but the resemblance often extends to matters of detail and turns of expression. For instance, Wyclif's complaints of the bishops *in partibus* who, instead of going to their dioceses abroad and converting the heathen, carry on an easy and lucrative business as suffragan bishops in England, has its exact

---

[1] C, vi, 169–72, 177–80 (B, x, 317–29).
[2] I am inclined to think that this prophecy is the source of Langland's lines, as it was well known in the fourteenth century and is often referred to by Wyclif.

counterpart in Langland's lines about the need for preaching the faith to the Saracens, the neglect of which is:

A peril to the Pope . and the prelates that he maketh,
That bear bishop's names . of Bedlam and Babylon
Who hip about in England . to hallow men altars
And creep among curates . and confess against the law
"Put not your sickle into another man's harvest."[1]

Or again, Langland's description of the rich ecclesiastic riding through the land on a fine horse with his sword on his thigh and his hounds at his back is repeated in Wyclif's writings in almost identical terms.[2]

It is not, however, in passages like these that either the originality or the heresy of Wyclif is to be found. The demand for reformation and the denunciation of ecclesiastical corruption were not peculiar to the Lollards; they are characteristic of the whole period. It was the custom of the Middle Ages to use strong language, and they had none of the modern prejudice against washing dirty linen in public. As Dr. Owst has pointed out,[3] many things that we regard as characteristic of Wyclif or characteristic of Langland were the commonplaces of the contemporary pulpit, and it is easy to find similar views no less strongly expressed in the writings of champions of orthodoxy like Bishop Brunton, and the Dominican John Bromyard, who took part in the Council at Blackfriars in 1382, which condemned

[1] B, xv, 537 seq.
[2] B, x, 306–16 and Wyclif, *English Works,* ed. Matthew, 121, 149, 151, 212–13, 434; *de Blasphemia,* 188; *Select English Works,* ed. Arnold, iii, 519.
Other instances are their common views on marriage and the evil of marrying for money instead of for love: Wyclif, "Of Wedded Men and Wives", *Select English Works,* iii, 188–201; *Piers Plowman, A,* x, 106; B, ix. 150 seq.: and their criticism of the Pope levying war on Christians, etc.
[3] G. R. Owst, *Preaching in Mediaeval England* (1926), pp. xii, 36, 131, and on Langland, 295–6. Also *Literature and Pulpit in Mediaeval England* (1933), ch. ix.

Wyclif's heresies. And it is here rather than in the writings of Wyclif, which were posterior at least to the first version of *Piers Plowman*, that we should look for the source of Langland's views.

Where Langland agrees with Wyclif is precisely where the latter was in agreement with English popular opinion. As we have seen, the second half of the fourteenth century saw the first complete emergence of the English national consciousness, which expressed itself in a widespread movement for reform in Church and State. This movement finds a clear expression in the proceedings of Parliament in the later years of Edward III and reached its climax in the Good Parliament of 1376, where for the first time the Commons took a leading part. Now, as Jusserand has pointed out, Langland's views reflect those of the Commons to such a degree that his poem often reads like a poetical commentary on the Rolls of Parliament.[1] "In religious, as in secular matters, Langland sides not with Wyclif, but heart and soul with the Commons of England."

"Like the Commons, he recognizes the religious authority of the pope, but protests against papal encroachments and against the interference of the Sovereign Pontiff in temporal matters. The extension assumed by the papal power in England appears to him excessive; like the Commons he is in favour of the statutes of Provisors and Præmunire, and wishes to have them maintained and renewed. . . . In questions of this kind Langland often agrees with Wyclif; but it will usually be found that both share on these points the ideas of Parliament."[2]

One petition in particular which deals with the evil effects of simony and non-residence shows a remarkable similarity to the dominant theme of Langland's vision of Lady Meed. In the past, say the Commons, benefices were conferred on

---

[1] J. Jusserand, *Piers Plowman* (Eng. trans., 1894), pp. 112 and 71.
[2] *Ibid.*, p. 128; cf. pp. 129–36.

worthy men who stayed in their cures and spent the goods of Holy Church in works of charity. "And as long as these good customs were observed the kingdom was filled with all kinds of prosperity, such as good people and loyal clerks and clergy, knights and chivalry, which are things that always go together, peace and quiet, treasure, wheat, cattle and other riches. But since the good customs have been perverted into the sin of covetousness and simony, the kingdom has been full of divers adversities, such as wars and pestilence, famine, murrain of cattle and other ills."[1]

And Langland expresses the same idea in poetical language:

Neither the sea nor the sand . nor the seed yieldeth
As they were wont . in whom is the fault?
Not in God nor in the ground . that they are good no
  longer;
And the sea and the seed . the sun and the moon
Do their duty day and night . and if we did also
There should be plenty and peace . perpetual for ever.

But

Now faileth the folk of the flood . and the folk of the
  land,
Shepherd and shipmen . and so do the tillers,
No more can they ken . the course of the seasons.[2]

Neither Langland nor the Commons desire revolutionary changes or the subversion of hierarchical authority, but a return to the sacred order on which society rested, according to medieval ideas. The Middle Ages were always striving towards this ideal and were never satisfied that they had attained it. And it was, above all, with regard to the reform

---

[1] *Rot. Parl.*, ii, 337 in Jusserand, *op. cit.*, 133–4.
[2] C, xviii, 90–3 ; B, xv, 360–2 (C, xviii, 103–4).

of the Church that this tendency shows itself. The real Age of the Reformation was not the sixteenth century but the whole later medieval period from the eleventh century onwards. It was inevitable that such a movement should produce extremists and enthusiasts who ultimately passed into schism or heresy, as was the case with Arnold of Brescia and Peter Waldo, and the Spiritual Franciscans and Ockham and Wyclif. Nevertheless the movement as a whole was essentially Catholic and found its centre and base in the reformed Papacy.

But in the fourteenth century this was no longer the case. The alliance between the Papacy and the reformers was temporarily broken and the disruptive element in the reforming movement got the upper hand. The Papacy ceased to be the centre of unity and became itself the victim of schism.

It was not, however, the Great Schism so much as the translation of the Papacy to Avignon that marked the turning-point, by destroying the super-national prestige of the Holy See. It is true that the popes of Avignon did not deserve the indiscriminate condemnation that was passed upon them by contemporary writers like Villani and Petrarch. They included men of high character and ability, such as Benedict XII and Urban V, who were not unmindful of their universal responsibilities. Nevertheless, the divorce of the Holy See from the sacred associations of the Holy City had a disastrous effect on public opinion. The charismatic aspect of the Papacy fell into the background, and Avignon came to be regarded simply as the centre of a vast bureaucratic and fiscal organisation which was governed by financial rather than spiritual motives. It was, in the words of the Good Parliament, *"La peccherouse cité d' Avenon"*, where "brokers of benefices" and worldly cardinals lived in shameful luxury on the exploitation of the faithful.

This state of things produced a situation in which it is far more difficult to draw a sharp line of division between the movement of Catholic reform and the heretical tendency to revolt than at any other period in the Church's history. This is seen, above all, in the Spiritual Franciscan move ment, which embodied so much of the spiritual ideals of the age, while its extreme forms produced the most extra· vagant types of medieval unorthodoxy. But it is also charac- teristic in a great or less degree of all the representatives of the religious thought of the age. A canonized saint like St. Bridget can denounce the pope in unmeasured terms as "a murderer of souls, more unjust than Pilate and more cruel than Judas",[1] while Dante can speak at times as if the Church had apostatized and had forfeited the divine guidance. On the other hand, some of the most character- istic doctrines of heretics, like Wyclif's theory of dominion and grace, are borrowed almost without alteration from the writings of orthodox prelates, like Richard Fitzralph, the Archbishop of Armagh.

In these circumstances it is not surprising that we should find many points of resemblance between the writings of Wyclif and those of Langland. Both were children of the same age, who had grown up under the same spiritual in- fluences and who reacted against the same abuses. Both, in spite of their hostility to the Friars, were strongly influenced by Franciscan ideas. And yet no two men could be more dissimilar in character and spirit. Wyclif, the famous doctor, with his ponderous learning and his bitter tongue, has all the faults and virtues of the Puritan reformer—a narrow mind, harsh, unbending, arrogant, austere, which, in spite of its genuine religious earnestness, lacks human warmth and spiritual sympathy. Langland, the poor clerk, had none of Wyclif's self-righteousness or his strength of purpose; he always pictures himself as a poor feckless creature

[1] *Rev.* i, c. 41.

labouring under a sense of inferiority and spiritual mal-
adjustment.

> *Woe-weary and wetshod . went I forth after,*
> *As a reckless wretch . that recks not of sorrow*
> *And fared forth like a losel . all my life-time*
> *Till I waxed weary of this world . and willed oft to sleep.*[1]

Yet he has passion and pity and a profound sympathy for
common humanity. He can see the squalor and absurdity
of life without losing sight of the spiritual realities that lie
behind the surface of existence. For all his bitterness of
heart, he was a man of charity, and a man of faith in spite
of his tendency to doubt and despair. And so, while Wyclif
became the harbinger of religious revolt, Langland embodies the spiritual unity of the English people at the very
moment when religion in England stood at the parting of
the ways.

For the English Church never really recovered from the
crisis of the fourteenth century. The next age was of moral
and spiritual decline. We had no San Bernardino to restore
the old alliance between the Papacy and the party of reform,
and no St. Joan to rally the nation to unity in the name of
God. Instead we had tough prelate-politicians like Beaufort
and Morton and Wolsey and the men who helped to burn
St. Joan and to pillory well-meaning reformers like Bishop
Pecocke. Only in the following century did the movement
of Catholic reform reappear with Colet and Fisher and
More. But it was then too late to avert the crisis. The
English way diverged from the Catholic way and ran astray
into the waste lands of sectarianism. The spiritual successors
of Langland are to be found not in the Catholic Church,
nor even in the Church of England, but among the Puritans
and the rebels, with Fox and Bunyan and Whitfield and

[1] C, xxi, 1–4.

Blake. But this popular tradition of English religion which was divorced from Catholic unity and even from the national unity after the sixteenth century already exists in its purest and most unadulterated form in the work of Langland. He shows us what English religion might have been, if it had not been broken by schism and narrowed by sectarianism and heresy. Langland himself was not unconscious of the impending crisis. In the last pages of his poem he foretells the coming apostasy, when the rich and the learned would follow the standard of Antichrist and only the fools would be left to stand by the unity of Holy Church. He pictures in prophetic words the new pagan pride of life that was to replace the old ideals of Christian chivalry:

Loud laughed Life . . .
And armed him in haste . with words of harlotry
And held Holiness for a jest . and Courtesy for a waster,
And Loyalty a churl . and Liar a gentleman,
Conscience and Counsel . he counted it a folly.[1]

And in despair Langland calls on his fellows, the common people, to make a last stand for the cause of Catholic unity:

. . . come with me ye fools,
Into Unity of Holy Church . and hold we us there,
And cry we to Nature . to come and defend
Us Fools from the fiend . for the love of Piers Plowman,
And call we to all the commons . that they come into
    Unity,
And there abide and do battle . against Belial's children.[2]

[1] C, xxiii, 143–7.   [2] C, xxiii, 74–9.